Small Creatures
and Ordinary Places

Small Creatures and Ordinary Places

ESSAYS ON NATURE

Allen M. Young

The University of Wisconsin Press

The University of Wisconsin Press
2537 Daniels Street
Madison, Wisconsin 53718

3 Henrietta Street
London WC2E 8LU, England

1   3   5   4   2

Printed in the United States of America

Library of Congress Cataloging-in-Publication Data
Young, Allen M.
Small creatures and ordinary places: essays on nature / Allen M. Young
232 pp.   cm.
Includes bibliographical references (p. 217).
ISBN 0-299-16960-X (cloth)
ISBN 0-299-16964-2 (paper)
1. Natural history.   2. Nature.   I. Title.
QH81.Y68   2000
508—dc21   00-008914

This book is dedicated to all children
and the adults they will become,
who deserve to respect, appreciate,
and love the insects—not because
our survival depends on them,
but simply because they exist.

Contents

Illustrations

Preface

I had not envisioned this book until several readers of my published essays, which had appeared in the *Sunday Magazine* of the *Chicago Tribune,* made the suggestion to write it. This collection contains, therefore, both previously published and unpublished essays—I have taken the liberty to change the content of some of the former. I invite you inside my brain to see and hear as I do our smaller kindred among us, the insects and other creatures of seemingly ordinary places. Far too often they are easily missed, ignored, taken for granted, and even disrespected or misunderstood. The relations of insects and other creatures to the environment upon which we depend are varied and complex, and they are crucial to our survival as well. They lived in our places long before the human footprint first pressed upon the earth, forcing our species to come to terms with their legions.

There have been times when people in this Great Lakes region really listened to the sights and sounds of the natural world, not only for clues to the timing of the seasons, but also for enjoyment. Even now, as we move into a new millennium as a species and the technological pace of our existence continues to quicken, we can find considerable comfort in nature close at hand, despite how steadily it is being pushed aside. Imagine summers without the flicker of fireflies or the soothing melodies of crickets, winters without cold-stunned butterflies or wild silk moth cocoons, springs without frog song. We must find a way to rejoin ourselves to these forgotten and increasingly threatened graces of our planet, to develop a healthy respect for all of earth's creatures. This, I believe, is humankind's biggest current challenge. Forget, for the moment, the rationales advanced for saving nature, from wonder drugs yet to be discovered to carbon sequestration. The simple yet awesome truth is that life is precious and deserving of our respect in all of its myriad guises.

I believe that a better, more enlightened, and peaceful society evolves when there is an appreciation for small creatures, since even very big ones like old oak trees depend upon many smaller beings for survival. I am not saying that this is easy to accomplish. We are often taught as small children to disdain insects and other "creepy crawlies." Yet small creatures have unique and interesting stories to tell us, stories that provide insights into the natural environment and how it changes through time. In particular, I marvel at the ways in which insects and plants cope with the northern cycle of the seasons, the timing of their life cycles integrally tied to the intricate workings of a bigger clock driving the seasons. Still, we know very little. There are many new frontiers of knowledge to be penetrated right here on this planet. Best of all, insightful discoveries about life can be made not only in far off exotic places, but close to home too.

Becoming curious about the lives of insects and other creatures often requires a new perspective on what thrives close by on a summer day. In this book I offer you a chance to go into your backyard, neighborhood park, field, or forest and look and listen in a new way. You may find yourself searching for insects, perhaps with other family members or friends. When you find them, you will pause to observe them close up and then leave them be. Simply take a good, close look, and walk away with new memories and insights now a part of who you are.

The center stage here clearly belongs to the insects. One of them, the often loathed bald-faced hornet, wends its way through these essays like a sentinel. Along with other paper wasps, the hornet is, for me, an especially appropriate symbol of the thread of life that ties together all seasons. Yet I do not place this ornery creature on a pedestal. Its role in the design of this planet's life systems is no more significant than the roles of all other insects. I simply notice paper wasps and thus use them as bellwethers for natural—and unnatural—changes.

My life has been blessed with many journeys into ordinary as well as exotic places, but I was never alone on any of these travels. My companions have been, and still are, legions of insects that grace our world with the wonders of the evolutionary process. But these journeys would never have gotten started in the first place had it not been for special people.

There were many who encouraged me in my pursuit of natural history over the years. I am especially grateful to my parents, George and Margaret Young, for allowing me to roam around looking for insects as a child. Several teachers and friends also helped me to continue this passion. My career in natural history was wondrously peppered with special people who taught me about the natural world, past and present, including Heinz Meng, Lynn Throckmorton, Ralph Yalkovsky, Arnold Nemerofsky, Thomas Park, and Richard Levins. I owe a special thanks to Doug

Balz, the former managing editor of the *Sunday Magazine* of the *Chicago Tribune* for opening the pages of his "book" for my essays. I am immensely grateful for my colleagues and associates at the Milwaukee Public Museum who very generously shared with me their knowledge of natural history over many years. I am also grateful to the late Jack Puelicher, retired chairman of the Wisconsin-based Marshall and Ilsley Corporation, for invigorating discussions of natural history and for his generosity in allowing access to his Willow Creek property in central Wisconsin. I only wish Jack had lived to read this book.

I also thank Linda J. Port for her encouragement and advice as the manuscript took shape. A special thanks to Richard and Susan Schmidt for their generosity and kindness in providing me many opportunities to experience the North Woods at their home near Eagle River, Wisconsin. Pat Manning, Mike Burdick, and Nikki Hammerberg helped with preparation of the manuscript. This book comes alive with the wonderful illustrations prepared and donated to the project by Judith Huf, a very talented volunteer in the Exhibition Programs department of the Milwaukee Public Museum. Paul G. Hayes, Dr. Lincoln P. Brower, and Steve Mencher critiqued drafts of the manuscript and made many helpful suggestions. I owe a very special debt of gratitude and heartfelt appreciation to Dr. Lynn Margulis, University of Massachusetts, Amherst, for reviewing parts of the manuscript. Mary Elizabeth Braun, former acquisitions editor at the University of Wisconsin Press, with her enthusiastic support, guidance, and interest in this book from the onset, initiated the process leading to publication and made it all very enjoyable. It has also been a great pleasure to work on this book with David M. Bethea during his tenure as acting director of the University of Wisconsin Press and several other wonderful people at the press. I am especially indebted to my copyeditor, Hannah Nyala, for her deep, caring involvement with this book.

To all of these and many others, I am extremely grateful.

Small Creatures
and Ordinary Places

Introduction

There is much to see during our very brief stay on this planet. Each and every one of us is a unique creature, a chance combination of genetic ingenuity and promise forged by the fusion of egg and sperm. Each of us could easily have missed out on being born. Ours is thus a privileged existence in a world made beautiful and wondrous because of the exquisite nature of every single living creature and the creative intellect and passionate core of human beings. Taking time to explore and unravel the secrets of this beauty is a challenge we cannot afford to leave unmet.

While our own species is an intimate part of nature's design, honed over eons of time by the capricious forces of evolutionary processes and happenstance, we often fail as a species to sense the presence of our companions, those legions of creatures, particularly the small ones, that grace this world. As individuals, when we do notice their presence, we commonly do so in an adversarial manner. I am very concerned, even distressed, about this state of affairs. Yet there is great hope for penetrating this mantle of bleakness and letting in the passionate, warming glow of enlightenment that always comes from engaging the natural world about us.

I do not necessarily have the answers on how to do this best, but I do have a singular, dogged conviction about the value of appreciating the world in which we live. This is what this book is really all about. It is not a cohesive account of natural history, but a collection of connected topical essays focusing on how creatures, especially insects, cope with the passage of the north-temperate seasons in North America. This book is neither an authoritative account of insects, by any measure, nor a field guide or treatise on temperate-zone natural history. Although the book does contain elements of such accounts to varying degrees, it is meant to be about things far less easy to capture in concise terms.

There is something intangible and refreshing about paying attention to the finer, often overlooked, small details of life's manifestations, as seen in and heard from the insects, and the diverse ways in which these creatures use the environment even as other creatures are using them. Most people, I would guess, have not taken the time to watch paper wasps building their nest, to sense the carefully paced timing between a new milkweed shoot pushing out of the earth and the early summer arrival of monarch butterflies, or to flip over foliage in search of caterpillars. These are not easy things to do or see. Technology has made it simple for us to get the idea and see the facts on television screens, for example, but this is several steps removed from direct sensory experience. Finding the elusive details of nature close at hand is a matter of exploring, of hard work and perseverance, a recipe for disappointment most days but for glorious rewards on others. In this book I attempt to place insectan ways of life into context and, using representative examples, show how some of the small creatures cope with the northern winter and exploit the short growing season of that region. These essays have strong roots in my many years of walking outdoors in the upper Midwest. I hope they inspire you to take the time to seek out and meet the insects close at hand come summer or winter, and to find as much joy in the region as I do.

The title of this volume, *Small Creatures and Ordinary Places,* is meant to reflect the life cycle that binds all living things into a working fabric of life. Reading this book is an invitation to compose snapshot portraits of creatures passing through the annual cycle of seasons. How do they prepare for winter, and how do they pass through it, exploding into a resurgence of life in spring? And what is the essence of winter anyway, if not a reflective pause to contemplate the events of autumn and summer past, and to wonder how this place—gripped now by brutal cold—will look by late spring? I see creative death propelled by the winter season; it is a time of massive shutdown of life's engines and a winnowing of numbers. Yet there is also the hope for renewal, the knowledge that dead organisms and matter are already fertilizing the land that will nourish new life come spring and summer. This is not to say at all that creatures do not die during other seasons; they certainly do. But winter is a special time. Insects and other small creatures have little opportunity to be active; therefore, the parallel activities of eating and exploiting of other creatures and being eaten and exploited themselves also pause. Being outdoors in winter thus offers a marvelous opportunity to contemplate what life drummed in this place just months before, and what will be here when the land warms up in the several months hence.

What too is the essence of summer? Might it have something to do with paradoxical harmony coupled with intrinsic struggle? Summer, after all, is the time in which vast amounts of plant tissues become insects and songbirds, a time to celebrate the outward signs of interrelationships between plants and animals. Both spring and summer, then, are times for the exuberant displays of life's renewal. Autumn's return warns us of winter's approach, and winter draws everything into a space of temporary death.

I have chosen to write about the specific creatures that have inspired me over many years. Someone else could rightfully choose a totally different set of examples and contexts, and those too would be appropriate, for coming to grips with nature—learning about it, respecting it, and holding it in high reverence—is a personal journey. What I have attempted to bring together in these essays is but a small sampling of life's complexity and perfection close at hand. The facts and knowledge presented here come from the hard work of many men and women who have devoted their lives to scientific studies of insects, plants, other animals, and whole ecosystems. But what was once, during the earliest phases of the ecology movement, a fairly exclusive club of highly motivated natural scientists and conservationists has in recent times attracted skilled people from all walks of life, individuals brought together by a common bond of a passionate, but not fanatical, reverence for life.

A major conceptual theme of these essays is how the cycle of seasons shapes the sexual reproduction habits of insects. The building of a paper nest by a mated foundress wasp, the precision songs of male cicadas and katydids, the patrolling of water by male dragonflies, the life cycles of butterflies and moths and much more are exquisitely sequenced and timed with the seasons. The drive underlying this precision is to reproduce sexually. The call of the cicada, the katydid, and cricket embodies a unique message about life's success on earth as a result of sex.

The key, I believe, is to appreciate how the northern cycle of the seasons has shaped the conservative timing of sexual reproduction in virtually all species found in this region. Sexual reproduction, and the mixing of genetic material and information it brings to a new generation every time, gives organisms the resiliency needed to cope with changing environments, especially when the boundaries of the seasons are whimsical and somewhat unpredictable from one year to the next. In their book, *What Is Sex?* Lynn Margulis and Dorian Sagan address the universal adaptive significance of sex. It is most important to remember while reading these essays that virtually everything a living organism does is in some way directed toward sexual reproduction. For in sex is etched the evolutionary blueprint for the survival of the species.

While I recognize and value beauty in nature, this book is not meant at all to beautify—or in any way to deny—the realities of life in the natural world, and herein rests another central theme of this book. Matters of sex, survival, and food can be brutally harsh. The smashing colors of a butterfly's wing, the metallic glistening of a dragonfly, the call of the cicada, and the gnashing of a bat's teeth on the tough cuticle of a beetle's body all convey a sense of the fight for survival, the quintessential game of life. The winking flash of the firefly's light bespeaks real struggle, the effort to find a mate without attracting an enemy. The ties that bind cicadas to trees hint at the threat of being discovered and devoured by a hungry bird. Everything we see and hear is a portal of further insights into the elegance of the interconnections among diverse species—some partners, others antagonists, but all part of the bigger picture of nature. These essays, then, are an ode to nature's deeper beauty, that which has little or nothing to do with physical appearance or graceful song.

All of the essays in this volume were written during the past six years, but the genesis for them began 47 years ago when I was nine, growing up in Westchester, a northern suburb of New York City. I would spend many hours exploring the remaining wild places near home, searching in the autumn and winter for silk moth cocoons and in the summer for the elusive true katydid, crawling through the woods for the cast skins of the annual cicada and digging up nests of yellowjackets. Then came a long spell during which I was drawn away from these forays to college and graduate school. But this was followed by three decades of good fortune: conducting scientific field studies in the American tropics. Only in the last decade have I returned to the wonderful escapes into northern nature that I enjoyed as an eastern youth. My interests are now anchored in the Midwest, near the western rim of a great lake. From this circuitous route of youthful lore to the serious study of natural science, to practitioner of natural science, and of late to writing about nature for a general audience, I have sought always to weave facts together with the often hidden beauty of the natural world. Each leavens the other.

I hope that the essays contained in this volume convey my conviction that the seemingly ordinary places and moments—a neighborhood street lined with old maple trees on a hot summer day or frosty autumn evening, a wind-swept stubble or a cornfield dotted with an occasional giant oak tree on a winter afternoon, a frozen lake, a meadow on a humid summer night, and more—reveal marvelous secrets and messages about nature, nothing short of extraordinary, when you begin to pause, look, and listen for them. These familiar haunts are home for symbolic messengers of deep, complex stories, those interconnections among all living creatures painting the portrait that is nature, giving form to its parts. It is important not just to peel back the layers of nature's complexity, but also to appreciate that all life is united by a common evolutionary bond, and every living creature influences the lives of all others. I ask you too, while gazing on the sheer aesthetic beauty of the forest, field, lake, and creek, to remember that such composite beauty is not without design and meaning. Perhaps most important of all, I believe that such places can reach deeply into the depths of the human spirit, quenching an endless thirst for true solitude and soothing comfort.

Humans in many ways see themselves both as individuals and as a species, as the dominant form of life on the planet. But the reality is exactly the opposite. Small creatures from arthropods to zooplankton (within the former, the insects) drive the systems of life shaping the ecological history of the world. Much of what is easiest to see in nature is, in some ways, the least significant story. The biggest stories of life take time to tease out, time and patience, and many of them revolve around insects. Because of their small body size, diverse physical designs, and habitats, insects have proliferated into many millions of species. They exert tremendous force and pressure on soil, plants, and other animals, as well as on each other and us. The inherent paradox here is that, in spite of their pivotal role in shaping the networks of life that define this planet, they are largely ignored, seldom understood, and usually unnoticed by people. I hope this book helps turn around this widespread lack of respect for the planet's most significant group of animals: though physically small, the insects are evolutionarily very big.

In these times of high technology and electronic noise, it is easy to miss out on nature. While these essays are somewhat timeless in that they could have been written a century ago, their creation today is significant for contemporary humans, who because of their love affair with technology have to work harder to be a part of nature than did those generations that came before. It is easy now to miss the call of the cicada or katydid, not to sense the joy of a child in a meadow lighted up with fireflies. It is equally easy to overlook the architectural elegance of a wasp nest or to dismiss the messages emitting from a patch of wildflowers. We are endowed with exquisite senses of sight and sound, of smell and touch; this book pleads with you to use them and feel nature's presence.

I believe that one of the greatest gifts of being alive is the ability to ask questions. Asking questions builds upon and enriches the innate curiosity embossed on the human intellect and lets passion bubble up to the surface. Intellect and emotion can become close companions, partners even, as long as we remember that asking questions has no age limit. We must instill this gift in our children and carry it to our graves. There are many mysteries in life, most of which we do not understand, but asking questions about nature puts us on course. Nature is for everyone, as is science. I am not particularly concerned about answers, but I am very concerned about process, how we get on the path, how we know the route to truth. This is not a matter of instructional technology, which can be a tool. But technology can also make real learning far too easy in some respects. What people need is an ongoing dialogue with nature, a chance to go into it and explore because appreciating nature is not a matter of simply consuming what is skillfully designed for a television screen. Experiencing nature is personal. Look at a caterpillar up close, turn over a rotten log all by yourself or with a friend. Dip a net into scum-frosted pond water. Flip a rock and then, like the log, put it back exactly where it was. This is when learning begins. This is when we access one of the greatest assets of being human: the intellect. To do this you do not have to be, or become, a scientist. And age is not an issue. But you must ignite your curiosity and go look.

We adults, I believe, can rekindle within ourselves an almost childlike fascination with small creatures, especially insects. Without too much effort, but with curiosity and dedication, anyone can become acquainted with some or all of the insectan citizens forming the basis of these essays. I wish you well in this novel pursuit. I invite you to venture outdoors, to woods or meadow in all seasons, to go deeper into the beauty of this world, to go quietly into the weed patch, garden, field, and marsh to see nature's details and experience firsthand the art, design, and behavior of our planet's smaller citizens.

Being alive on this planet is a precious gift. Your life is your one and only chance to be enriched by the natural beauty and lessons all around you. Every moment of every season of every year is unforgettable in this way. You do not have to be a scientist to better understand the portrait of nature. You can embark on your own journey and see for yourself many details of the great gift of the universe: life. Please do so. I hope this set of essays helps.

Spring

L ast summer, leaves and twigs snapped and cracked beneath my feet along this path. Just three months ago I slogged through a foot of snow here. This place was brittle and bare then, its deafening silence offering few clues of things alive. But today this wooded glen is dripping and soft, its mulch a water-soaked sponge underfoot—winter's thawing legacy.

I try to forget the surrounding city's stoic embrace of gray, metallic clatter. Slipping into this sodden place, a small pocket of relic forest closed in by urbanized landscape, reveals some persistent signs of what long ago was the year's awakening in sprawling, majestic woodlands. This five-acre slice of forest is skirted by old warehouses, modest homes, a railroad line, and an expressway. Yet it still has a few ancient oaks, many maples, beech, other assorted trees, and a springtime pond.

On this day, with its rain sparkle blending with the slow, steady chirp of a lone wood frog, it's easy to sense the awakening of earth's wild citizens. What's really special about going into these woods just now is that it is the very cusp of the season, when the trees are barely beginning to bud and nature's presence seems scant. Scant that is, unless you look closely at the land for stirrings of life.

I can never guarantee exactly what I might see in the woods at this time of the year. For sure, there will be some bird watchers—the same feisty group that comes here every year to witness the spring northward migration. I prefer to relinquish upward gazing to them and focus on more earth-bound signs of nature's rebirth. Nature's bold strokes, symbolized across the continent, even canonized perhaps, by huge old trees, owls, raptors, and big cats, are precipitously held together by intricate linkages among many small wild beasts. Surprisingly enough, more than 80 percent of this planet's animal life comes packaged as small arthropods

alone, and the interconnections among myriad other small creatures adds an even more complex dimension to the design of these woods.

Many people feel more at ease with the larger, more obvious signs of nature, even in spring. But the true nature loyalist seeks out the tiny, far less prominent beings and their intertwined lives. Taking the time to expose nature's unfolding subtleties in spring's thaw kindles an appreciation for this land's capacity to reseed itself and sprout new life. What is truly marvelous about spring—oft noted only in passing, as a cliché, and rarely comprehended much further—is that nature's awesome tapestry is woven together once again, as if the whole woods is some superorganism coming out of a deep sleep.

Spring, however, can be very different one year to the next. Like a petulant child, the season thrives on inherent unpredictability and guile. In some years, it arrives "early" and in others, "late." Sometimes its display is gradual and muffled, a stretched unfolding of freshened new life sliding at a snail's pace into summer. At other times it is a thin and rushed but glorious and vibrant ribbon whisked from winter's grasp and flung into summer. Such capriciousness aside, spring's personality is always an elegant symphony, orchestrated stanzas of things being born, shaped, and blended by weather and each other.

Only inside the woods, when meandering toward the flooded center of this place, can we truly begin to sense the ancient seasonal cycle of birth, growth, harvest, and death that has needled philosophers and others for centuries. Those who ponder life's essence, its soul, find ample fodder for the task in spring. Streaks of sunlight cascading down through a pale green veil of interlacing buds and new leaves give a soft glow to the bottom of the woods. Patches of an incredibly blue sky fill spaces behind dead and threadbare branches. Even though this place is still cold and damp, the growing green roof above hints of many sultry, steamy days to come only a few months ahead. By summer's debut the depth of these woods will darken under a full-blown canopy of expanded, seasoned leaves. A flawless mosaic of many sizes and shapes, this living shawl will give shade and coolness to this glen and its rich ground cover of accumulated sticks and leaves. Across the mulch an occasional smudge of lush, crisp skunk cabbage catches my eye—the venerable and pungent plant whose spicy odor fills the air when its succulent leaves are snapped off underfoot by passing deer, raccoons, red foxes, or people. A staggering of sunspots hitting sap flowers on tree trunks hints at secrets within the bark.

Suddenly, less than twenty feet away, a flutter of blackness appears, as if a shadow passing, drawing my attention to an illuminated tree trunk. A skittish mourning cloak, one of spring's first butterflies, has just alighted on the frothy brew of a fresh sap flow. As tough and cunning a beast as any fox, this small angle-wing butterfly has survived the brutal winter in a cold-stunned state. Richly cloaked in chocolate-brown, yellow-tipped wings, two-thirds the width of an average man's fist in span, the butterfly flits through the woods in search of its first meal of the new year and finds it on this tree. Nuthatches and sapsuckers have already gouged holes in the trunk in search of their own food, and these wounds are bleeding sugar-rich sap that ferments on contact with the air. This fragrant concoction always lures insects, mostly flies and honeybees, but also an occasional angle-wing butterfly, like the mourning cloak, question mark, or comma. From the moldy sap, male butterflies get energy needed to fly about in search of a mate. Females search for scattered willows, elms, and birches on which to place eggs as new leaves unfurl.

As if by some uncanny clockwork, almost invariably when I spot a mourning cloak, I also hear a red-winged blackbird—two of the most familiar harbingers of spring. By summer, the blackbird's song will be blotted out by the mixed concerts of many other birds, and the mourning cloak will seldom be seen against a backdrop of many other more colorful butterflies; their presence here today is like a benediction, and the homely sap flow as rich a canvas as can be spread. Nature, it seems, always sits on an invisible, rolling landscape of adaptive opportunity, with each alternate summit being a different option to meet the challenge of survival when the growing season begins. A month or so from now, when I might stumble upon a clot of churning mourning cloak caterpillars in a willow bush along the border of this woodland, I will be able to tie the presence of those caterpillars back to this sap flow and the handiwork of these earlier sapsuckers. A shifting, restless patchwork of interconnections is steadily chiseled onto a backdrop of increasing warmth and often abundant rain.

A run of spring days and weeks gushing with warm, nourishing rains yields a bountiful summer resplendent with lush greenery, mosquitoes, songbirds, and butterflies, followed by bumper crops of wasps, grasshoppers, and crickets. The fields will be blanketed with wildflowers, and roadside pockets choked with an exuberant range of wild and exotic flora. A cool, dry spring charts a different, less demonstrative destiny. Spring cannot be divorced from the winter just past, nor can summer's face be separated from spring's events. All are connected at every level. Nor are the connections merely superficial.

A wooded glen such as this one cradles hallmark clues of nature's ancient march toward summer. Consider a small patch of mulch on the forest floor. Sooner or later, the sun strikes this spot, warming it up. As the mulch heats, minute creatures stir, igniting a chain of events that will draw even more life to this spot. The soil beneath the mulch warms up too, and a carpet of spring beauty, one of the season's earliest wildflowers, resprouts and blossoms. Its tiny pale bluish-lavender flowers will lure six or more species of wild bees native to these woods. Not every spring beauty will be pillaged by these elusive bees for nectar and set seed. Certain flowers that bend over too much in a cluster, concealing access to themselves, will be passed up on a bee's steadfast patrol. The more upright flowers have a better chance of being noticed by bees and setting seed. Far from mere horticultural trivia, these traits illustrate nature's elegantly fine-tuned ability to shape the future destiny of a species, and remind us that every springtime woodlands is a chancy ecological chessboard.

Our wild honeybees are a good case in point. These woodlands were once filled with many more kinds of wild bees—not the familiar domesticated honeybee brought over from Europe by the Pilgrims, but a large assemblage of native North American species. Considerably smaller than the over-revered, aggressive honeybee, these wild bees efficiently pollinate many species of wildflowers and trees, and their few remaining species play a key role in the overall design of these struggling lands.

These woods also point backward to the Midwest's richly diverse natural past. The few surviving huge oaks in this glen stand as silent reminders of what this place must have been like three or four hundred years ago, long before the cities now skirting this great lake came into existence. Today's woodlands almost everywhere are but mere wisps of earlier, more diverse assemblages of creatures. That vital synergy between plants and animals—be it wild bees as pollinators of our native flora; squirrels, rodents, and birds as scatterers of its seeds and fruits; or bacteria, fungi, arthropods, and other small creatures creating the mulch that nourishes the collective beings of the forest—was far more elaborate in design and scope in the distant past. This midwestern wilderness existed over millennia of spring seasons after the last retreat of great glaciers sculpted the bowels of this land 10,000 or more years ago. Today the woods offer some of the best clues about this ancient heritage. That rabbit carcass up ahead, lying along the path, its decay hastened by bacteria, mold, maggots, and mites churning in its rotting flesh, is part of this dwindling legacy. So too is the small vernal pool nearby.

A deep depression has filled with very cold crystal water, the melt-off of snow mixed with rains, and a family of wood ducks glides silently across its mirrored dark waters. The drake sports a striking metallic-green head, outfitted with white lines and red eyes. The less striking hen is leading a line of chicks, six in all. Ponds like this one are a necessity not just for wood ducks, but for other ducks as well. Wood ducks lay their eggs in tree holes, usually oaks when available, high above the secluded water or even away from water altogether, but once hatched, amazingly, the fluffy chicks drop to the ground, bouncing slightly, unharmed, and follow mom to water. This seemingly insignificant little pool makes all the difference in a wood duck chick's chances for survival.

Kneeling down at the water's edge or crawling along that big partly submerged log jutting into the water allows a glimpse of other creatures who use this pond. A fairy shrimp, a remarkable crustacean swimming oddly on its back, glides into view just below the surface. Ethereal, translucent, its delicate body gracefully slices through the motionless, cold water while its coal-black eyes sit squarish on its head and gaze upward, each eye mirroring hundreds of tiny facets like a television screen. Fairy shrimp do not live in permanent ponds, lakes, or rivers. They reside only in water-filled roadside ditches or springtime ponds, so their existence from one year to the next is nothing less than tentative and depends entirely on their ability to wrest a living from these transient places. In about four weeks, the shrimp mature and breed, dropping their eggs into the bottom mud and debris, and then die, leaving the eggs well hidden even after the water disappears. Over the winter the eggs begin to develop inside the frozen debris, hatching in spring as tiny larvae, and the cycle begins anew. Fairy shrimp, feeding through their flattened, leaf-like feet, treat this pond bottom as a smorgasbord: filtering minute rotting plant matter and other suspended organic particles from the water. In turn, many other creatures feed on the shrimp as the whole system moves inexorably from this season to the next.

It might be helpful to remember at this point that the snapshot I have created here—one facing forward into the year—is every bit as tightly linked to what has already happened. In the summer just past, squirrels, birds, and wind dumped payloads of seeds and twigs to the forest floor, peppering the depression where this pond now rests. As spring slid into summer last year, many kinds of birds repopulated these woods, feeding on arthropods, especially insects, to nourish themselves and their fledglings. Rains of feces and other bird wastes, including broken insect parts and even the carcasses of dead chicks, provided an added bonus of nutrients to the mulch, fueling even bigger blooms of cryptozoic animals, bacteria, and fungi. A baby deer died here as well, and its plump, swollen carcass became a writhing mass of fly maggots soon after bacteria had softened the flesh. Weeks later, beetles, mites, and ants worked over the melting meat, aged like a vintage wine by tenderizing maggot action. By summer's end the elements of the decomposed animal returned to the mulch and soil, where at least four species of ants had large, elaborate colonies. Ants probably inadvertently buried seeds in the mulch where a precious treasure chest of fairy shrimp eggs lay in the debris and dried mud, waiting for the cool temperatures of autumn and the cold of winter to arrive. Each creature contributes its existence to the overall web of life. Each lives, each dies, and none outranks another in value.

The alternating cycles of summer's drying and spring's inundation of temporary woodland pools generates non-overlapping hatches of crea-

tures. As each cycle progresses, the basic substrate in these pools, such as accumulating leaf litter, is changed by the action of creatures, modifying it for a subsequent generation of life. Drying out reduces the food quality of litter over time, perhaps increasing as a result the competition for limited food and space by some creatures dependent upon these pools. When voracious agents of carnivory, in the form of odonates and diving beetles, are added to this situation, these pools quickly appear to be anything but stable, calm systems of life devoid of environmental stress. Nature's demands become apparent. And the personality of this springtime pond— whose size, depth, and capacity for life is contoured by snow, rain, temperature, and organic debris—changes from one year to the next.

By early summer, this pond will shrink again, leaving first a receding mud hole and then, by midsummer, a bone-dry bed of caked soil covered with plants that looks as if it could never have hosted as many creatures as it does this afternoon. Bigger ponds that stick around longer in a protracted spring accumulate even more residents. Their fleeting food chains become more complex, linking many species, and a much richer array of creatures inhabits them by the time the pond has shriveled into a shell of sticky mud. Time stamps its indelible watermark upon springtime ponds as it does for other assemblages of life blanketing our woodlands, marshes, and meadows. More time allows nature more opportunity to experiment with the design of whole ecosystems and the ties one system has with others, like the matter of how a vernal pond is linked to the woods and vice versa.

The fairy shrimp shares this pond with other life. Peering closely again into the water, I spot a long, thin brownish creature suspended head downward, a larval diving beetle, a ferocious carnivore of fairy shrimp and other small animals, even tadpoles. Its powerful sickle-shaped jaws strike at lightning speed to snare prey. Because of its appetite, only a small number of these shrimp will survive; many will be converted into diving beetles. Meat-eating diving beetle larvae are far less numerous than their prey. Each one must consume many fairy shrimp in order to become a beetle. As this pond dries up, adult diving beetles will mature and fly away seeking permanent ponds, sluggish streams, and lakes in which to breed over the summer—a feat fairy shrimp cannot rival. But occasionally the eggs of some pond creatures will stick to the feet of ducks visiting this pond, thus seeding other seasonal ponds further north as the waterfowl migration continues. This pond also will serve as a nursery for frogs, toads, and salamanders, who will in turn function as prized game for garter snakes or the occasional hognose snake and ubiquitous raccoons that live in or pass through these woods. The red-tailed hawk patroling high above will be hunting for snakes and rodents.

The actions of one insect, then, creates opportunity for others. Woodland life takes shape as the springtime pond expands and contracts with the passage of seasons. It is a complex theater production with many acts and curtain calls driven by a troupe of diverse creatures, each one with a specific role to play. A garter snake who eats a wood frog cannot be divorced from the insects that fed the frog, or from the survival of the hawk that hunts for the snake. This lesson can strengthen our understanding of nature. Simply noting the presence of the strong, powerful hawk often instills respect and reverence in us for all of nature's large powerful creatures—be it the hawk, other top carnivores such as owls and big cats, or mammoth trees. Much harder to grasp is the often overlooked, but towering collective strength of smaller creatures. Theirs is not a strength of brute force, but rather a quiet one rooted in their endless, intricate connections to the world they help create. Without the underpinnings of nature's multitudes of small creatures, whole forests would collapse. All species, including our own, would suffer and eventually perish.

Understanding nature is truly a quest. We know very little about creatures we encounter on a walk in the woods, and we remain ignorant about many species who live in small woods and seasonal ponds. We do know, however, that come summer, these woods are home for at least ten species of butterflies, ten times that many moths, three of large green katydids, one type of cicada, hundreds of species of beetles, and so forth. And I can guarantee that even though we do not have names yet for many of the fungi, soil microorganisms, bacteria, protists, and arthropods that live here, each of them is helping to maintain the ecological soundness of these woods by recycling energy, air, and water through them—the very requisites for our own survival.

I believe that all humans have a duty to respect, protect, and enjoy nature, and that nature is good ointment for the soul. But finding positive ways to integrate human values with conserving the natural heritage is not an easy task. A useful first step in heightening our awareness of nature and its importance to our collective existence is learning to observe and watch. It takes time, patience, and a touch of passion to explore the natural world, but the rewards are infinitely vast.

What we need most, I think, is a renewed sense of perspective, a reminder about the placement of our own species within nature. Being in the woods in spring gives a real sense of continuity with the natural world, and only this—a committed stewardship—can slow or stop the destruction of what little is left of our natural heritage both at home and afar. This is the lesson echoed in the call of the red-winged blackbird, in the dull basking flash of the mourning cloak, in the awakening woodland pool with its stirring belly of transient life.

Spring's shifty personality thus teases us with a challenge: to be more cognizant of the real story in which all creatures grab hold of ecological

17

opportunity to survive. But much of this narrative slips past us unnoticed. It is relatively easy to see the trees budding, to spot a cluster of spring beauty poking through the leaf mulch, to smell the pungency of skunk cabbage, to hear the crackling rush of a squirrel in the underbrush, and to feel quiet joy at hearing the call of the spring peeper. It is much harder to let these and other sights and sounds define a roadmap in our psyche that will lead us to those elusive ties binding all beings big and small into the glory of life evident everywhere—even in this little woodland.

We can never know the whole of nature. At best, we can only take a hearty stab at getting beyond ourselves enough at least to sense wholeness. But just because we can't experience the whole does not mean that we cannot do as much as possible to understand that nature, even garbed in spring's fickle moodiness, is good for the body and spirit, and worthy of respect and protection. Similarly, we cannot always know what is to be found along a path in the woods, what the dip net in the pond will bring into view, or what we'll see under a rotten log in the mulch. Our meetings with nature are often random, a chance encounter deep in the woods, alongside the pond, or near the contested boundary where woods meet fields. No matter, for it is taking the time to search, listen, and learn that enriches our ability to welcome and value the northern spring.

Mourning Cloaks

One of the clearest memories I have as a twelve year old in 1954 is of taking a walk one spring day to an area of old greenhouses perhaps a quarter of a mile from our home in the lower Hudson River Valley region of New York. Walking between two of the glass buildings, I suddenly saw a good-sized butterfly alight on the ground, its chocolate-brown, jagged-edged wings bordered in yellow and glistening in the sunshine. As the butterfly held its expansive wings flat against the ground, I edged closer and noticed a line of blue dots inside the yellow margins. I was seeing my first mourning cloak butterfly. Only months before I had found a color picture of it in my *Golden Guide to the Insects*. The picture of the mourning cloak (*Nymphalis antiopa*) matched exactly what I was seeing before me.

One of the greatest gifts I ever received from my parents was that copy of the *Golden Guide*. The little paperback book, with its fine color paintings of various exemplary North American insects, became my Bible into a lifetime and a career of worshiping the marvels of the evolutionary process. Perhaps in no other group of creatures are the perfections and ingenuity of adaptive features and behaviors so amply expressed in a seemingly infinite number of forms, all reflective of a long history of continued success by this group of animals in coping with environmental change and its complex, multifaceted forces and pressures. I am still deeply grateful to my parents not only for the book, which opened my eyes to an amazing world, but also for their wisdom in allowing me to pursue this interest. There was something exciting about seeing the butterfly's painting in the guidebook and then searching for the real thing in nature. Part of this wonder, I am sure, was the thrill of the process. The rest, no doubt, was the unexpected and unheralded moment of sudden discovery. I relearned this lesson repeatedly. No matter how steadfast my efforts might be, discovery often came at the least anticipated times. Even as a child, then, I was thankful that the people who had come before me had worked so diligently to write these helpful books, offering encouragement for a young naturalist in search of insectan game.

I cannot think of a greater joy than the freedom to follow a path of discovery into the outdoors. Exploring nature truly is a trip that has no age limit and requires no costly travel or expensive gear. It is, in fact, one of the easiest journeys to undertake, one for which all you really need is an inquisitive mind studded with patience and acuity of the senses—and the simple existence of a fellow creature like the mourning cloak.

In a flash my first mourning cloak was gone that day so long ago. The magnificent creature graced me with its presence against the familiar screeching of a red-winged blackbird in the distance and the sturdy feel of my *Golden Guide* in hand. From it I had learned what the caterpillar and chrysalis of the mourning cloak look like and how to recognize its mass of eggs adhering to the branch of elm or willow. From it I also knew that mourning cloak butterflies are seldom seen. Seeing one is far less common, for instance, than spotting several monarchs in a patch of purple coneflowers, a roadside band of yellow sulfurs sipping salty broth from a steamy mud puddle in midsummer, or several tiger swallowtails guzzling nectar from the throats of thistles.

A good spring day such as this one holds promise, however, that I might just succeed in catching a glimpse of a mourning cloak in these sodden woods. On this day in April, the earth is warming up, but it is still way too early for most other butterflies to be on the wing. Pockets of snow lie about, even though the air is warm and the sun bright. Spring, though, is one of the best seasons to find mourning cloaks; they seem to disappear come midsummer. Sunlight falls in shafts through the leafless tree limbs. Over to the left some old birches stand sedately, their trunks pockmarked with woodpecker holes. A few of the holes are oozing sap. Tree sap is rich in carbohydrates, life's prime source of energy and fuel, so a dripping, smelly sap flow from an old birch acts as a collecting spot, a watering hole, for not only winter-tired, angle-wing butterflies such as the mourning cloak, bees, and flies, but also an occasional, newly awakened queen bald-faced hornet.

Ah! A brownish butterfly just lit on a birch about twenty feet away. Edging closer, I see it walking around, flapping its wings. A mourning cloak. As the butterfly walks, beams of sunlight burnish its wing scales to iridescent. How deeply brown and vibrant those blue spots make the top sides of the insect's wings stand out. The undersides look drab and dull in comparison. And there lies one of the mourning cloak's secrets to survival: when the wings are closed, the insect resembles a chip of tree bark or broken, dark-stained wood—inert, lifeless, easy to pass by. When captured in a net, the mourning cloak uses the coloring to tell another lie: it plays dead and falls into the netting, with its wings tightly closed, staying motionless for up to a minute or two before making a rapid escape. In nature, even colors—and the meanings attached to them—are functional.

Sometimes I see mourning cloaks basking in a sunspot on the ground, wings fully stretched out in a very purposeful posturing. The dark wing colors may help the chilled butterfly to capture and soak up the sun's warmth since darker hues absorb heat more readily than lighter colors, so by alighting on a flat surface and keeping the wings stretched out, the butterfly positions itself to absorb as much heat as possible. Thus it may be no coincidence that many deep-woods butterflies have dark brown wings that help them to stay warm in the sun-flecked shade of the lower layers of the forest.

The cryptic underwing coloration, I believe, has something to do with the butterfly's wintering habit. The mourning cloak, which gets its name from the somber yet beautiful earthtones of the upper surface of the wings, along with a handful of other closely related "angle-wing" butterflies, has the curious, even mysterious, habit of passing winter as an adult butterfly. This is highly unusual in the butterfly world, since most temperate-zone butterflies overwinter in the chrysalis stage. A few others, such as fritillaries, do so as partly grown caterpillars. Only a minority, the angle-wings, overwinter as hardy adults. One of the reasons I am so intrigued by the mourning cloak and its kin is that it is widely out of phase with the life cycle of most others of its kind. Come late summer, most butterfly caterpillars heed the shortening days by completing their growth and molting into pupae or chrysalides. The chemistry of a chrysalis, which in many species resembles a chip of wood, dried leaf, or twig, includes a recipe for cold hardiness. Certain hydrocarbon substances abound in the creature's fluids, lowering the freezing point in the developing tissues and preventing death from cold. By contrast, in the mourning cloak a similar resistance to brutal cold is embossed into the chemistry of the adult insect rather than in the chrysalis, and it functions well enough to allow the butterfly to withstand the cold and blizzards so common in this region.

The mourning cloak on the birch tree has now wedged its way into a buzzing throng of flies at the sap flow. When autumn arrives, it will seek out wind-sheltered crevices under loosened bark on old trees or in woodpiles, attics, and barns to settle down for the long winter. Once, many years ago, I found a cold-stunned but live mourning cloak in the attic of a city house. In the same place I also encountered an equally cold-numbed queen bald-faced hornet, another insect that passes winter as an adult. Clearly, the bark-mimicking design of the insect's wings makes a lot of sense. Hungry birds, chipmunks, and squirrels rip open old logs, rummage through wood piles, and poke around under loose tree bark in

search of food, mostly insects and spiders. A motionless mourning cloak, lying flat on its side, though, does not look like an animal at all. The design of the wings, I believe, most likely helps these creatures avoid being found and eaten in winter.

One of the most appealing traits of this butterfly is its habit of sucking up fluids from soupy, fermenting sap and crushed overripe fruits and berries. I find it fascinating that a butterfly would prefer to dine on nature's decay rather than the nectar of flowers. This is not to say that mourning cloaks do not visit flowers, and, indeed, I have seen them on the blooming lilac bushes alongside my house. But we expect flies to be more closely associated with the product of nature's decay than butterflies. Any foray into the tropics illustrates the contrary fact that many kinds of butterflies feed solely on these sources of energy-rich fluids. The butterfly ahead sits lightly on the tree trunk with its proboscis probing the sap wound, keeping its wings closed as it feeds. It may well stay put for several minutes, despite the risk of becoming mildly intoxicated by the fermented sap. Intoxication would not be a good thing for a butterfly, though, since its thick body would make a tasty morsel for any passing chickadee or chipmunk.

Mourning cloaks, like wasps and ants, also take advantage of another kind of sap, more prevalent in summer than in spring. Many of the plants in a northern field in summer support sizable colonies of aphids, tiny sap-sucking insects (also called plant lice) that are sometimes tended by ants. The ants act like shepherds, protecting their flock from predatory beetles and other carnivorous insects, while feeding on the honeydew secretions produced by their livestock, and mourning cloaks sometimes feed on this honeydew as well. What surely lures the butterfly to the sap flow is the pungent smell of the fermenting substance. Butterflies have a very keen sense of smell. I am intrigued by fermenting sap and fruit in forests, and the means by which they attract insect life, a matter of microbial ecology of which we know very little although the basics are familiar enough. A sapsucker or woodpecker gouges a hole in a live tree, causing sap, the tree's "blood," to flow. Rich in sugars, the exposed sap (or later in the summer, the trickling juices of crushed fruit) becomes a ready target for agents of fermentation, yeast and bacteria and mold. Only after the exposed juices have been invaded by other creatures do they become suitable foods for insects like the mourning cloak.

Consider too the time of the year. In these woods, save for some patches of trillium, spring beauty, and a few other wildflowers, there are few quick energy-rich foods available in spring. Yet the woods are waking up and so are mourning cloaks. I have even seen them alighting on snow after a string of exceptionally warm and balmy days in February and March. Come late winter and early spring, animals are eager to find food.

The microcosm of a spring woods sap flow is a life raft for the mourning cloak, a chance for the winter-strained insect to recharge its batteries, energize its muscles, and take flight in search of important game in the quest for survival. We know very little about spring sap flows and their role in shaping the destiny of woodlands. But surely they are important, perhaps more so at the end of some winters than others.

We also know nothing about what fraction of a mourning cloak population in a forest such as this one actually makes it to spring. A good guess is that depending on the severity of the winter, varying numbers of the butterflies survive, and in all winters I am sure that it is still only a small fraction of the entire population. Years ago I had the opportunity to return to the same patch of woods over a couple of spring seasons to observe mourning cloaks. Each spring, I captured some of the butterflies I saw at sap flows and baits of fermented beer, painted code numbers on the undersides of their wings, and set them free. I had hoped to resight these marked butterflies in the following days and weeks. After no resightings, I concluded that they move around a lot in search of food and mates. I also concluded once more that we know far too little about this species, despite its widespread occurrence across the United States, as well as the mountains of Mexico, Guatemala, and El Salvador.

We know very little about how and when mourning cloaks mate. My best hunch is that, soon after stirring awake from their chilled slumber, the newly hatched butterflies from a second-generation brood produced in late summer or early autumn opportunistically mate in the brushy borders skirting a woodland such as this one. Although awakening mourning cloaks may wander far and wide, they quickly settle down to the business of breeding, becoming more residential to achieve this end. Like many other butterflies, they do not back away from aerial encounters. Instead they establish a "territory," usually along a trail or path, perhaps on the side of a building, and chase away other butterflies, even birds and bats. This behavior suggests that mourning cloaks have not only excellent vision, but also a well-developed sense of space and boundaries. Although I did not note the sex of the butterflies I have seen showing off this way, it is very likely that they were males setting up their separate spaces to court females, a well-known phenomenon among many types of animals. Keeping and defending a place helps ensure that mating can take place. What is often disguised behind a veil of frailty, then, is a very strong butterfly capable of combat with intruders much bigger than itself.

No one knows for sure, but male mourning cloaks may attract females into their spaces and court them. In many butterfly species, one mating is sufficient to fertilize all of the eggs in a female's body. But male butterflies can and often do mate several times, each time with a new partner. A springtime wood like this one provides a unique opportunity for this butterfly to get a head start on breeding, well before most other butterflies have taken wing. Successfully mated female mourning cloaks, their bodies heavy with eggs, can then move about the landscape in search of the correct plants on which to place their broods.

There's a small meadow not far away that seems to suit them well. While the females do lay eggs on some very tall trees, such as elms or this birch, caterpillars are also found on the low bushes of the swamp willow in these softly rolling hills near the edge of a great lake. The field looks like a heap of dried, brittle weed stalks and brush dotted with small thickets of upright wooden stems. This is swamp willow. Right now the bushes are still threadbare, and the rolling landscape appears dead and forlorn. But not for long. The earth is warming up and within a matter of a month or so this field will be drumming with new life. In a few more weeks, the bushes will have tender new leaf buds, well before many other plants in this meadow. A mated mourning cloak butterfly imbibing sugars and broth from a woodland sap flow will soon sprinkle these small willow bushes with clusters of tiny eggs. She will arrive and carefully scan the budding vegetation of a field, cueing in to the branches of willow already studded with tiny leaf buds. Alighting on the branch, she will walk over the buds, tapping her antennae on them, then move back down the twig and begin to lay eggs—not singly the way many butterflies do, but in clumps. A butterfly may affix one large mass of eggs around a twig and then a second group at a different site on the twig. When first laid, the barrel-shaped eggs are yellow; they turn orange within a day and deep purple several days later.

There is a reasonably good chance that mourning cloak caterpillars will be in this field within the next month. As I've already mentioned, the mourning cloak gets a head start on the season, well before most other butterflies are on the wing. Its timing is quite exquisite in this regard. The eggs hatch into tiny black caterpillars by the time the new willow foliage is almost unfurled. While still tender and soft, willow makes a good fodder for baby caterpillars. Other common food plants in this region are elm, birch, and poplar.

The caterpillars become very noticeable when they are almost fully grown, with black branching spines and a set of reddish spots on their backs, and a mass of them on a willow bush or poplar tree can be impressive. Once I found a clump of about 150 in a stand of three-meter-tall willows. The larger spiny caterpillars were actually splintered off into several smaller subgroupings occupying different adjacent twigs. Many cast-off skins from an earlier molt still clung to the branches. On another occasion in the city I found about 50 crawling down the trunk of a large

elm tree. They scurried along rapidly, purposefully, leaving the tree in search of places to transform into chrysalides.

Willow leaves are filled with some nasty-tasting substances, making them challenging to chew up and perhaps, as a side benefit, making mourning cloak caterpillars distasteful to enemies such as birds. Red on black color patterns in nature usually spell trouble for those who dare to eat the bearers of such colors anyway, as anyone who has encountered the striking red hourglass marking on the black widow spider knows. Animals bearing toxins in the wild usually tell you so by such colors. About the only other insect that feeds side by side with mourning cloak caterpillars are bright red and black polka-dotted leaf beetles. Later in the summer others will appear on this scene. From time to time I have been lucky enough to spot a viceroy butterfly caterpillar feeding on the willow. This creature, resembling a twig, spends winter in a small silken tube fashioned inside a leaf in autumn and comes out to resume feeding in spring. Unlike the mourning cloak, in this species the gaudy signs of distastefulness appear in the adult butterfly rather than in the caterpillar.

It takes somewhat longer for mourning cloak caterpillars to mature than it does for most butterflies. I do not know the reason for this, but it may well have something to do with the metabolic inefficiencies that ensue when a caterpillar is faced with chemically formidable foliage as its meal. But being a caterpillar is a risky affair altogether anyway. Even supposedly distasteful, spiny mourning cloak caterpillars are acceptable prey for many types of birds—the red-winged blackbird and the Baltimore oriole among them—and some insectivorous animals. Paper wasps and the caterpillar hunter beetle also hunt them, and both eggs and caterpillars are attacked by a variety of parasitic wasps and flies—decreasing their chances of survival. But this is a natural process, part of the overall design and complexity of a field come spring and summer. It is a natural cycle of exploitation that has been fine-tuned and adjusted over eons.

Many people have wondered why these caterpillars flock together as a group while resting and feeding. There are several theories about the function of this gregarious behavior but the complete answer remains elusive. Certainly it starts out as a result of the eggs being placed on a twig in a tight, orderly cluster. Young caterpillars can conceal themselves, even in groups, on the undersides of leaves, but as they get bigger they become exposed to the very keen hunting skills of birds and small mammals. Clearly, then, it is advantageous to amplify the colorful signal or message about being distasteful by staying in group formation. But even distasteful gregarious caterpillars can fall victim to some enemies, and when one is found so are many others. At present we simply know very little about the natural history of these insects and why they distribute themselves on the food plant as they do, though the presence of certain leaf beetles is surely also a factor in their behavior. Willow-eating leaf beetles secrete repugnant chemicals that cause mourning cloak caterpillars to avoid leaves on which the beetles, in their larval stages, are feeding. Otherwise a willow tree is a wide-open field for these caterpillars. And, despite the odds, many do survive.

During early summer and again near autumn, I often spot several freshly hatched adult mourning cloaks flying around. These are broods of new butterflies from one or more former caterpillar groups that dined in these willows, evidence that their predators—both birds and mammals missed them. Of course, these larger animals are not the only enemies of caterpillars. There are literally legions of parasitic flies and wasps who complete the maggot stage of their life cycles within the living body tissues of caterpillars, including mourning cloaks. These parasites lay eggs either directly upon the outer cuticle of the growing caterpillar or, as in the case of some flies, on the leaves where the caterpillars are feeding. The eggs in the latter situation are inadvertently devoured, uninjured to hatch out later inside the gut. These particular enemies do not discern mourning cloaks as being distasteful and show no regard for caterpillar colors.

Many years ago, as a teenager, I gathered about five dozen mourning cloak caterpillars from a small elm tree near our house and carried them into our attic. There I set up several water-filled milk bottles holding sprigs of elm branches. With a loose cheesecloth netting around the whole area, this became a butterfly nursery of sorts.

The caterpillars seemed to eat constantly. I could hear the concerted clicking of their sturdy mandibles slicing through the bony, tough elm leaves no matter what time of the day I came to visit. Of course, I also soon discovered the patter of caterpillar fecal pellets, often called frass, piling up on the floor—one of the small details of caterpillar life not often readily apparent in the wild. This was the first time I had set out to raise that many mourning cloaks all at once. With their voracious appetites, it was a challenge to keep them well fed on a daily basis until about two weeks later—when all of the caterpillars suddenly disappeared. I began searching the exposed wooden beams and side panels of the unfinished attic for chrysalides and ended up finding many of the drab brownish and angular vessels but certainly not all of them. The chrysalis hangs down from a tiny button of silk securely affixed to a solid substrate; it is very easy to pass by as it blends into the muted wood and shadows. Seeing this told me something interesting about gregarious caterpillars. While mourning cloaks thrive as clustered eggs and caterpillars, they clearly scatter to form the chrysalides. Since I did not find chrysalides clumped together in the attic, I presumed this behavior would hold true in the wild as well. In nature, the caterpillars, when fully grown, wander away from the food plant, dispersing widely over the terrain to form chrysalides in secluded and hidden locations. Indeed, I have tracked and watched on a daily basis a rookery of mourning cloak caterpillars in a willow bush only to, very suddenly, have found them gone, not a single one left on the plant. Having a knot of these caterpillars holed up in an attic gave me a chance to witness a massive hatch of the butterflies a few weeks later and I was able to set them free through an attic window: a near-perfect exercise for a budding scientist.

The complete cycle of the mourning cloak has not been fully studied, to my knowledge. Yet this place, I do know, will have a fresh crop of newly hatched butterflies by midsummer, and most likely a second brood by early autumn. And while we know very little about the seasonal progression in the population cycles of the mourning cloak, the following pattern appears likely for most years in our area. Overwintering adults lay eggs early in spring and this brood matures into a wave of fresh butterflies, hatching from early June through mid-July, depending on the prevailing weather patterns of each year. These butterflies, a summer brood, mate and lay eggs that mature into a second pulse of fresh mourning cloaks during August and September, and it is mostly the survivors from this brood—individuals like the one on the sap flow today—that overwinter. I remain convinced that the best times to see mourning cloaks are right now, in early spring, and again in autumn. In midsummer, they seem to be less conspicuous; perhaps this has something to do with there being many more kinds of butterflies on the wing and many creatures vying for our attention. But it also must have something to do with the pulsing of their broods through the seasons.

I am always pleased to spot a mourning cloak on a tree sap wound; it is not always easy to find one. Despite the frailty we usually assign to a butterfly, I see an uncanny sturdiness in the mourning cloak, a creature able to survive the rigors of a northern winter. Here in its realm, I appreciate how the apparently simple observation of a stately, dark-winged butterfly flitting through the woods can set us on an adventure into the deeper layers of nature's complexity. The presence of that single butterfly today reflects events that took place last summer and autumn and testifies to a safe passage through winter. In that one butterfly resides a promise of continuance beyond this time, of more mourning cloaks, more renewals, another spring, another summer.

The mourning cloak, I believe, holds many lessons about the diversity of life around us, most of which usually go unseen and unnoticed. One of these lessons is especially poignant: every woodland, field, or meadow is powerfully knit together by the action of animals. The mourning cloak cannot exist without the sap flows; it cannot exist without woodsy crannies in which to overwinter; it cannot thrive without swamp willow. Earth's little creatures, like this dark-winged winter-hardy butterfly, enlighten us about the interconnections among the places and species that bind life together.

Spring Peepers

Even after many years of studying nature, I am still amazed at how clear particular first experiences remain in the recesses of my mind. Part of this, I am sure, has to do with the many reminders of them I've since encountered. Take, for example, spring peepers, a quasi-tree frog about half an inch long that is widely distributed throughout much of eastern North America. The spring peeper (*Pseudacris [Hyla] crucifer*) is without question one of my favorite frogs.

I remember cold spring late afternoons 40 years ago, crawling on my belly toward a golf course drainage ditch swelled almost to overflow by a thaw. From the low, matted dead brush sticking up through the slow-moving flowage came the soft purr of the peepers. Their endearing persistent chirping filled the dusk spring air long before many songbirds and the calling insects appeared on the scene. My goal was always to catch some for a closer look, but usually I failed. Many times I came very close to a spot along the ditch where I thought a spring peeper might be, only to discover that the frog's call had played tricks on me.

The dilemma reminded me of how frustrated I'd been while trying to find a male snowy tree cricket stridulating away on a hot summer evening in a bush. The creature's song pulled me closer but at the last moment, or so it seemed, the cricket itself was not at all in the vicinity of the foliage where I'd felt sure it was perched. Nor was this limited effectiveness due simply to the inexperience of a teenager, for even now, after many years of practice, I still find it difficult at times to pinpoint the locations of frogs or crickets by their calls.

Spring peepers are just downright hard to find, especially when they are singing under a dusk sky in spring or fall. But every once in a while I have gotten lucky and spotted one. A slight movement, perhaps a readjustment of the calling posture from a grass stem to a dead leaf, would give the frog's position away. That tiny, slow movement of a leg coupled

31

with the dark brown X on the animal's light brown back, called attention to its presence. No amount of experience can negate the need for luck in these situations, though, for only through sheer coincidence can even a trained observer be staring at the right clump of grass stems just when the creature moves a bit on its perch.

Perhaps with more tenacity and persistence, I could have increased my success rate a little bit, but not much. Whenever I did find a peeper, I would sometimes enclose it in my hands and place it in a jar to observe up close, setting it free where I had captured it later. The few times I have held a male spring peeper in a jar, it sat motionless and silent. Captive peepers seem pathetic somehow, wan, far from the posturing and camouflaged beauty they exhibit on the muted mulch outdoors. My goal was not to keep the frogs, but rather to find one, keep it close at hand for a little while, and then return it to the wild, but the peepers, of course, could not have known that.

Did you ever examine a tiny tree frog up close as it sits literally flattened against clear glass? Holding the bottle or jar up to the light, you can almost see straight through the animal's delicate body. You can make out its fine bone structure, trace the coursing of its gut, and catch yourself counting the pulses of its quick-paced breathing. It is possible to learn quite a bit about the life of an amphibian by holding it up in a jar against the light. Sometimes I have even caught the gleam in its large eyes. Catching the frog in the first place, in order to have this experience, is the hard part.

The capture would appear to be easy at first—especially when you're standing at the edge of flowage, peering down into a water-filled thicket throbbing with the concerted calls of perhaps a hundred peepers. As you move closer most of them stop singing, but a few persist. Still there is about a 90 percent chance that you will not find a single one. And it is not because they are submerged in the dark cold water, because most spring peepers sit in leaf litter or low brush at the edge of the water to call in a breeding chorus made up solely of eager male frogs seeking females. In the lingo of the biologist, the males are chorusing to assemble females for breeding.

After having spent the winter hibernating in the leaf litter and rotting logs that fill the woods, male frogs head for a pool or ditch after the first thaws. Since the peeper is a forest frog, small in size and vulnerable, it breeds in the fishless temporary pools rather than in permanent ponds, lakes, and streams. Females follow males to the breeding pool, and mating takes place at dusk and just after dark. Mated, gravid female peepers then lay eggs singly in the water, attaching each one to a piece of submerged plant debris.

Spring peepers are not the only amphibians to occupy the ephemeral

niche of spring pools and sporadic drainage ditches. A much larger species, the wood frog, gets there first to breed, arriving even before peepers. In addition chorus frogs and at least two species of salamander breed there too. All things considered, the vernal pools provide a considerable food base to support a reasonably diverse population of frogs. Only bullfrogs and green frogs eschew these pools, primarily because they have a two-year growth phase and require permanent water for breeding.

Spring pools, however, even when fishless, are notoriously tricky places for frogs, especially small ones. The game is to develop quickly and leave before the water dries up as spring turns to summer. The fragile, bulbous-headed spring peeper tadpoles usually develop within four to eight weeks by grazing on algae and nutritive detritus adhering to submerged rocks and stems. At the end of this time, they are fully terrestrial and scatter as a new generation into the surrounding woods. Because they do not have toxic skins, as do some tree frogs, and because of their small size, spring peepers are prized food for a variety of animals, from the big predaceous diving beetle, certain dragonfly naiads, and leeches in the pools to sandhill cranes, bluejays, shrews, ground beetles, and centipedes on land. The peeper, even though a vertebrate animal, is noticeably smaller and more fragile in design than some insects and other arthropods haunting these woods and pools, but groups of calling males at spring pools still set themselves up for being discovered and eaten by birds, mice, and shrews—animals capable of hearing their chorus. Once the adult frogs scatter in the forest, they become somewhat less vulnerable.

The places that nurture young peepers are complex and fascinating. Spring ponds especially, it seems, teem with a peculiar assortment of animals, all with habits designed to allow them to develop rapidly before the water goes away for another year. Some dragonflies, for example, mature only in temporary pools, a good indication that these bodies of water can support major carnivores. Together with diving beetles, libellulid dragonflies or odonates tend to be "sit and wait" attackers, while diving (dytiscid) beetle larvae vigorously tread water as very active hunters. The main prey of both groups are larval anurans (tadpoles). Dragonfly nymphs gravitate toward frog eggs and tadpoles, while dytiscids pursue larger tadpoles in these pools. Together the diving beetle larvae and odonate nymphs or naiads can exert considerable pressure on frogs in these pools.

One thing I have come to appreciate over the years is that seemingly sloppy and haphazard pools of standing water created by spring thaws are in fact key natural features of our landscape, whether located in forest or on old farmland, and they support an amazingly diverse array of life. The temporary pool's recurrent wet and dry phases within each year, together with its tendency to appear every year in the same place, gives it some semblance of seasonally interrupted permanency, and the unpredictable beginnings and endings of its wet phases establishes a habitat that can only be occupied by certain creatures.

First and foremost, the animals that live in spring pools must have the means of dealing with their ephemeral condition. Creatures that cannot migrate when the water dissipates have to burrow into the mud and survive for a long time, even when the mud becomes hard-baked by summer's heat. Whether mature or not, these animals have to stay inactive until the following spring when the pools fill up again. This obviously is quite chancy. A winter with light snowfall means a shallow pool or even no pool at all. Other animals, unable to withstand staying inactive down in the hard earth through summer, have the choice of migrating to more permanent bodies of water by the time the pools dry up. Either way, creatures that live in these pools must synchronize their life cycles so that the appropriate phase or phases are completed before dryness sets in.

For two spring seasons many years ago, when I was a graduate student in zoology at the University of Chicago, my thesis research advisor, Thomas Park, took us to temporary pond sites in suburban Chicago as part of his field zoology course. As we waded through the frigid water in hip boots, seining for creatures in the deep brown water, I was impressed by just how many kinds of animals appeared in the samples. We found small snails, chironomid midge larvae, water boatmen, diving beetle larvae, damselfly larvae, various crustaceans, and bright red aquatic mites. Very quickly I realized that these ponds, which became bone-dry by early summer, nurtured a lot of life in a relatively short breeding period. They also hosted very high numbers of some species and very low ones of others. Researchers have found that even among species able to breed in more permanent water, those who choose to do so in the temporary pools— where certain predators are absent—reach greater numbers even when the time period for breeding is quite compressed.

While spring peepers and other amphibians make their way from the surrounding land into woodland temporary pools to breed, other colonist species, in the form of insect eggs adhering to the feet of passing waterfowl, drop into the pool from the sky, while still others awaken from the softening mud below. This rich influx of life establishes an ecological battlefield within the little pool, a network of interconnecting creatures competing for limited resources and contending with short breeding times and carnivory. All these biotic interplays help enrich the decaying leaf mulch that slips into the pool as it forms with the thaw. What happens is that a miniature ecosystem of sorts develops in the water, complex enough in its own organization and design, but not disconnected from the surrounding landscape and sky. Spring rains add more to the pools. Sunshine first helps fill and then drain them. Spring peepers simply enter into this arthropod-dominated domain, their eggs and tadpoles becoming food for larger animals looking for an early meal. Many frog eggs may go into these pools; later, far fewer adult frogs are matured from them.

The life challenges of spring peepers offer important lessons to humanity, I believe. When resources are unpredictable from one year to the next and fleeting at best, the creatures exploiting them are rushed to breed and leave. Temporary pools, then, despite their humble appearance, are critical. Rich in rotting mulch and small lifeforms, they are key entities in the long-term success and well-being of forests, and thus cannot be dismissed lightly. They support the existence of not only midges, bugs, beetles, and frogs, but that of many larger creatures as well. What many of the approximately 200 species of returning songbirds often need the most in late spring are large stores of insects on which to nourish themselves and feed to their fledglings. Temporary pools, with the capacity to warm up faster than deep-water permanent ponds and lakes and thereby to produce populations of springtime flying insects quickly, are vital links in the sustenance of these bird populations. The adult insects fly off attempting to reach other bodies of water and fall victim to songbirds returning to these parts on the northward migration.

When I listen to courting spring peepers in the forest, I worry that we're ignoring this lesson. Many common human activities—filling in drainage ditches, shaving earth off the land and changing its natural contours, and emptying wetlands—destroy temporary pools and threaten the frail network of creatures that need them. In the spring peeper, a small and easily dismissed creature to many, I see a symbol of the need to conserve the pools, to reaffirm their vital role in the cycles of life that define a healthy northern woodland and old field. Both peepers and pools play crucial roles in the great recycling project that is nature. Thawing snow and ice first creates a broth or brew of rotting plant and animal matter, which in turn supports legions of mold, bacteria, algal plants, and eventually animals. The spring peeper, in one sense at least, is the recycled detritus and scum of this place; later on the fledgling jays, mice, and dragonflies will become part of the reworked nutrient profile of spring peepers.

By midsummer the breeding places and the chirping song of the spring peeper will be gone, and the peepers too will have moved, but not far. Clinging to the foliage and stems of forest shrubs, they will be eating flies, ants, spiders, and other small insects, participating not as springtime balladeers and breeders, but as little carnivores in the design of life here. This is the marvel of metamorphosis. A creature is born as a grazer of pool scum and organic garbage. Then at a certain special moment, triggered and commandeered by chemistry, temperature, and sunlight, it becomes an adult, and now a carnivore. This transformation illustrates nature's capacity to grasp opportunity; thus a spring peeper's existence in this woods asks us to grasp the basic principles of competing resources and food supply. On one level, survival is a matter of anatomical and genetic architecture, physiology, and behavior. On another, it is a matter of how well the peepers have met basic requirements of existence: food production, reproduction, avoidance of extinction.

Consider for a moment the overall survival plan of an amphibian species. Although they may mate on land, amphibians need water for their eggs and hatchlings. Now consider the spring peeper, an ecological perfectionist who specializes in the art of the temporary. Spring pools and flooded ditches present an opportunity for which there are relatively few takers, but the peeper seizes and makes the most of it and thus allows its species to move as a population once a year from an aquatic existence to an air-breathing terrestrial lifestyle. The very same creature goes from eating scum to being a stalker of game.

The beauty of natural history is that we must be fairly dedicated to understand such a transformation. Appreciating this planet's countless smaller creatures, even those quite close at hand, requires time and patience, but out of such effort grows a respect for all living things. Standing in a forest such as this one on a bone-chilling day near dusk allows the forces that have sculpted the network of life here to begin to make sense. Encountering the secretive spring peeper helps reveal the inner workings of this habitat. Often it is the smallest creatures that give us great insights into nature, for they function almost literally as the living bricks and mortar of a woodland, field, or forest network of spring pools.

I find great joy in walking the woods in spring, just when life is awakening after the long cold, and often come here again and again. At first there appears to be nothing afoot and stirring. Then suddenly the air is filled with a symphony of peeper song and its hopeful message that life has survived winter. These descendants of past growing seasons sing of life's renewal, a continuance of the species beyond now. The spring peeper's music coats the surface of what is happening in these woods; otherwise, except for the patter of rain, the whoosh of a breeze, or the scurrying of a squirrel, all is very silent. If the peeper music ever stops, fades away in spring seasons yet to come, the earth is in big trouble.

We are already losing our frogs. As has recently come to light, amphibians worldwide have been steadily vanishing since the 1960s. Because amphibians are good indicators of environmental damage—serving as the veritable canary in the coal mine—this is cause for serious alarm. Our forests are changing and not for the better. It is virtually impossible to find one that has not been contaminated recently by the by-products of human activities. Pesticides, fertilizer run-off, and other chemicals are killing off frogs and other wildlife. Toxic chemicals and pollutants are erasing whole food chains in mulch and thaw waters, splintering the complex interconnections that once linked detritus, bacteria, insects, and tadpoles into a cornerstone of life in a tiny, temporary pool. We are changing the chemistry of snow and rain with atmospheric discharges, bulldozing wetlands and forests. It will be a very sad spring for all of us when we no longer hear the deep woods chant of the spring peeper and other woodland frogs.

So I take this opportunity to enjoy the sounds of the spring peeper where and when I can, one spring to the next. Sometimes when winter has been slow in coming, fooling the frogs into a false sense of spring so that they breed early, I might even hear them in the fall. In summer, when their songs are drowned in the cacophony emerging from many other small creatures, I must simply trust that the peepers will come again with spring. But the seasons are fickle here in the north. Like much of nature, they steadily ask us to bend, to pause, to pay attention to the minutia we're free to ignore elsewhere. They remind us that we can't predict the return of the peepers by the calendar or the almanac or any of our other tools; we have to watch the weather and simply come here, again and again, listening until we hear the fleeting melodies of frog song. They, along with the rest of the life sounds in the forests and fields, right now are setting the mood, tone, and tempo of an unfolding acoustical drama. We are called first to attention by the spring peepers, whose impending silence welcomes warmer days; then, as summer arrives, the repertory of returning songbirds and frogs from permanent water will sound. Much later the insect musicians will enter, and although by this time the peepers' melodies will have faded, nature remembers them and keeps their promise alive: after winter comes the spring.

Summer

Walking through a meadow on this summer morning near the western rim of this great lake, the scene suddenly shifts back 40 years to another meadow and a distant hot summer. I am pushed ever so gently across a hallowed threshold, engulfed by a living time machine: the wonder of a lower Hudson River Valley meadow's summer magic long ago merges with the seasoned perspective of what many fields here in the Midwest have taught me since.

Each walk through a meadow in summer is a trek toward enlightenment about the wonders of the natural world, how a meadow or old field comes to be, how it works, and how it is tied to the landscape. This is not to say that a meadow holds little interest in other seasons, for there is much to see and learn here throughout the year. But in summer a meadow boldly displays the full range of its many wares, catching our eye and asking us to seek the secrets sprawling here. Summer for me is best reflected in the metallic-sheened glory of a field's riotous tapestry of insect life. Embedded within are the intricately webbed interrelationships among the myriad creatures living here.

Most meadows I am familiar with are low-slung places, marshy at times but not true marsh, and often corralled by forest. Because a meadow is filled with a mixture of herbaceous plants and low woody brush, it is an excellent place to find all sorts of insects and spiders. When you walk slowly through a meadow on a hot, steamy day, heat drums in your ears and pulls your attention many directions at once. I have known this for a long time, of course, but my first summer forays into a meadow more than 40 years ago are still embossed, like the trace etchings of bark beetles on old wood, on my mind.

I used to spend endless hours exploring a meadow across the road from our house in New York. Bounded by a river, an oak tree-lined road with homes, and a distant woodland and swamp, this meadow brimmed with beautiful flowers such as Joe-Pye weed, milkweed, Queen Anne's lace, and goldenrod, all held motionless in August by a stifling heat bath and humidity thick enough to slice with a butter knife. The dense sultry air danced with buzzing bees, wasps, and flies and rang with the incessant drumming of cicadas, the collective legacy of summer's natural harvest. Amidst all this beauty and symphony was a spatter of butterflies, a riotous, shifting patchwork of russets, yellows, and deeper tones bobbing among the sea of flowers. The magenta heads of the plentiful Joe-Pye weed especially seemed to lure throngs of black swallowtails, great spangled fritillaries, monarchs, red admirals, and many other butterflies. My reference point for exploring was a tiny brook that ran through the meadow and snaked off into the distant woods. The brook's gurgling crystal-clear water, a ribbon of shimmering silver, yielded its own legacy of insect life, including incredible metallic green damselflies with coal-black wings.

At night, even though I could not see the meadow, I could hear it stirring with life through my open window. All sorts of noises leaped in. I eventually learned that sleek cone-headed grasshoppers, hidden head downward in tall grasses, pounded the humid night air with their constant "zip-zip-zip" one-line melody. Leaf-green bush katydids gave raspy calls from small pockets of swamp willow and tall crowned weed stalks. Not surprisingly, I was easily enticed to venture out armed with a flashlight to explore the nightlife.

Searching the meadow at night, seeing what the beam of the flashlight caught when cast this way and that through the tall, dew-crusted brush, always had an air of the clandestine about it. On a clear night, bright stars and the moon aided my hunt for insects, and at such times, everything else seemed distant. The glare of nearby streetlights and lighted windows slipped away; insect songs muffled the roar of passing cars. This nighttime chorus was embellished by the very different and loud calls of true katydids perched in the highest foliage of the old, stately oaks and maples that filled the neighborhood. Somehow all this gave the summer night a magical quality, as if these creatures were claiming their dominance over the landscape. The meadow's complexion changed drastically from day to night, as if two wholly different sets of creatures, mostly hidden, lived on the same spot. Which indeed they did.

Looking back across those many years to that distant meadow, I am now thankful that our house had a big porch in front and no air conditioning. We sought the coolness of the porch when summer's heat seemed unbearable, and there were treated to the music of the night, the serenades of katydids and crickets. Screened windows and porch sittings brought us close to this natural wonder; we did just fine without freon-treated air. We functioned well keeping a close relationship with our meadow. It never occurred to us to try to block it out of our lives.

Every foray into our meadow—whether undertaken in the dark or broad daylight—was mystical and addictive to me. I didn't overthink the approach: it was more a matter of haphazard meandering, of heading this way and that, inching my way along the brook's edge, charging into the tall brush, or seeking the woodlands at the far perimeter. I have never tired of the quest or found a meadow that didn't intrigue me. And my associated passion for insects has simply moved apace as well, never diminishing in the least, but flourishing always and in the process giving me an unexpected gift: insects have melted away the years, making one composite rich experience of many summers and many meadows.

There is much to learn and understand about a meadow, of the interconnections among its species and its living ecological glue, and the lessons by no means add up to a completely peaceful, simple story. Survival games are waged by all of the creatures that dwell here and much of what goes on is a matter of life and death. Nor is it straightforward or elementary. But, because any meadow is not the same from one summer season to the next, much less from one day to the next, every effort to learn something about it is often rewarded with discovery. This is so, however, only if I choose to look hard. It is one thing to gaze at a meadow, relishing the beauty of its flowers, the lazy soar of its butterflies, and everything else that is easily obvious to the human eye and ear. It is another matter entirely to pay attention closely enough to begin to understand what is really going on here.

Even in the depths of a glorious summer, meadows are moody. A sunny day bathes the place in a warm, colorful glow electrified with the buzzing of bees, wasps, and flies, while a day of steady overcast yields gloom and enforcing silence even as it helps ensure new life to come in the weeks ahead. An early wet, warm spring gives the meadow crisp, lush foliage and crest upon crest of flowers. This well-orchestrated floral exuberance sets the stage for bumper crops of wild bees, butterflies, beetles, grasshoppers, bugs, and more. By contrast, in a dry cool year, the meadow's face has less sparkle. Yet even when summer's arrival is late, as it was this year here in the Midwest when our faith that the season would even arrive was put to the test, the meadow, groggy from winter and a cool spring, like the forest and wetland, stirs to life and blooms.

Still, while no meadow is the same as another, and every meadow changes through time, each challenges us to explore and understand. The meadow in which I stand now is no exception. Even the mundane matter of siting—determined by the joint forces of soil, mulch, land contours, climate, and neighboring woods, farms, and lake bluffs—ties into the larger story. Rock gives way to soil over time. Glaciers reworked the rock along the western lake edge, thickening the soil and endowing it with a natural fertility fortified by a rich organic mulch that accumulates on top of the soil. The rolling landscape, fierce winters, and gusty spring storms continue to create cascades of branches, leaves, and animal carcasses (from tiny ants to deer) which infuse the soil with life-giving substances. Millions of bacteria, fungi, tiny mites, and insects then massage the earth, establishing a healthy bed for seeds, shoots, tubers, and suckers, the collective underpinnings of the meadow's thick and bountiful plant life.

I am one for leaving meadows be, to allow them their own course of evolution. Some people argue for mowing them, for aesthetic reasons or in the belief that this somehow duplicates the patchy effects of grazing by herd mammals in ancient times. But mowing shaves off everything to the same level, eradicating the foliage needed by butterflies for their eggs and caterpillars. Mowing also paves the way for invasions of exotic plant species, whose vigor often pushes aside native species. The complex etchings of life in the meadow were established in millennia preceding the ice ages. Many factors, including fire, floods, animal grazing, and drought, have shaped the ecological mosaic that is a meadow. Mowing it removes this rich, ancient heritage, cuts off the supplies of nectar needed by butterflies and other insects, and shreds up potential pupation sites for caterpillars.

Less than three months ago, this particular unmown meadow was little more than a fresh green stubble poking through the brown, matted carpet of last season's growth. Now, with summer marching toward us, the full glories of this place emerge. Only in the past few weeks have the sounds of katydids, cicadas, and crickets been heard in full force. Their concerted clatter this afternoon offers a soothing respite from the electronic noise of human technologies, hinting again at the larger patterns of the natural world. Strong flying insects, especially butterflies, moths, cicadas, and flies, move between forest and meadow, their lives intimately tied to both places, not just one of them. Cicadas born of forest trees court in the sunshine of the meadow, perching in shrubs such as swamp willow or pockets of wild cherry trees. Tiger swallowtail butterflies, growing up as caterpillars in the ash thickets along the border with the woods, plunder the rich stores of nectar from meadow wildflowers. Near dusk and after dark, hoards of mosquitoes and other swarming flies exit the woods and fill the air above the meadow; brown bats and green darner dragonflies, eager to graze upon them, tag along behind.

Sometimes the boundary between forest and meadow literally blurs with the movement of animals. Energy flows back and forth in a subtle, yet bold process that transgresses the borders—and the very notion of them—with apparent abandon. In other instances the line between meadow and woods stays sharp and clear. There are forest frogs with habits very distinct from meadow frogs and treetop-dwelling katydids that spend their entire lives (one summer) in the forest. There are also a remarkable number of insects here that were raised well beyond both the meadow and the forest.

A big ten-spot dragonfly darts swiftly back and forth just above the patch of goldenrod, systematically plucking off flies and bees attracted to the yellow, pollen-laden flowers. These chocolate brown and powdery white dragonflies grew up as carnivorous nymphs in a pond somewhere on the other side of that distant woods, well away from here. Adults are then lured into the meadow by its vast legions of flying insects. Land and water conjoin in the design of a dragonfly's habitat. The meadow centers survival—makes it possible—even to creatures who only visit temporarily.

Locust borers, slender black and yellow beetles that blend in well with the flowers, are scurrying across the goldenrod flowers too. This insect depends on both the tree-studded bluffs of the lake and the meadow for its survival. Locust trees line the rugged lakeshore, and locust borer larvae bore through the iron-tough wood of the tenacious colonizing tree. Although there are no locust trees in the meadow, adult locust borer beetles are equally happy to feed on the pollen and nectar of goldenrod blooms.

The true backbone and integrity of this place, I believe, lies buried within its colorful displays. Like all natural places, meadows are vast plundering grounds where every creature seeks to exploit others for food even as it is also becoming food for others. There is no escaping, no turning away from, this basic axiom of life. And yet there is a sense of balance about it, albeit one we may never fully understand.

The stunning beauty of many creatures in this meadow, like the magnificent viceroy butterfly sipping nectar at Joe-Pye weed blossoms nearby, helps to reaffirm this deeper story. The viceroy's bold colors make it stand out, an easy target for a watchful bird. But viceroys are rarely eaten because of their bitter taste, which depends upon the swamp willow. On rare occasions, I find a viceroy caterpillar, an angular brown and white mottled creature, eating willow foliage. Mother viceroys carefully place their eggs on willows, and the caterpillars obtain the plant's defense poisons as they graze, without any ill effects to themselves. The poisons are carried through the chrysalis stage into the adult butterfly, and their purpose seems clear enough. Yet here we can see one lesson of the meadow coming into focus. Shrubs like willows, which grow well in the meadow, defend themselves against the onslaught of insects, most of which eat fresh foliage, by producing poisons or chemical smoke screens that discourage attack and feeding. In response, some insects, like the viceroy butterfly or the bright red milkweed beetle feeding on milkweeds, overcome this defense and not only feed on the plant, but also exploit its poisons to protect themselves. These creatures then fall victim to parasitic flies and tiny wasps that, despite the toxins, feed on their caterpillars. The connections are dense, multilayered, and incredibly intricate, yet there is a sense of ecological balance to a meadow. Every resident here has a set of interlinked purposes for existence.

Take, for example, that cluster of yellow sulfur butterflies gathered around the edges of that mud puddle. We used to believe puddling butterflies were drinking water, thirsty in such mercilessly hot weather, but now we know better, thanks to science. Those tiger swallowtails and sulfurs are there not to drink, but to obtain precious traces of salts concentrated in evaporating water. Males need the salts to make the scent necessary to court females. So the meadow's story is not simply about basic connections—the provenance of food, water, and energy—but about all the obscure, quirky activities underlying them. Just coming here isn't sufficient; to hear the meadow's lessons, we have to exert some effort.

To that end, I raise my sturdy sweep net and swing it back and forth just a few times through the goldenrod and then dump its contents on a white sheet. My zigzagging walk toward the goldenrod flushes out hoards of red-legged grasshoppers shooting off like bottle rockets in all directions, and the sheet is littered with insects in a matter of seconds. There must be at least ten species of spiders, a dozen species of leaf hoppers, two kinds of crickets, and 20 species of beetles. Although it appears chaotic, there is ecological balance in this little smorgasbord. Multiplying the speck of biological diversity crawling across the sheet at this moment by several thousandfold gives a good inkling of the meadow's complexity, most of which does not quickly meet the eye. The life on this sheet proves the point: the landscape speaks to us when we probe it.

A bald-faced hornet is weaving and dodging like a menacing black-and-white helicopter through very tall Queen Anne's lace searching for soft-bodied insects, especially moth caterpillars, to sting, slice up with its strong jaws, and shape into tiny meat patties to feed its brood. No doubt there is a large hornet's nest in the stand of tall trees across the way. Hornets and wasps need forest trees and field bushes to build their elaborate paper nests off the ground, and open meadows to find the food for themselves and their brood, which is bulging by late summer. Wasps, who rely on vast amounts of caterpillars for sustenance, dampen the spread of garden pests and forest defoliators. They also trip pollination devices while rummaging for nectar, thus helping our native meadow plants to set seed. Seeing such things and learning to respect them, I begin to understand the meadow. Sun, rain, mulch, and soil establish plant life. Dead plant matter is recycled into bacteria, fungi, mites, and much more. Insects like caterpillars, leafhoppers, leaf beetles, and grasshoppers are recycled living plant tissues. Spiders, wasps, assassin bugs, dragonflies, and others are recycled foliage insects. Songbirds are recycled insects and spiders. Field mice are recycled seeds, fruits, and insects.

But the meadow is no utopia, and the ways of the insectan world are not peaceful. Nature's game is conflict and competition: being eaten, avoiding it, or eating something else. Insects offer important lessons about the point and counterpoint dynamics of these natural contests. What is truly beautiful about insects, truly breathtaking, though, is their design and behavior. It is the agility of a dragonfly catching flies on the wing. It is the logistical triumph of a heavy bumblebee collecting pollen from a flower. It is the means by which many caterpillars feed on noxious plants without getting ill and dying. It is the exquisite, precise architecture of a wasp nest and the industrious, efficient organization of an ant colony. It is all of these things and very much more. And it is almost beyond my comprehension. When you seek out such details in a meadow, the place indeed comes alive in ways hard to imagine in advance.

As much as I enjoy spending long summer days wandering across wild landscapes such as meadows in search of insects, however, I also regularly experience wonderful moments of insectan discovery close to home— sitting on a deck overlooking my backyard in August, for example. Although we seldom construe them as untamed, yards can also be wild spaces, even when gussied up with manicured grasses and ornamental beds. My backyard is a shamble of some lawn and a generous dose of wild plants, some native, others maverick exotics here on their own means. And I like it precisely because it still feels a bit like a meadow.

When August days are really hot and humid and the air a wall of thick stuffiness, I am out on the deck watching. The afternoon air is richly charged with a steady, piercing buzz, the songs of unseen cicadas perched high above in an old silver maple tree. On these days, steamy and stifling, long and lazy, my narrow yard with its wild edges of thick foliage resembles a Rousseau-like tableau of a tropical paradise minus the big game. No matter, for my quest has always been small game anyway. Bouts of heavy thunderstorms and steady, even heat create an envelope of mugginess, uncomfortable for most people but absolutely perfect for wildlife. In the yard, the weed patches are taller and the foliage unusually lush. Even my little patch of tomato plants near the rear of the yard is rivaling me for height: topping six feet. The whole effect is one of satiation, a bit of land redolent with life's potential.

Of course, as is the case for meadows and forests too, not all summers are this way. Some are dry, others cool, and at these times, the landscape's vitality is noticeably toned down. Life's eagerness to blossom is dampened. The best summers for my purposes are the ones with record-breaking heat waves and rolling thunderstorms. These are times of great insect activity, mirroring the propensity for life to excel when heat and moisture prevail, and the bustling meadow brims over to fill places like my yard or the city parks.

Sometimes, when I am on the deck, I notice yellowjackets and other paper wasps gnawing on its frayed, worn wood. They are crafting slivers of the tough fiber as construction material for their paper nests with no apparent concern for the fact that the deck is less "natural" than a tree at the meadow's edge might be. Late summer encourages work; wasps and other colonial insects such as bees and ants everywhere in these parts swell their nests with expanding ranks of workers, and raw materials become fodder, whatever their provenance. All of this is done in the name of life's continuance, a living, breathing promise for its renewal a year from now.

I cannot get over the beguiling surrealness of my yard on a hot muggy day. The scene by high noon is a shifting portrait of color, sound, and movement. Yet the air is heavy and the foliage dead still—at first glance, that is. Imperceptibly almost, the harvest picture comes alive: etched in the bold strokes of the deafening din of screaming cicadas, the helicopter antics of paper wasps stripping the deck, the crisscrossing of an occasional bumblebee above the grass, the buzzing bees and bottle flies pilfering pollen and nectar from a patch of purple coneflowers and black-eyed Susans hugging the sun-baked side of the garage, and the sudden arrival of a tiger swallowtail or a red-spotted purple butterfly. Taken together, in all their riotous glory, these summer insects are saving graces for my yard and me. So even when we live in cities, we still exist—in a very real, thorough way—*in* nature.

Of course, even in a semi-wild yard like mine, the richness of insect life nowhere approaches the complexity of that found in a meadow or old field. Life in the yard is compressed, fragmented, and kaleidoscoped. It is also interrupted and often poisoned with chemicals that come against my wishes. True, I can find an occasional caterpillar of the question-mark butterfly on one of the young elm saplings or an adult male of this species setting up its territorial mating space on the lilac bushes alongside the house. But the insectan cycles of life require bigger spaces occupied with many more species. Still, I am thankful for what I do see and hear in the yard come late summer.

Looking for insects in the backyard, as anywhere else, requires a healthy dose of time, patience, and sharpening of one's senses. I have learned to hone mine, to will my body to pay attention to the smallest details, the slightest movements, the non-sounds even. I come here often, training my ears and eyes to connect with what seems invisible, elusive. And I don't only come when the weather is warm either.

Five months beyond August, when ice and snow blankets the yard, I will be sitting on this deck, bundled up in a parka, bent on catching a glimpse of nuthatches working the dried buttons of the coneflowers, still high on their stalks, eating what seeds remain in them and the grubs buried in their fibrous tissues. Many of the birds that use my yard and the meadow year-round depend upon the seeds and insects that proliferate under the broiling sun of summer and its veil of humidity.

Sitting out here in the deadening cold of December, I always feel reassured, through the rattle of a few dead leaves still clinging to the branches, that next summer will bring forth a fresh band of insectan musicians in both the yard and the meadow. Deep in the soil, beneath the mulch, and tucked away in minute crevices in high branches are the safely ensconced young of cicadas, crickets, and katydids. Not all life perishes in winter; creative death in the cold elegantly changes life's suit and holds a promise for its full regality come next summer. The bone-chilling winds of winter call to mind the sun-drenched days of August.

But for now, today anyway, my thoughts are with the messages of summer, not winter. I look forward to the end of the day, when the heat begins to ebb and the golden sky in the west fades into dusk, filling the evening air with gnats. This is when the cicadas give their last call, and when moths and crickets awaken. It is also when the stillness and humid night air spits out fireflies. It is summer near the edge of a great lake.

Quite naturally, I suppose, I never want my insectan adventures to end here. Opportunities abound everywhere, all the time. This is a true joy— being able to step into the interconnected links of a continuous experience, walking always ever further into an ongoing adventure in meadow and yard. Tomorrow, next week, or next month, I will add more lines and shadings to my sketch of a meadow's intricate, shifting portrait. As I see more and think deeply about that which I have seen and hold with great awe whatever I have not, and if I manage to get beyond the surface beauty and the obvious, my sketch will be refined into a portrait that, by its own design, can never be completed. But forays into meadows and yards with such intent lets nature take over the pencil, paintbrush, and sketch pad, steering me toward understanding the heart and pulse of these hallowed places near the bluffs of this great lake.

Obviously I am very grateful for summer because it exposes insects in all of their fine details and perfections. But summer also helps me to appreciate the underpinnings of our natural world and our own species. All of this planet's larger creatures, from trees to deer to humans, depend on insects and other arthropods in one way or another. Being in a meadow or probing our backyards brings us face to face with the exquisite details of these bonds. And this is plain good therapy, medicine for both mind and spirit. This, to me, is part of what summer means.

At our latitude the growing season is relatively short and compressed.

All of life's theatrics here—breeding, sowing seeds, and planting eggs, eating and being eaten—illustrate the drive to continue one's own kind. Every activity is rushed and hurried. The key is to sense this purposeful, determined journey through its fine details. The signs are everywhere. Wildflowers drum with the buzz of bees, flies, and beetles; caterpillars, some subdued and others flashy, become chrysalides or fresh adults; paper wasps line the eaves of an old barn with a row of compact papercomb nests; the night air rings with the calls of crickets and the dabbled light show of fireflies. The area around streetlights crackles with the sounds of bats gnashing the bodies of moths and beetles. When these things are happening, life is guaranteed to go on. It is when they stop happening that we will be in deep trouble.

Summer may well be thought beautiful, warm and rich with life, benign and welcoming, but it is also the time in nature when the real beauty is brutal, hidden, and downright sneaky. For in summer, life is focused on one goal: to satisfy, as quickly as possible, the singular craving to be nourished and to make babies before fading away for a another year. This then, this frenzied struggle to wrest a living from lavish resources before they are gone, is the very essence of summer.

Monarch Butterflies

Perhaps you, like me, find pleasure looking to nature and natural history for living symbols of the seasons. Doing so gives human society an insightful collective identity through which to understand the ebb and flow of life. Our natural heritage, a continually changing mix of native species and transplants from afar, offers a challenging backdrop for such thoughts. The key, it seems, is to choose common symbols that tell deep, significant, uncommon stories about how existence wends its way from one season to the next in an unending cycle.

Some would opt for summer's symbol to be a bird, mammal, or wildflower, and there are many appropriate ones from which to choose. I, of course, would choose from among insects instead, not simply because I study them but because they comprise by far the largest slice of the diverse animal life on the planet. A useful symbolic summer insect ought first of all to be readily available in the out-of-doors. Beetles fill that requirement, since they are the largest group of insects. But while beetles have a stellar reputation as a diverse and intriguing group of creatures, most around these parts are small and difficult to see from any distance. A notable exception is the spectacular display of a flashing firefly—commonly called a fly, but in reality, a beetle to the core. A symbolic insect for summer, however, should secondly be easy to spot from a reasonable distance, especially in daytime. One excellent candidate meeting both criteria is the regal monarch butterfly, which belongs to the second largest group of insects, the Lepidoptera. This large orange and black creature is both common and easily spotted. Many of us know it well and have seen it drifting along above the milkweeds and other flowers, flapping its graceful wings a few times then swirling into a glide guided by air thermals alone.

The monarch butterfly is found across the entire continent, due in large part to the fact that its caterpillar food, a diverse group of herbaceous plants called milkweeds, is also widely distributed. Although the monarch and its food sources originated long ago in the American tropics, both moved northward in response to Ice Age changes in climate.

Milkweeds experienced great ecological success in North America over thousands of years, especially in what is now the United States, thus providing a solid foothold for the monarch to follow suit. A gravid mother monarch is an excellent chemist, knowing exactly how to recognize a milkweed by leaf texture, color, and scent. This strong dependency between plant and insect has been a marvelous lesson for many children in schools and nature center programs.

I do not remember exactly when it was that I first discovered monarchs. I do remember distinctly, though, the early thrill of riding my bicycle to a weed patch along the river near our home and finding many butterflies there, including monarchs. Several years later when our family moved to a neighboring village, Briarcliff Manor, a friend, Robert Heubner, and I set out together in search of them. Behind Bob's house there was a drainage ditch near the road and every summer plenty of milkweeds grew there. I would flip over the leaves wherever I saw large holes, hoping to catch the monarch caterpillars feeding. These hunts sometimes proved successful. It was especially nice to have a friend along to share the fun and the frustrations.

Perhaps you know this lesson as well as I do. Maybe you have seen a leaf-munching monarch many times. It's an easy caterpillar to identify after all, especially with its gaudy alternating bands of yellow, white, and black. The caterpillar chews the succulent, white latex sap-filled milkweed leaves and grows up in a matter of weeks. Then it shrinks a bit, spins a button of silk on a twig or stem (often not on a milkweed), snares its rear clasper in it, hangs down, and splits its skin, exposing a beautiful green chrysalis. There is a very tricky hitch to this procedure, one that must be deftly surmounted if the creature is to survive. At the very moment the cuticle splits away and shrivels up where the caterpillar has snared its hind claspers into the silk button, the new end of the chrysalis must be quickly tethered into the silk. Otherwise the soft, fragile chrysalis falls to the ground and dies. Since the original anchoring point of the caterpillar's cuticle is no longer working, the transfer must happen quickly and smoothly. As the outer shell of the plump chrysalis hardens, sets of tiny gold markings appear, making the creature, now neither caterpillar nor butterfly, a living jewel. If all goes well, within a few weeks the jewel will tarnish and crack open. A butterfly will emerge, expand and dry its wings, getting ready to soar off into the sunshine.

I have gleaned many of these basic principles of butterfly survival from hands-on experience: collecting caterpillars in the wild and rearing them in jars or plastic bags to see what develops as they grow and reach pupation. This is one place where having a wild garden in my own yard comes in handy. I thoroughly enjoy encouraging the monarch to be at home on land that technically belongs to me. As I cut grass with my old hand mower, a monarch butterfly suddenly floats into view, descending gracefully into the yard, and alights on a coneflower blossom. Soon a second one arrives. Several years ago I deliberately planted some pieces of milkweed's starchy tuber along one side of the yard opposite a patch of wildflowers. It took a year or two for the plants to appear, but the underground tubers slowly metastasized into a web of sprouting plants, eventually creating a milkweed patch that would attract monarchs.

This summer was the first time I discovered monarch caterpillars on my milkweeds. I counted this a small victory, even though all but one caterpillar disappeared long before coming close to being fully grown. Although I have seen small spiders lurking inside the young, furled leaves, yellowjackets probably snared them. I'm still happy with my observation, and see it simply as part of the greater story of life. Being a butterfly in fact, is a very chancy life at best. True, when there are lots of milkweeds and good weather, monarchs survive in greater numbers, increasing the chance of spotting them sipping nectar from purple coneflowers and black-eyed Susans in the yard come July or August. But even when they seem plentiful, the fact is that only a small fraction had actually survived to the butterfly stage. This is the case even though monarch caterpillars use the latex poisons in the foliage they eat to acquire a distastefulness repugnant to some enemies, such as birds.

Butterfly and moth caterpillars especially are highly attractive food targets for many kinds of parasitic flies and wasps whose existence depends upon finding these hosts on which to lay their eggs. In some situations, as in the group of parasitic flies called "tachinids," the eggs are sometimes laid on the caterpillar's food plant, close to where the caterpillar has been feeding. The flies are lured to these places by a special scent emitted from the plant tissue wounded by feeding caterpillars. Here the eggs have a good chance of being ingested along with plant tissue as food. Otherwise a parasitic fly or wasp uses the unique radar built into its antennae, the organs of smell, to locate the caterpillar and lay eggs directly upon its cuticle. Caterpillars employ violent head and front-end movements to chase away approaching flies or wasps, but the action does not always work. Either way, ingested or external, the parasite's larvae feed on the caterpillar, eventually weakening and killing it. The larvae then mature and pupate in the host or outside it. So even if monarchs as caterpillars are sometimes distasteful to birds, they are certainly not avoided by parasitic flies and wasps. In fact, strong signals associated with supposedly repugnant strains of milkweed might make it more likely that monarch caterpillars are attacked than caterpillars of other butterflies feeding on less noxious plants.

Considering the many natural enemies, from birds to spiders, ants, predatory bugs, and parasites, it is very unlikely that a monarch caterpillar will actually become a butterfly. But this circumstance is not to be mourned or disdained, for without such natural processes, much of our landscape would be gobbled up by caterpillars. Still, finding a monarch butterfly sipping nectar in a garden, perhaps looking fresh and vibrant from its chrysalis, is a testament to a grand act of survival against the odds. This is equally true for most butterflies and other insects as well.

While it might seem counterintuitive to claim that the presence of a beautiful butterfly in the garden or meadow represents intense warfare, this is in fact the case. Like all plant-eating insects, monarchs and their caterpillar food plants, the milkweeds, are locked in vital combat. In a common human manner of speaking: monarch the antagonist seeks to convert milkweed, the protagonist, into more butterflies, at the expense of the plant's energy that would otherwise have been used to make more leaves, flowers, and seeds. Scientists have discovered a wide range of defensive weapons in plants designed to thwart insect rampage. In the milkweeds, a latex-like sap with cardiac glycosides is the primary chemical defense, a repellent to most insects but amazingly an attraction for monarchs. The sticky white sap that oozes from a cut milkweed leaf or stem contains these glycosides and other key substances in the plant's chemical arsenal against insects. The stuff looks impenetrable by its appearance alone, but imagine how it can gum up an insect's mouthparts. Unlike most insects, the monarch and a small host of other species have successfully circumvented this line of milkweed plant defense, allowing them not only to eat the plant, but to incorporate the milkweed's chemical defense system into their own.

Caterpillars that feed on plants rich with milky, latex sap sometimes do surgery on a leaf before eating. A caterpillar snips a main vein of the leaf with its mandibles, slowing or stopping the flow of the latex to the area of the leaf where it will dine. Doing so facilitates feeding, even though the caterpillar still ingests small quantities of the liquid defense system. Monarch caterpillars munching on milkweed foliage, flowers, and stems, as with colorful milkweed beetles and bugs, ingest the glycosides along with the nutritional components of the tissues, absorbing them into their own bodies. Through the life cycle, the defensive chemicals pass through the chrysalis into the adult butterfly. Not all milkweed species and populations have identical chemical defenses, and some monarchs as adult butterflies are less distasteful to birds and animals than others—monarchs are by no means all equally immune from being eaten in the wild.

Another butterfly often seen every summer in these parts, one which looks a lot like the monarch, is the viceroy, an inhabitant of damp fields and meadows where one of its familiar caterpillar food plants, the swamp willow, thrives. Although somewhat smaller in wingspan than the monarch, the viceroy's wing colors and color pattern are very similar to the monarch's. Viceroys lay their eggs on willow leaves in summer, so the mottled, twig-like caterpillars, very different in appearance and behavior from the yellow, black, and white banded monarch caterpillar, can eat those leaves.

As with milkweeds, some species of willows are well endowed with chemicals that give the viceroy caterpillars and the adult butterflies a bitter taste to some animals attempting to eat them. Other willows are less defensive. For both monarchs and viceroys, the more bad-tasting their meat, the more likely their chances of surviving some natural enemies, but certainly not all of them. Because of similarities in the adult stage, the distastefulness of the monarch to predators in some instances may reinforce the unsuitability of the viceroy when their populations overlap in summer and vice versa.

The viceroy caterpillar is very distinct from the monarch caterpillar in other interesting ways. A late summer generation of young viceroy caterpillars prepares for winter on the food plant. Each caterpillar spins a silken tube inside a small willow leaf, anchoring the leaf to the stem with silk. The little caterpillar then passes winter inside this tube which, during the winter months, resembles a small dry leaf and thus perhaps escapes the attention of hungry nuthatches and other birds. When spring arrives and the willow produces new leaf buds, the caterpillar abandons its winter refuge and resumes feeding until fully grown and able to make the twig-like chrysalis on a branch.

I find this relationship between the monarch and viceroy intriguing from an evolutionary viewpoint. Each of these species belongs to a different group of butterflies, indicating different evolutionary origins and histories. Yet they have converged in some ways to resemble one another as adults living in the same or similar places and at the same time of the year. Their association certainly indicates the power of taking a new direction in environmental adaptation. Other butterflies closely related to the viceroy do not look like it at all, suggesting an opportunistic divergence. But close relatives of the monarch, other "milkweed butterflies," that is, do seem to be similar, suggesting that the viceroy adapted more to copy the monarch than the other way around.

For now, for this day, I am pleased simply to see the monarch butterfly in this summer landscape for, entirely aside from its outward beauty, it tells a much deeper story, exposing the inner beauty of its interconnections with other species and the role of ecological chemistry in the life struggle. This beauty reminds me that much of what is natural is an ecological battleground, a changing flexible network of interconnections among diverse species, a delicate system evolved over very long periods of time and too precious to be busted apart or tampered with by people with their penchant to conquer the landscape and its inherent wildness. Indeed, the monarch butterfly has much to say, much to tell us. It is a symbol rooted in lessons crucial to human survival.

There are other stories about nature reflected by the life-sustaining bondage between butterflies and plants and exemplified by the monarch. The northern summer is rife with optimistic opportunism in nature. Caterpillars, belonging to thousands of species of moths and butterflies, graze on a diverse bed of fresh foliage that gradually ages over summer like vintage wine. These grazers are plundered by carnivorous paper wasps, ambush bugs, ground beetles, and jumping spiders. Native bees and honeybees, during acts of pollination, pillage flowers for nectar and pollen and scrape stems and twigs for nest-building resins. Dragonflies near dusk descend on gardens, cleansing their airspaces of gnats and mosquitoes. After nightfall, they are replaced by bats on the same patrol. Ants churn up soil or mulch and bury seeds there. Songbirds stalk cicadas, katydids, and moths, plucking them from branches and foliage high above. The monarch, in its own natural tightrope game of survival, symbolizes all of this and much more.

The emerging message from these details of a butterfly's precarious existence says a lot about how insects in general guide evolution's paintbrush on a larger scale as well. A monarch butterfly is recycled milkweed tissues. Milkweeds are recycled soil nutrients and rotting vegetation. The ripe seeds in a milkweed pod become colorful seed-eating milkweed bugs and beetles. Milkweed flowers, rich with nectar and pollen, like purple coneflowers and black-eyed Susans, become bumblebees, honeybees, and butterflies. Those ethereal yellow crab spiders hanging in the flower heads are the recycled body fluids of snared bees, butterflies, and flies. Yellowjackets, spiders, and ambush bugs are recycled butterfly and moth caterpillars.

But the lesson does not end here. The monarch butterfly's migratory habit instills further wonder at the uncertainties of survival. Because of its tropical origins, the monarch is not able to withstand the winter season. Most butterflies cope with winter as a sheltered caterpillar or chrysalis; some survive as eggs, even fewer manage as winter-hardy adults. But not the monarch, a creature far more akin to the heat of summer than the deathly cold of a northern winter. Taking advantage of its tropical affinity, the monarch butterfly undertakes its famous migration every autumn from all points east of the Rockies to certain mountain slopes and defiles in Mexico to pass the winter. Here they hang by the millions from the branches and trunks of tall fir trees. So while the monarch cannot survive the northern winter in any stage of its life cycle because it does not possess the cold-hardiness of our resident native butterflies, it is still strong enough to make massive long-distance migrations comparable to those of our songbirds.

By the following spring, after mating, monarchs leave and head north, eventually laying eggs on freshly sprouting milkweeds in the southern United States. The first generation descendants of these colonists make up the bulk of the monarchs that usually arrive in the northern states by June, when milkweeds in these parts have appeared. It is really not until mid-June here, though, that milkweed plants have resprouted to a size of which a female monarch, recently mated, would take notice for laying eggs. Just how many monarchs arrive here each spring is tricky to sort out. Certainly it has something to do with the numbers surviving at over-wintering sites and the productivity of that first wave of new butterflies produced in the southern states from the offspring of the original mi-grants. But weather is also a factor. The interplay of warm fronts and cold fronts also shapes the size of the colonizing contingent of butterflies arriving here.

In the course of the summer season in the north, two or three over-lapping generations of monarchs are produced. Late-summer monarch caterpillars are physiologically different from early-season ones. The dif-ference has something to do with the shortening length of days by late summer, a signal causing changes in hormones and cell differentiation inside the caterpillar's body. As a result, the adult butterflies from these caterpillars are better designed structurally and behaviorally for long-distance migration than early-season butterflies. They have stronger wing muscles and larger fat reserves in their bodies, giving them the strength and sustenance needed to make a successful journey of a few thousand miles.

Because of the monarch butterfly's inability to spend the winter in North America east of the Rockies, the creature is best viewed as an an-nually colonizing species returning from a tropical mountain setting every spring to repopulate vast stretches of this continent. And, as such, the monarch is indeed an impressive beast: a colonist that evolved its coloniz-ing ability thousands of years ago. Milkweeds as a group probably spread into North America from the American tropics during the cycles of glaci-ation. Monarchs, as predators or parasites of milkweeds, followed suit. Colorful milkweed bugs and beetles, adorned with vivid red and black colors, and a colorful tiger moth all did the same thing—predators fol-lowing their prey, stalking their quarry. (I am reminded of the Arctic lynx and snowshoe hare locked into this formidable kind of combat as well.) But while milkweeds withstand winter either underground as starch-rich tubers or above ground as tough, wind-blown seeds, monarchs, with their still strong tropical roots, migrate, and it is highly unlikely that they will ever become cold-hardy.

Every spring and summer here in the north brings forth an onslaught of many similar seasonal colonizers. Winter thaws flood creeks and streams, creating new piles of mud and debris. The contours of the land change. New earth is ready to be occupied. Butterflies, dragonflies, songbirds, and waterfowl return from the south, bringing with them suites of bacteria, spores, seeds, and microscopic animal life. Colonizers piggybacking on colonizers. Nature's opportunism at its best. The ability of colonizing plants to thrive at the margins of habitats, in a sort of ecological no-man's terrain, has earned them the names of weeds or at least weedy species. Dandelions, creeping Charlie, garlic mustard, thistle, buckthorn, purple loosestrife, and honeysuckle are some of nature's loose cannons, imported from other parts of the world, and they are blamed along with other such exotic pests as the gypsy moth, the eastern tent caterpillar, and the zebra mussel for smothering out native species. Most of our serious pests, be they plant or animal, are imports. Some of them, like the gypsy moth, once considered to be a possible basis for a silk industry in this country, were brought here on purpose. Others have arrived unintentionally. Unfortunately, when imported species are introduced, they can proliferate early on because they often have few checks and balances, if any at all. In their native habitats, the same species are not pests largely because each one has its own natural enemies. Only when species are moved well outside their usual geographic areas are there problems. It can take a long time for a new balance to be struck.

The monarch butterfly, a non-invasive species that followed in hot pursuit of its caterpillar food plant is, therefore, not a pest. Its arrival was largely a matter of geographic range expansion in the same hemisphere—rather than one species being brought in by people from outside of its natural range. The antagonistic partnership between monarchs and the other splashy insects that eat milkweeds may have dampened the spread of these plants. But milkweeds survived this attack, in large part because of their long history on the continent. They have natural pollinators that help them make good seed. Enough passage of time, on the magnitude of many thousands of years, has allowed this to happen. Monarchs are thus part of the fabric of our native natural history. It will take a long time for many of our present-day pests to become part of our ecosystems, if they ever do. And a lot may be lost along the way.

Yet, contrary as it may be, at some point I find it intriguing to consider invaders in a different light. While I am not an advocate of allowing exotic species to push aside members of our native floras and faunas, I wonder: will it be appropriate at some point to rethink our view of nature, to perhaps simply view it as one big experiment of changing species, a view that embraces the eventual integration of exotic species into the landscape? Earth's history has not been a constant. Life is in a continual flux. Over many millions of years there have been cataclysmic changes, the shifting of continents, formation of land bridges, volcanic eruptions, movements of the seas, and much more. Other changes are gradual.

The Central American land bridge, which existed approximately 12 million years ago, allowed for a great interchange of flora and fauna between the two great continents of North America and South America. Could one not argue that such events reshuffled the ecological context of species by spurring numerous invasions of plants and animals into regions well beyond their original geographic ranges? Today, by and large, we consider much of the floras and faunas of the Americas to be natural assemblages, save for modern invasions of exotic species. So is the real issue one of time?

This is not to say that we should condone or encourage invasions of exotics. In fact, we should try to stop them from happening, especially when people, directly or indirectly, are the agents of transport. But perhaps the better part of prudence would have us actively cultivate a more long-term perspective. Rather than spending millions on the chemical eradication of the pesky gypsy moth, might it not be wiser to adopt the view that eventually natural control measures will subdue this insect over time as nature's continually changing complexion assumes new faces? As much as preservationists would like wilderness to be natural and pristine at any one point in time, it is never anything more than natural over time.

This view is also compatible with what we know about the monarch butterfly, which, in its initial spread across North America from the neotropics following the invasion of milkweeds into the continent by biogeographic events thousands of years ago, was an exotic species, a colonist attempting a foothold on new land. In this case, the insect succeeded, to a point. Every year it must renew its colonist status, undertake its extraordinary migratory habit. Thus I see the monarch as an ecological bridge between our landscape and others far south of here where non-migratory monarchs live. When a monarch drifts into close view in the garden, I cannot evade these deeper thoughts about the earth and its colonists. For I as an ecologist, like historians, remain intrigued with colonists and their struggles to stake out new land.

I hope the bigger picture is beginning to emerge, the story of how these colonist butterflies fit into the cycle of seasons and just how precariously they live. The structure of nature in summer is an ecological minefield. Ups and downs in butterfly numbers, and those of other creatures for that matter, from one summer to the next are neither unexpected nor odd. But a downward-sliding trend over a string of years could be symptomatic of real problems in nature. Such a pattern has been emerging for the fragile monarch, ringing the alarm bell with good reason. Trouble here shows up as habitat losses, and butterflies are excellent barometers of environmental health, given their strong ties to plant life.

The monarch butterfly is in serious trouble, not because children or nature-center naturalists are rearing caterpillars in jars, but because people are destroying its habitats, both in the north and in the far south. The same squeeze play is decimating some species of the migratory songbirds that spend summers here and the northern winter months in Central America and points further south every year. Conversions of old fields, meadows, and marshes into new residential subdivisions and strip malls along with invasions of exotic plants are erasing large stands of milkweeds in the north that have supported rich monarch populations for many years. Increased logging activities in the high mountain passes where monarchs spend the winter have altered the delicate balance between air temperature and moisture, killing millions of the butterflies in recent times. Closer to home, meanwhile, researchers recently found that about half of the monarch butterfly population in the United States originates within a narrow band of the cornbelt between Nebraska and Ohio. In this intensely agricultural zone, with its herbicide-resistant corn and soy bean crops, milkweed plants are being destroyed in vast quantities by herbicide applications every growing season.

How is it that we can know the heartland is the birthplace for such a large monarch population? The answer has to do with monarch caterpillar diet and milkweed chemistry. Local rainfall patterns and climate help shape the ratios of certain carbon and hydrogen isotopes in milkweed tissues, and these ratios change from one geographic zone to another. Milkweeds in the Midwest therefore have characteristic chemical "fingerprints." When milkweed is eaten by monarch caterpillars, these chemical ratios stay intact and appear in the adult butterfly's tissues. By comparing these chemical fingerprints in butterflies reared on various populations of milkweed and doing the same analysis for these telltale birth signs from overwintering butterflies in Mexico, researchers were able to determine that impressive numbers of monarchs winding up in Mexico were born in the heartland. Because of this fascinating revelation coming from tedious research, we now know that farming practices in the Midwest are threatening the survival of the monarch butterfly.

As heartland milkweed populations decline from herbicide applications to control weeds in fields of corn and soy, so too will monarchs enter an enforced decline. The likely result? We stand to lose the world's most impressive and massive insect migration, one linking our lives and enjoyment of summer with the American tropics. There will continue to be resident, non-migratory populations of the monarch in the American tropics, assuming minimal or no loss of their habitats there. What could vanish is the awesome phenomenon of a butterfly's long-distance migration, erasing from summer one of the season's most welcomed creatures in our gardens. This would be a shame, for while we know a lot about the monarch butterfly, thanks to Dr. Lincoln P. Brower and his colleagues, there is much more that we do not know. As a symbol of summer, this creature brings together the best qualities. Outwardly large and beautiful by butterfly standards, making it comfortably familiar for all of us, the monarch embodies the bigger, more troubling lessons about our tenuous natural heritage overall, in one broad sweep across the continent.

We need symbols of our growing season, as brief as it is, that help us to cherish summer and its harvests of life, symbols that cauterize into our collective psyche the complex issues of nature expressed as the diversity of life gracing this planet. Monarchs exude a rare beauty as well as tell us about the harsh realities of our threatened natural heritage, even small pieces of it; they urge us to remember we are all equal players in the collective soul and well-being of the planet. They also help awaken our sense of passage.

Seeing that first monarch starts summer for me; finding a frost-killed monarch caterpillar on a yellow, withered milkweed plant in autumn gives closure to the season. Because our growing season near the western rim of this great lake is relatively short and its end remains an unpredictable event from one year to the next, or even over a string of years, some insects like the monarch get trapped in years of early frost. When this happens, some fraction of the population dies before having the chance to head south for the winter. Conversely, when the frost comes late, there's a good chance more will survive to become butterflies and make the journey south.

Monarch butterflies, wherever they are found, are part of a welcome, enduring sense of nature's permanency exposed by summer. There is great comfort in the cyclic predictability heralded by the appearance and reappearance of a graceful icon from one summer to the next. I personally hope to live to see many more steamy and stifling August days near the edge of this great lake graced by the lazy, floating approaches of monarchs landing on coneflowers and milkweed blossoms. Such vivid splashes of color fuse in my mind with their daytime auditory complement, the call of the annual cicada from high above these weed patches, and bring me a joyful message: all is well, for this one more summer at least.

Annual Cicadas

Once again, I am sitting on my deck near dusk casting careful glances across the yard. It has been one of those steamy late summer days, and now the almost deafening pulsating buzz from a throng of cicadas in the tree tops provides an acoustical curtain call to the day, welcoming nightfall.

Here in the Midwest, this time of year often brings sweltering days, clapping thunderstorms, picnics, and plenty of bugs. Today the cicadas, sometimes mistakenly called locusts, are screaming louder than usual, urged on by the stifling humidity. Little else stirs in the yard, especially at high noon, when the weather is like this. My eyes burned earlier, stung by rivulets of sweat rolling off my forehead, blurring my vision, and making me even more cognizant of the cicada whines that seemed to unite all the trees as far as I could see from the deck.

I focus now on two very large silver maples, waiting for a band of catbirds to come walking across the lawn, stealthily silent in their movements as they approach the exposed roots of the old, twisted maples. Their dusk strolls are well timed for the quarry they seek. Precisely at this time of the day at this time of the year, big fully grown annual cicada nymphs tunnel up to the ground surface, crawl up the tree trunks, split their crusty skins, and become winged adults.

No one really knows for sure just how a cicada nymph measures time and decides the fateful moment of pushing itself out of the earth and darkness, but it is surely a marvel of nature's precision. It is also a necessary but risky transition in a creature that spends most of its life, which spans years, underground in an effort to survive long enough to become a sunshine aficionado whose life above ground lasts only a few weeks. One thing is certain: a plump juicy cicada nymph, about the thickness of a man's thumb, is filet mignon to a catbird. And this seasoned neighborhood, with its old stands of maples, ash, white oaks, and a few surviving elms, is fertile territory for cicadas—a veritable fastfood restaurant for catbirds.

So while old big trees like these can breed lots of cicadas, a cicada's life is a very tenuous matter. In any summer, most fall victim not only to the sneaky catbird, but also to other birds, raccoons, field mice, and perhaps squirrels. People too kill cicadas, even in the absence of fear, crushing them underfoot both deliberately and accidentally whenever the nymphs stray onto a driveway or sidewalk. Nonetheless, by summer's wane my yard is littered with several dozen of their discarded brownish shells or cast "skins." Sometimes I even find several nymph shells clinging to a nearby wooden fence. Cicadas are a crucial part of my yard's natural history.

I am speaking specifically of one particular kind of cicada, the annual cicada. Its scientific moniker is *Tibicen carnicularis*. This creature, with its black and green mottled body, large green eyes, powdery white belly, and crystal-clear wings, gets its name because it shows up every year in July and August. Saying it "shows up" is a bit misleading, though, because *seeing* one of these elusive insects is uncommon at best. It's one thing to spot a nymph, with its stout brownish husk, clinging to a tree trunk, ghost-like and eerie with bulging eyes and digging front legs, but just try spotting an adult. Mostly we find adult cicadas only when one falls out of a tree, blown down by a gust of wind or rain. The enigmatic cicada, then, is always more often heard than seen.

Their presence, however, speaks eloquently of nature's persistence. Even in neighborhood yards and city parks, cicadas are interconnected to the rest of the fragmented nature in our midst. Tree-lined streets and small pockets of woods in parks give a sense of permanence to cities and suburbs while at the same time attracting interesting wildlife. This is good for insects, yes, but also good for people, nourishing the intellect and spirit, offering some closeness to nature, and reminding us that we are deeply ensconced in an ancient history far older than the human presence. The cicada helps us sense permanence and see slightly beyond ourselves.

I cannot even begin to imagine a midwestern August or September without their sound. Our barbecues celebrate summer the best when the cicada's acoustical barometer is reminding us of just how hot and humid it really is. Cicadas bear witness to weddings. We bury loved ones within earshot of them as they call overhead from cemetery shade trees. Family porch chats at dusk slip into inky darkness as katydids and crickets take over where balladeering cicadas leave off, daytime choruses giving way to soothing nighttime melodies. We know cicadas in auditory memories too deep to explain, too ordinary to need explanation. We know them like we know our own breath—a constant presence about which we "know"

nothing at all. The "knowledge" is subliminal, transcendent, a fact of biology and existence communicated to us by sound alone.

There is a bold lesson here. The annual cicada is a watchmaker, instilling its own sense of time upon us. It is a fine-tuned being, ticking off the rhythms of summer slipping toward yet another autumn, and its appearance, made known to us by its song, is staged ever so precisely. It is almost as if a mysterious timepiece has been engraved into the chemistry of the young cicada over thousands of years; the nymph in its subterranean existence bears a genetic code bridging two worlds, one below ground, one in the sunshine. The cicada could therefore in some ways be construed as nature's own "Phantom of the Opera," but there is no ugliness or misbehavior here, only natural beauty, one elusive little beast uniting underworld and tree tops.

In both worlds, darkness and light, the cicada plays out a specific ecological destiny. Nymphs churn up the soil, breathing fresh life into it and promoting the well-being of a whole suite of soil creatures, including bacteria, fungi, mites, and ants. By feeding on sap from roots, they may even stimulate plant growth. Certainly the stout-bodied nymphs are prey for moles and other burrowing animals, and their cast skins litter the soil and mulch, creating minute pockets of sugar proteins that enrich the soil for other life. In both worlds too, the cicada's clock is synchronized to that of the seasons, the steering device for all of nature here in the Midwest. And, whether in woodlands, city parks, or lawns, cicadas are tied to trees, whose own annual rhythms also follow the march of the seasons.

Once again, I must turn to the language of synchrony and ecological clocks. Sitting on the deck and listening to the annual cicada builds connections for me. The life of this species connects distance, height, and time. The cicada covers considerable distance flying from one tree to another, so much so that I could never track one. It closets itself high in the trees, high enough to be seldom seen. And it weaves time together, in a plain, but elegant pattern: first living in the ground for seven to nine years sucking sap from plant roots and then emerging into the sun for a few short weeks. Despite this life cycle, adults appear in peak numbers by late summer *every* year.

The life strategy of the annual cicada in this regard is very different from that of the enigmatic periodical cicada, a complex of three species, the adults of which appear above ground once every 13 or 17 years depending on the location of their broods across North America. While the annual cicada is a reliable sign of middle and late summer, its loud buzz often gives an illusion of great numbers, but their densities do not reach the impressive levels of the periodicals or the rich hatches of cicadas found in Costa Rican rain forests. During the tropical summer, which curiously is about the same length as ours, these big-bodied cicadas provide a very large slice of the insect biomass available to many birds, mammals, and lizards.

In contrast to both periodical and tropical cicadas, annuals place a batch of eggs on a tree branch in late August. The eggs will hatch into tiny ant-like nymphs destined to mature at different rates of growth. This process, coupled with new batches of eggs being produced every summer, creates a potentially large bank of overlapping generations of the annual cicada churning through our soils, with staggered hatches of new adults every summer. The advantage of such a cycle can only be surmised. Northern climates and seasons, of course, can be quite unpredictable from one year to the next. In such a setting, an insect with a built-in long life cycle might well enhance survival by staggering adult hatches, thereby catching some good years and bearing the brunt of off years as well.

Plants and their responses to the annual cycle of northern seasons play an especially important role in shaping the cicadas' fate. Unsurprisingly, the life of the annual cicada is closely tied to signals given off by trees and other vegetation. A subterranean cicada nymph's timing to crawl up and out of the ground for the final molt into a winged adult is perhaps more than a matter of the animal measuring time mediated by soil temperatures or other cues. Could it be that the changing length of the day defining the middle of summer triggers a chemical change in plant sap which is then picked up by a cicada nymph sucking on a root? Could there be some deeper signal yet? Whatever nature uses to keep time, the cicadas "hear." The creature knows when to make its entrance and its exit. As a species, it submits also to the arrival of autumn, which brings a sharp downsizing in the insectan world more broadly.

Cicadas, however, are not simply natural creatures. Their presence in my yard is as much a matter of human history as natural history. The annual cicada was originally part of the complex webwork of creatures that developed in healthy forests. Then early settlers cleared forests and planted shade trees such as oaks, maples, and others to line their dirt streets. Cicadas, katydids, robins, bluejays, orioles, catbirds, squirrels, field mice, wasps, wild silk moths, and other forest creatures moved into these stands of planted trees. All of this happened as villages and towns expanded and aged into cities, pushing aside more and more open land. Back then, like today, the cicada's presence in these places, as well as in isolated patches of woods on farmlands, reminded people of the broader scheme of nature. Often dubbed the "Dog Days Harvest Fly" by early settlers, with good reason, the annual cicada's call reminded everyone that harvest time was approaching. Wherever trees endure, then, cicadas, birds, and other lifeforms endure, coaxing us to bear witness to the seasonal personality of the land on which we too ultimately depend for our very existence. It is a story they sing out to us every year.

While some would argue that the cicada's strong buzz is anything but appealing to the human ear, I sense something deeper in that whining buzz and try to listen for the patterns in the conversations. Sometimes an individual cicada sings, followed by another in a neighboring tree, as if the two were simply talking back and forth. At other times, several others chime in as soon as one starts up. The air becomes electrified with a mounting cadence, a pounding shrill. What was a solo performance or dialogue expands into a full-blown concert, difficult not to notice, like it or not. Such fiercely energetic activity speaks of the ribald, a frenetic preoccupation with procreation, courtship, and the sowing of seeds for future generations.

Summer's own path of inception, blossoming, and decline guides nature's fate. As little as a month ago, my yard was silent of cicadas. Now the place is a cacophony of insectan serenades. In another three months, silence will again embrace this yard. What is going on in the treetops above me is steadily ensuring that the summers to come will also be filled with cicadas. A lot can happen before a cicada nymph digs its way skyward out of the earth many seasons from now, creating new opportunities for marauding catbirds and mice. Birds cued into singing males through dense foliage will chase after cicadas in treetops. Birds are very good listeners. Sometimes I hear a loud squawk high above in a tree and look up to see a cicada thrashing about, locked in the beak of a bird and screaming about the situation. Some flies, too, locate singing cicadas and lay their eggs on their bodies. The maggots hatch out, burrow in, and feed on the cicada's meaty flesh. The "cicada killer," a giant solitary wasp, provisions its earthen burrows with cicadas immobilized by its powerful sting, and then lays an egg on each captive host—a tasty and complete food supply for wasp grubs. Sand traps on golf courses are favorite nesting places for the cicada killer.

Still, all is not grim in this backyard scenario. Tucked away in those high branches of silver maple are cicada eggs, placed there by the few who survived long enough to breed. In a few weeks, the eggs will hatch, assuming they are not discovered by ants, and the baby nymphs, themselves hardly bigger than the average ant, will drop to the ground and dig in deep. Obviously, trees are pivotal to cicadas' existence.

Cicadas in tree tops use a tube-like, sturdy mouth to tap into branches and suck up sap. Their nymphs tap tree roots in the same way. Tree sap is a watery broth of sugar, protein, fat, and minerals, foodstuffs that give the energy, strength, and endurance cicadas need to drive their powerful wing muscles. Because sap is mostly water, cicadas spend a lot of time urinating, so it is not at all unheard of to be sprinkled with their rain of clear fluids on a cloudless day, especially when many of them are sitting together in a tree and you are under it. Biblical accounts of blood rain from the skies are likely referring to the red urine from cicadas perched in legume trees native to the Middle East, some of which have bright red sap.

It is a good thing they have access to such rich food sources, because cicadas use a lot of energy. The male makes its boisterous song by rapidly vibrating its stomach muscles, causing a pair of stretched drums to move, creating a pulsing sound that is amplified many times over by the largely hollow body cavity. The fine structure of the drums and the beating rhythm of the strong muscles give each species of cicada its own unique song, which helps avoid confusion during mating in places where one species overlaps with others. Females, by contrast, have no drums and their body cavities are designed instead to hold hundreds of eggs, fertilized when cicadas copulate in silence in tree tops. The personality of a cicada's song is shaped by weather one moment to the next. Cicadas sing loudest when it is hot and humid under clear blue skies. A sudden change, such as a shift in the winds off the lake dropping the air temperature, shuts them down in an instant.

Although I have made the case that cicadas can handle the vagaries of life at the edges of human society, they are also vulnerable to our poor decisions. Timing in nature is a matter of chemistry clocked with external cues from the environment. How cicadas behave has a lot to do with how the plants they depend upon respond to these cues, but we do not yet understand the mechanism keeping the system functional. One thing is sure: the annual cicada, like many creatures, needs trees and other plants. When the plants go, so will the cherished and expected sounds of summer.

I personally plan to keep my silver maples for as long as I live here. But what happens when people cut down their trees or when diseases, encouraged by rapidly changing landscapes, kill off the trees around us? What happens when a little woods, a quaint tree-lined street, or a field dotted with shade trees gets paved over for a parking lot, supermarket, shopping mall, or highway spur? Then cicadas die, often by the thousands.

Is the message of the cicada's seemingly desperate call not only a warning of summer's passage, but one of interdependency, of the interconnections that bind us, wildlife, and trees into a meaningful ensemble? When the big trees go, and we lack a vision to reseed the landscape, to sow that which we reap from nature, the cicada's song will surely go. Losing cicadas is not a trivial matter. It is both a real and symbolic breakage of the interconnections that make our summer whole—and possible. It is also a tangible blow to our ability to see evidence of life's interconnections close at hand. A cicada is recycled, reworked plant juices. This is also true for many insects. Catbirds, bluejays, and others are largely the reworked flesh of cicadas and other insects. So too the cicada killer wasp. Shade trees are hosts for cicadas and other insects and nesting and food-hunting grounds for many birds. Soil and mulch together provides home for countless tiny creatures, many of which help feed shade trees. And from here, the interconnections among creatures branch out even more. The beginnings of the picture of nature's design and complexity are readily apparent even in my yard in summer. But they are easily missed.

When I hear the annual cicada, I am reminded again of how much of the insect world truly goes unnoticed, even when it is close at hand, every summer. As big and noisy as it is, the annual cicada is largely an invisible beast to most people. Its life cycle makes it relatively inaccessible. We know its song, yes, and we bend to the same rhythms that bring the nymphs out of the ground. But we often pass right by the animals themselves and never see them. Perhaps, where the cicada is concerned, the act of listening itself is enough. So I sit here on the deck, watching the fading sun and letting the waning light speak to me in the language of the annual cicada. The rattles and chirps of songbirds also rise above the background noises of people and their machines, and I wait impatiently for the cricket songs to start. I feel soothed and ready for night. The acoustical continuity between daylight and darkness reminds me, from the deck in summer, that we are all the keepers of nature's presence.

In the annual cicada's whine I feel a message of synchrony. Late summer here hosts a collective and concerted symphony, one that paces itself with the progression of the season. It is a rhythm that prepares the creatures who share this place with us for continuance. Life goes on. Caterpillars are struggling through a last generation under an onslaught of predatory bugs and brood-feeding wasps; katydids and crickets seem frantic in their swelling night calls before a frost sets in, no matter how far off; yellowjackets zing mean and nasty toward our picnic foods and the crushed apples in the orchard. The call of the annual cicada illuminates these happenings, creating a bond, if we choose to acknowledge it, between us and the insects as summer reaches its peak and slides toward autumn.

Soon enough, autumn's chill will muffle the cicadas and crickets into silence for another year. I am already thinking ahead, toward the sounds of next summer, and other summers far in the future. I think too of the magic cicadas bring us, reminding us where we came from and steering us wisely into the future with a renewed respect and awareness for a natural permanence close at hand. I think toward the future as the cicada calls toward it, both of us bound together in a shared existence whose full magnificence I may never fully comprehend. This is fine, the cicada's racket seems to promise: it is enough just to listen.

Paper Wasps

By late summer here, I am amazed that the forest and meadow near my home are still lush with foliage. The same holds true for my garden. Given the gross population figures for insects, by late summer the landscape should be heavily defoliated. But it is not. True, on occasion, I may find a tree or shrub pretty well stripped of its leaves, but the effect is very scattered and patchy. Swinging my sweep net back and forth through a patch of weeds in the field illustrates the point. Along with the hoards of caterpillars, beetle larvae, adult beetles, and sap-sucking bugs I've tipped onto my white sheet, there are lots of small spiders, an ambush bug or two, and a few wasps. Carnivores are mixed with herbivores, tiny pieces of life scurrying off in too many different directions to count.

Without the aid of the net, 90 percent of this life would have gone unnoticed by me, even during my close inspections of various plants. With it, I see the links between living plants, the creatures that munch on them or suck their sap, and in turn other creatures that plunder the plant feeders. Of all the creatures here, I am most fond of wasps, paper wasps in particular. By far the major carnivores of caterpillars and other soft-bodied, largely indefensible insects, wasps compel me to think about carnivory. The paradox of paper wasps is that while they can be dangerous when their nests are disturbed, they are highly beneficial to gardeners and farmers. They are equally important in the natural control of caterpillars potentially injurious of shade trees and forests.

While there are many kinds of wasps, including sand wasps and mud daubers, those which intrigue me the most are the paper wasps, the ones who build those familiar, papery nests usually suspended from a branch or fitted inside an abandoned animal burrow. In order to understand such sophisticated and socially complex insects, it is helpful to place them within the diverse and huge world of the insects. First, remember that insects comprise more than 80 percent of all animal life. Insects are divided up by human assessments of their traits into large groupings called orders. One of these orders, the Hymenoptera, so named because of the two pairs of membranous wings tethered together by tiny hooks, includes wasps, bees, and ants. It is within these sub-groups, called families, that true social behavior (as it exists in insects, called eusociality) can be found. Although there are 80 families of hymenopterans, only four—vespid wasps, sphecid wasps, bees, and ants—exhibit eusociality. Therefore, the majority of Hymenoptera, like most insects, are not eusocial. To give a sense of scale, more than 100,000 species of Hymenoptera have been described by scientists, out of a possible 300,000 species in all.

Taking the huge diversity of the insects and coming up with human-made systems of order that serve as a basis for better understanding the group as a whole is a daunting challenge. So scientists work for years putting names to insects and other creatures, hoping to create some order reflecting the evolutionary patterns of diversification. Clearly such a task is enormous and constantly changing as new information becomes available. The challenge, of course, is to bring together genera and species that are truly closely related into the same or similar groupings, and to recognize others that are truly different and worthy of being members of other groupings. Such circumstances apply to the large number of species of Hymenoptera which, together with butterflies, moths, and beetles, make up a very large portion of the insectan world's rich diversity.

Like butterflies, beetles, and flies, hymenopterans have four stages to their life cycles: egg, larva, pupa, and adult. Eusocial hymenopterans build nests, lay eggs in them, and provision larvae with food collected on foraging trips. In these species, a dominant queen is typically the sole egg-layer and governess over the whole colony. Depending upon species, the colony consists of various divisions of labor often referred to as castes. The most familiar caste consists of workers, individuals with diverse assignments such as protecting the nest and feeding the larvae.

Paper wasps belong to the family Vespidae and are referred to as vespid wasps, and this family contains six subfamilies. *Polistes,* which will be my main character for this foray into the world of wasps, belongs to the Polistinae. Yellowjackets and bald-faced hornets are members of the Vespinae, which are very closely related to the Polistinae. Another group of eusocial insects outside of the Hymenoptera are the termites, of the order Isoptera.

A paper wasp or hornet consists of a powerful set of meat-crushing and wood-pulping jaws or mandibles attached to a liquid-processing gut; it has strong legs, wings, a stinger capable of searing pain, and excellent senses of vision, touch, and smell. They use the sting strictly in defense of the nest and its occupant colony. Food is pursued by foundresses and, later, by workers in the colony. All hunt by using their mandibles to subdue arthropods, chiefly caterpillars, in order to feed their larvae. Wasps are very agile fliers capable of all sorts of tricky aerial maneuvers associated with hunting, nest-building, and defense. They are also highly efficient gatherers of flesh, which they most reliably find, process, and feed to their brood. This act alone largely defines their role in nature. They slice up caterpillars with their sharp, powerful mandibles, maxalating the prey and getting some nourishment in the process from the oozing hemolymph or insect body fluids. As adults, they are more prone to eating pollen or lapping up nectar and juices from crushed, sweet fruits. So, like it or not, paper wasps such as yellowjackets, like fireflies, picnics, whining cicadas, and blistering heat, are inseparable from the midwestern summertime.

I am awestruck at how the paper wasp's nest-building anticipates the growing season. A queen wasp instinctively knows when it is time to begin its nest, even when the food needed to sustain the future colony is nowhere present or accessible for the time being. But the initiation of a new nest in late spring is an investment that pays off as prey numbers bloom later on, allowing the wasp colony to mushroom in size. Great care goes into choosing the appropriate place to build a nest. If you look closely around the outside of your home on a warm spring day, do not be surprised to discover a plump mother yellowjacket "inspecting" any exposed wide cracks in the foundation or between loose bricks or siding. This is business as usual. Sooner or later, she will find an opening somewhere, perhaps an abandoned rabbit nest with a cavity behind it big enough to become a wasp nest site. She may also choose the ledge above your front door.

My story of paper wasps has much to do with the one called *Polistes fuscatus*. The fascinating life cycle of this particular species was studied by Dr. Robert L. Jeanne of the University of Wisconsin–Madison, one of the world's leading authorities on social wasps. *Polistes* builds a relatively small, open paper nest, an easily recognizable cluster of brood cells, usually attached to the eaves of buildings and branches. These wasps use woodpulp paper to build their open comb nests suspended from a stalk, also known as a petiole. One outstanding feature of *Polistes* is the presence on nests of uninseminated worker females during most of the colony cycle, but people seldom pause long enough to notice this. They are usually too busy knocking down the nests of these beneficial wasps. Fortunately for the wasps, their nests can be hard to spot at times.

Species of paper wasps in the genus *Vespula*, the familiar yellowjacket and bald-faced hornet, on the other hand, build large, elaborate, enclosed paper nests shaped like footballs or spheres and often concealed by foliage. Interestingly enough, hornet nests are also not at all easily spotted or discovered during summer. It is only in late autumn or winter that the

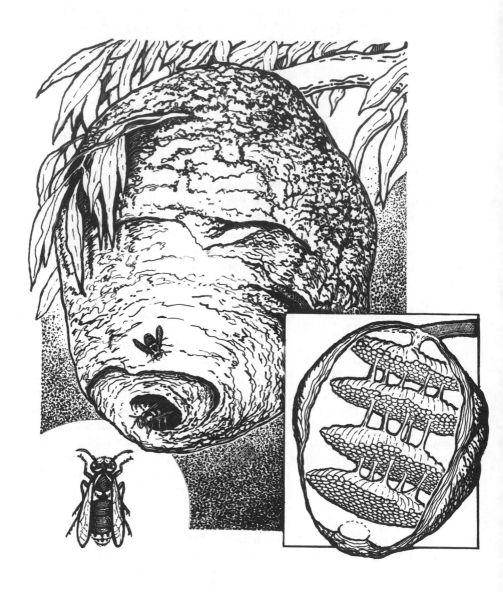

nests are easily seen in the bare branches of bushes and trees. People are often surprised to discover just how close at hand a bald-faced hornet nest was all summer long when they make such a startling discovery, well after that fact. Clearly, despite our highly entertaining popular lore about their vicious tendencies, in reality wasps toil about their own business, their homes seldom seen and usually out of our way.

In *Polistes* the queen wasp is about the same size as the other adult members of the colony. Yellowjackets, of which there are 16 species in North America, and the bald-faced hornet have large queens and small workers comprising their colonies. While some yellowjackets are pestiferous, scavenging food from picnic tables, others are nonpestiferous, passing up our food and heading for the preferred prey of carnivores. The latter habit is generally true of *Polistes* as well.

Naturally, of course, it makes sense to be careful when an active paper wasp is encountered in the yard or on the house. One never wants children or pets to be in harm's way. By late summer, a bald-faced hornet nest in a low bush near a heavily used driveway or sidewalk can also be a threat. But nests high in trees or otherwise removed from people-traffic areas usually present no danger. Exceptions, of course, are the subterraneous nests of yellowjackets or yellowjacket nests in the walls of houses. Many people have encountered the lightning fast, easily provoked fury of yellowjackets while mowing the grass, sometimes right over their nest entrance. And since some yellowjackets in late summer are very attracted to the scent of heavy cosmetics or the sweet smell wafting from open soda cans, hot dogs, and potato salad, common sense must prevail at picnics and barbecues too. But in most situations, it is not necessary to destroy a wasp nest. Consider my situation. As recent as this past summer, I had a colony of yellowjackets living in the foundation of my house. The entrance to their nest, hidden away in the cinder block, was only about four feet from the side door leading into the kitchen. Not a single yellowjacket appeared in the house all summer and no one ever noticed their daily comings and goings.

I have become quite comfortable, in fact, with having wasps use my house. For the several years I have lived here, a curious summer ritual involving *Polistes* has taken place. Almost like clockwork, beginning in spring and taking a whole summer to finish, a queen *Polistes* wasp builds a nest on the outer lip of a skylight window on my house. The uncanny thing about this is that a new nest appears each year at the exact same spot on the window, although some summers have bigger nests than others by the end of the season.

The nest always appears at the southeast corner of the window. *Polistes* shows a definite preference for nesting to the south, giving colonies maximum exposure to the sun's warmth. Keeping warm helps the colony stay active and grow faster throughout the season. This is especially important in temperate climates where warm sites for nest construction are crucial during spring, and perhaps helps to explain why the same sites tend to have new colonies over a string of spring seasons. On cool evenings, I sometimes slowly crank open the small window, and there are the wasps, clinging in slumber to the paper cells fashioned over several weeks, a growing brood nest. At such moments I ponder the events leading the mother wasp here in the first place, just as her mother came the year before, her grandmother three summers ago, and who knows just how many other generations before that.

When this process begins anew each year, the mother wasp is usually a lone ranger, working by herself to begin the nest and care for her first-born. But rapidly, as summer advances and a dribble of newborn worker wasps covers the nest, the situation changes dramatically and with real purpose. Colonies are founded by either a single female or by two or more females coming together to begin a nest. When cofoundresses join forces to start a colony, it is probable that they are sisters, mated in the fall, who have overwintered together, usually under roof shingles or other well-sheltered crevices. How the story unfolds each year depends on what kind of weather embraces the landscape.

New colonies are typically founded in May in this area, and the first offspring do not appear until the latter half of June. Thus a major feature of the colony cycle in *Polistes* in this region is the absence of offspring on newly founded nests in spring. Therefore, when there is more than one wasp on the nest before this time, they have to be overwintered sisters coming together as cooperating cofoundresses of the new colony. By the time the first workers appear in June, cofoundresses have established a dominance hierarchy with the queen, the sole egg layer, at the very top. As workers are produced in the colony, the subordinate cofoundresses disappear from the nest.

Last summer, the nest on my window was a modest comb of about 30 cells, and by season's end had produced new queens and males. Prior to this, with the exception of the queen, a virtual egg-laying machine, the nest's membership consisted exclusively of many worker females. But in autumn, as days shortened, a fraction of the final pulse of nursed brood (eggs, larvae, and pupae) became new queens and males. These vigorous, fresh wasps vacated the nest and mated, and the newly fertile queens scattered to seek shelter from the impending winter in crevices. The rest of the wasp colony died off, and the wasp harvest and life cycle was complete for that year.

Thus the stage was set for what I now see before me on this summer's eve. Two months ago a surviving queen wasp was stirred to life by warming temperatures, promising the renewal of the life cycle for another year.

An exquisite lesson in midwestern natural history was unfolding, molded and shaped by the finicky interplay of the sun's warmth and rainfall. This wasp's survival and ebullient success, mirrored by the growth of its nest, thus reflects the bountiful harvests of life that result from hot weather and abundant rainfall early in the summer this year. Less than a month ago the paper nest consisted of only a few elongated grayish cells suspended from a black, gummy petiole attached to the upper lip of the window. The winter-weary wasp fashioned the nest by shaving slivers of wood from a nearby fence, mashing the pulp in its strong jaws and mixing the tissue with saliva. This pasty mass was then carefully spread, molded, and dried into perfectly shaped paper cells. These wasps are the world's original papermakers!

While most people spend time on the deck to get a tan or simply to relax while perhaps sipping a cool drink at high noon, I enjoy being here to watch paper wasps shaving wood fibers from the rails and the frayed wooden armrests of two old lawn chairs. I often wonder if these hard-working females are from the nest on my window. Even when my eyes become blurred with the sting of heavy sweat dripping from my forehead, I stay put, enjoying the wasps flying nearby, and feel great comfort in knowing that these creatures are plundering minute scraps of lumber from my deck and recycling them into sturdy paper nests somewhere in the neighborhood. This is one of life's small pleasures to which I look forward as summer approaches and peaks.

Wasps, of course, use materials other than processed wood for their nests. The dead stalks of meadow plants such as milkweed are sometimes put to very good use when winter gives way to spring. Once on Cape Cod I watched a very robust queen yellowjacket cut off strips of fiber from a dried, bent milkweed stalk. She moved over a short distance only, up and down the stalk, head bobbing as she sliced off the precious fibers. The previous summer's wild produce was being recycled for a most worthy cause—the building of a nursery for this season's offspring. Thus the dead organic debris from last summer's bounty plays an important role in steering the course of new life in a new summer.

I am not at all sure that we can begin to fathom just how much labor must be done by a foundling queen wasp in spring when it begins to build a nest. After finding a suitable site, the first order of business is to fashion a tough, sturdy petiole that serves as the attachment point. The production of the petiole in *Polistes* is in itself a fascinating piece of natural history. Again, thanks chiefly to the studies of Dr. Robert L. Jeanne, we know that this tough structure attaching the nest to its substrate is largely a labial gland secretion from the wasp which hardens on contact with air. This fibrous and resinous structure is also coated by the wasp with sticky substances made from tree sap oozing from fresh wounds or storm-broken trunks. The petiole, together with possibly other auxiliary ones built later as the nest increases in size, must be strong enough to support the steadily increasing weight of the growing wasp colony over the summer. It is equally challenging to attempt to fathom how many forays into the surrounding area it must take for the lone mother wasp to collect enough wood fiber to build those first few brood cells.

Quite naturally, during this crucial phase in the establishment of a new wasp colony, a lot can go wrong. For one thing, sudden severe cold weather can kill the queen, or she may be eaten by a hungry bird. Assuming all goes well though, she builds these cells and places one egg at the bottom of each. The paper cells of the comb nest are an incredible example of insectan precision in design and construction. Crosswise the cell is perfectly hexagonal, with all six walls very straight and even, and within each successive growth stage of the nest, the cells are all the same size.

Wasps building their nest ranks very high as one of nature's most spectacular displays of ingenuity. The process begins with the first few workers, sterile females, being produced in a new nest. They take over much of the nest building from the queen. Workers knowingly cooperate in making the nest. Each wasp knows its task and how to do it. Nest-building knowledge, as with other aspects of wasp behavior, is built into the genes, ensuring that the nest of a species of *Polistes* or the bald-faced hornet will come out the same every time. The brood cells will be the correct dimensions, the walls the appropriate thickness, and their arrangement compact and orderly. The size and shape of the final nest, by the end of summer, will not be the same in all cases. Each nest is designed to fit a particular place. In *Polistes* the final nest is a single tier of brood cells, while in bald-faced hornets and yellowjackets, there are several tiers of brood cells, arranged much like the floors of an apartment or house.

Just as humans design a building to bear a certain weight load when it is ready for occupancy, so too does the paper wasp compute the parameters of the growing nest necessary to bear the eventual heavy load of a large brood that will accumulate by late summer. Humans and other primates, it is clear, have by no means cornered the market on effective parental care of offspring. In the wasp house there is no living room, dining room, bathroom, or den. The entire nest is basically a nursery. In this arrangement, the needs and comforts of adult wasps are subjugated to the needs of the brood. In the brood is the promise of continuance, a renewal of paper wasps through many summers yet to come. No effort is spared. Because larger paper nests with multiple tiers of brood cells require greater care and protection, bald-faced hornets, for example, build a multilayered envelope of paper around the entire nest. Not only does this envelope, with airspaces between the layers, protect the colony from

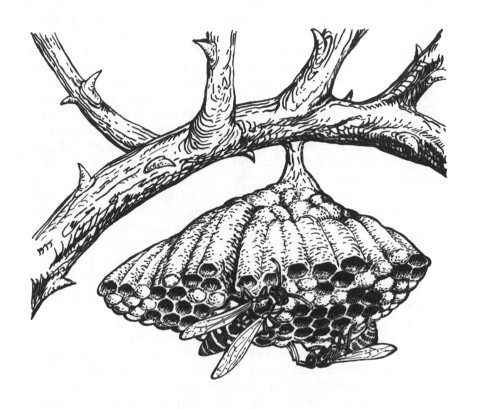

rain, it also keeps it cool. *Polistes* has the advantage of smallness. Its nests readily fit under the eave of a building, in a cool dry location. Both display great sophistication and talent. Their task is enormous, requiring the concerted effort of many individuals working as a team.

How does a wasp colony keep itself whole and on track as it grows and expands over the summer? This question has puzzled researchers studying wasps, bees, and ants for a long time. There are some partial answers. Paper wasps, like social bees and ants, have sophisticated language and communication mediated more by chemical scents and body movements than by sounds. I do not mean to imply that these animals do not communicate acoustically. Rather, they are champions at the use of specialized airborne chemical messengers. The system creates a sense of cohesion and order to a wasp colony. Different chemical scents from various glands communicate different kinds of information. Different signals share information on food-gathering, defense of the colony, recognition of nestmates, and the care of the brood. Adult worker wasps further communicate certain kinds of information to the brood through a food-sharing process called trophallaxis in which workers regurgitate morsels or balls of chemically worked-over flesh to brood grubs in return for sustenance.

Certainly the well-developed vision of wasps must also play a key role in communication, both within the colony and with other creatures, as any attempt to get close to an active *Polistes* nest will rapidly illustrate: the workers usually are quick to assume a threatening posture on the open comb. This response, which can be very dramatic and intimidating, is provoked in large measure by sighting an approaching threat to the nest. *Polistes* on the defense swiftly rear up on their strong legs and move over the brood cells in jerky motion while flicking their wings—annoyed and ready to attack to protect not so much themselves but the developing brood. For with that brood resides the reason for everything paper wasps do. Colonies therefore work very hard to produce as large a brood as possible during the relatively compressed summer season here. The bigger the brood, the more likely that a colony will, by the end of summer, produce not just one, but several queens to mate, pass the winter, and make new nests the following year. This mission is the sole purpose of the nest and its inhabitants.

As a result, workers not only hunt for food, build the nest, and nurse the brood, but also do anything else necessary to ensure the survival and maturation of the brood into new wasps. I have even watched workers bring drops of water held gently between the mandibles, one big drop for each wasp, apparently to give to the brood when conditions were very dry. It would be difficult for me to list a full inventory of all the behaviors of paper wasps as they are very complex, agile, and intelligent creatures whose flexibility holds the key to their survival.

As I have already mentioned, although in *Polistes* a sole queen, or foundress, can begin a new nest, often two or more foundresses establish a nest together. Larger nests tend to have multiple foundresses, one of which may serve as a queen-wasp replacement if the original foundress or cofoundresses perish early in the growth cycle of the colony. In contrast, a yellowjacket or bald-faced hornet colony is begun by a single, inseminated queen in the spring.

Assurance of new colonies next spring in *Polistes fuscatus* is strengthened by the fact that some workers late in the season disappear, rather than stay with the colony. They quickly seek out overwintering sites, and those that survive become new foundresses the following spring. These particular wasps tend to be smaller in size than those that stay with the nest and typically leave very successful colonies filled with a lot of brood. Foundresses also exhibit other very specific behaviors that aid in the survival of the brood. Multiple foundresses appear early in the growth cycle of the colony; later their functions are assumed by workers that emerge from the brood. Foundresses and workers use vibratory signals on the nest as part of an elaborate communication system, particularly between adult wasps and larvae. The appearance of larvae in the colony triggers conversations between the caretaker adults and the young through specific body movements and gestures by the adults. Using these various signals, larvae in their cells exhibit responses, many of which relate to feeding. Since antennae are the smell organs of insects, much of what they do is governed by chemical signals.

Foundresses exhibit three kinds of body oscillations in communications with larvae. The three body movements are done in sequence: antennal drumming, abdominal wagging, and lateral vibrations. Antennal drumming by the adult wasp tells larvae in brood cells to withhold salivary secretions before getting a liquid meal from adults returning to the nest with maxalated prey. Abdominal wagging and lateral vibrations signal larvae to secrete saliva and withhold it in sequence. Antennal drumming consists of the wasp dipping its head over the larva in the brood cell and rapidly hitting her antennae on the rim of the cell. Abdominal wagging consists of slow side-to-side movements of the abdomen against the nest while walking across the brood cells. Lateral vibrations occur when a stationary wasp rapidly moves her abdomen against the nest, making audible sounds. What is much less clear is how the larvae respond to these specific signals, but we do know the sequence of behavior that ensues when prey is brought into the nest.

In a single foundress colony, the three movements are completed rapidly, and larvae are fed maxalated food. When multiple foundresses are present, the sequences are often disrupted and feeding delayed. One intriguing and marvelous component of adult–larvae communications is trophallaxis. Trophallaxis plays an important role in the social organization of the wasp colony, strengthening the essential co-dependency of adults and larvae. In adult–larvae trophallaxis, maxalated insect flesh and regurgitated prey hemolymph are fed to larvae by adults. When an adult worker wasp feeds a larva a ball of flesh, the larva gives off a tiny droplet of saliva which is eaten by the adult. The saliva is very rich in concentrated sugars generated by the larva's ability to synthesize carbohydrates from proteins, the bulk ingredient of its food. Larval saliva energizes workers efficiently, enabling them to forage effectively for larval food in their comings and goings from the nest. This surrender of saliva by larvae occurs most frequently in nests with large numbers of offspring workers present. Another form of trophallaxis is the transfer among adult wasps of hemolymph ingested during the maxalation of prey to feed the larvae. This interadult trophallaxis follows the dominance hierarchy among foundresses, with the egg-laying queen getting fed first by the subordinates. In addition, various glands in the body of the wasp are sources for the synthesis and storage of many different substances used in chemical communication.

Another interesting facet of *Polistes* behavior concerns the role of certain lipid substances in the cuticle (exoskeleton) used in the recognition of nestmates and non-nestmates. Non-nestmates, having a slightly different set of these lipids, elicit aggressive behavior by foundresses and workers on the nest. This signaling system also elicits cooperation among nestmates. Paper wasp behavior and the various mechanisms underlying it are very complex and subjects of considerable research. Such studies help to elucidate the interplay of chemical, visual, and vibratory cues in providing cohesion to the wasp colony, which becomes more and more important as the nest expands over the summer.

What I witness all day long now is a constant flow of aerial traffic around the window, resembling in no small way a Lilliputian holding pattern of airliners over Chicago's O'Hare Airport. Wasps are hovering everywhere, or so it seems, ready to land on the nest, while others are taking off. There are no collisions. And off they do go, flying straight toward the trees in search of food. Unlike bees, which are often confused with wasps and vice versa, wasps for the most part are carnivores. This is really the secret to understanding the very beneficial roles wasps play in nature, even affecting our own lives in very positive ways. The business of hunting and gathering meat and bringing home this booty to feed the babies, only one of a long series of instincts embedded in the wasp's brain, seems an endless task from one day to the next, all summer long—a task with an ancient history.

Wasps are indeed remarkable beings in having been around for millions of years and, as examples of truly social insects, in having evolved ingenious means of coping with their environment. The head of a wasp is a complex behavioral library, where an assortment of unique chemical signals are made and stored for release in communication. No doubt their habit of building conspicuous paper nests packed with lots of brood, a tasty food target for birds and small mammals, must have played a key role in the development of the stinging behavior so well known and feared. The sting is not really meant for people, of course. We sometimes just get in the way of routine wasp activity.

Paper wasps do give us a visual warning about their stinging prowess. Some species here, such as yellowjackets and bald-faced hornets, sport colorful patterns on their bodies. For the group overall, a dark brown or black background color is accentuated with bands and blotches of yellow, red, or white, or some combination of these hues. It is no accident that wasps, with their painful stings, have these bold color patterns. In nature, such colors typically signal danger to an aggressor. Paper wasps are fearless, or so it seems, and prone to attack at a slight provocation. Would-be attackers learn quickly to beg off by the very recognizable color patterns; if they don't desist, they are in for a memorable encounter.

All these components of a paper wasp's existence—from body color patterns, powerful stings, exquisite nest-building skills, and superb hunting prowess come together to ensure the survival of the brood and the species from one summer to the next. Every action that takes place from the moment the queen begins her new nest to the end of summer ensures the survival of the colony. At first, when the nest is very new in early summer or late spring, wasp life indeed seems simple and straightforward. Into each brood cell the mother wasp deposits a single egg that soon hatches into a soft, white grub, a baby wasp. The firstborns of early summer produce the nest's first wave of workers who build more paper cells and hunt for food to feed the budding nursery as the queen enlivens her pace of egg-laying. This building process is repeated over and over again everyday, with more and more worker wasps accelerating the expansion of the nest. Soon the nest is a bulging comb of many brood cells, a virtual baby factory.

Over the summer, the nest swells in size many times, its ultimate bulk determined by the mood swings of the midwestern growing season. When early summer is blessed with hot weather and lots of rain, as it was this year, the more profuse and lusher foliage produces bigger soft-bodied, leaf-eating insect populations, wasp food. No matter that in the weeks ahead the weather may shift to cool, dry days. It is that first pulse of sultry summer weather that charts the course of nature's unfolding story every year.

As already mentioned, caterpillars provide a large portion of the wasp's diet. During the day, worker wasps scour foliage for caterpillars. With their keen sense of vision and smell, wasps are extremely clever in spotting their prey among dense foliage. They can even find clusters of small-scale insects, which they pluck off and roll up into pulpy morsels for the brood. They target the familiar cabbage butterfly, an exotic species that is pestiferous and lays eggs on garlic mustard, a very tenacious exotic weed that creeps into my yard. They also, no doubt, prey on cutworms and the monarch butterfly caterpillars that occasionally turn up on my milkweeds. Sometimes I find myself wondering just how far from the nest these workers travel to find food for the growing colony. I, of course, hunt these clever hunters at eye level or lower. But perhaps they fly high into the tall trees in search of their quarry as well. Wherever they go, the wasps' carnivorous behavior helps keep in check the legions of bugs that would otherwise gobble up vegetation. So a summer endowed with a healthy wasp population is a good thing. They control the garden and tree pests attacking our native species. It is much less appealing when the wasps potentially dampen the attack on exotic weeds like garlic mustard by eating the ubiquitous cabbage butterfly. But on balance, paper wasps are good for the land, and good for us. Every summer they recycle tonnages of pest insect flesh, allowing us to reap the benefits of beautiful flowers and sweet corn.

Armed with such insight, just imagine what could happen if the paper wasps in our midst disappeared altogether from the summer scene. Many shade trees would be stripped of their dense cooling foliage by hoards of defoliating insects, leaving less shade for outdoor weddings, funerals, and livestock. Our landscape would soon turn into a parched, summer wasteland picked clean of its refreshing lushness, and this in turn would diminish other wildlife, such as songbirds, which depend on healthy trees for their own survival. Wasps rescue our trees, crops, and other plant life from the ravages of insects. Our collective experience with wasps, unfortunately, is synonymous with pain, which is really too bad given their undeniably beneficial role in the bigger picture. Wasps are truly our allies, not our enemies. We are lucky they are here.

Paper wasps, even with their dreaded sting, are not immune from danger. Their existence, like much of nature, is a precarious balancing act. Many queens die off during an unusually brutal winter. An early summer of heavy rains can flood foundling yellowjackets' nests, drowning the queens and their young colonies. Some birds artfully dine on wasps while skillfully avoiding the sting, or by yanking out the stinger altogether and tossing it. Mold and bacteria can wipe out whole broods. So although some of our summers may have more wasps than others, there's little threat of our gardens and parks being overrun with them.

What intrigues me still is the mystery of a *Polistes* nest turning up at this exact same spot on my window each summer. This is not something that all paper wasps do. It is more prevalent in the open nest of *Polistes*. Yellowjackets and bald-faced hornets, for example, seldom return to the same place to build a new nest. How does a new queen in some wasp groups "know" to build in the exact same spot as perhaps her own mother did the year before? Does a newly hatched queen in autumn pick up a scent from the nest that stays with her all winter long as she sleeps in some protected niche away from the old nest? And does this scent also help her to locate her original birthplace the following spring? By autumn's end, however, the old nest is empty and a ragged mess. What little is left of the comb often withers away during the winter, so it's not a simple matter of rebuilding a nest on an old foundation. Instead, a lone wasp must return somehow to the same spot at the window and establish a new nest. There is real beauty in watching close at hand this tight cycle of the paper wasp continue for another summer.

Many people, discovering a wasp nest on their house, would choose to dispatch it swiftly. I prefer to see the presence of the nest as a welcome attachment to the natural world. The nest, as it grows and flourishes as summer moves along, is an ecological barometer: its steady growth, the bulging brood, the mass of wasps peaking out in late summer, and its inescapable crash in autumn hence, bespeaks the bigger story of nature in the northern Midwest. In spring and early summer we plant, sow seed, and then dutifully and joyously nurse our gardens all summer in anticipation of welcomed blooms and harvests later, the spoils of our labor before the killing frosts.

Lest I appear to be gazing at wasps through highly rose-tinted sunshades, let me quickly say that I know all too well firsthand the lightning strike of a white-hot wasp sting, and those all too predictable assaults by yellowjackets at a picnic on a sultry summer afternoon. It's hard to imagine a creature more difficult to embrace than the wasp. Needless to say, for most people, it is real stretch to appreciate a wasp's beauty. We are easily moved and awed by the color design of a butterfly's wing, the regality of a purple coneflower or soaring eagle, or the melodic cry of a distant loon on a lake at dusk. Other creatures, like wasps and dragonflies, compel us to look deeper for their inner beauty. But surely natural beauty is also in the wasp—especially in the intricate design and construction of a paper-wasp nest or in the adult–larvae feeding loop.

Stinging abilities entirely notwithstanding, I cannot begrudge wasps their role in this very ancient scenario of life. Like all living creatures, their life cycle is exquisitely in tune with the birth, progression, and end of summer, the growing season. Their ticking clock of what to do and when is engrained from earlier lifeforms in past eras, written into the design of all creatures. In the tropics, where there are many more kinds of paper wasps than anywhere else, wasps fly all year. But to the north, we have only our wasps of summer to appreciate and understand. Rather than see them as menaces, I see them as key players in the bigger, marvelous chessboard of life on earth. And while I naturally avoid their painful sting at all cost, I nonetheless appreciate wasps and their well-engineered nests as a reminder of nature's annual schedule.

Paper wasps make our lives more livable. Their impact on us is a collective matter, the action of whole colonies, not unlike massive colonies of ants churning up soil or converting a rotten log in a forest to mulch. But paper wasps are not citizens of ground cover and they are not big exploiters of organic debris. They are flesh-eaters, driven consumers of living flesh, with an occasional meal of nectar and pollen or fermenting fruit juice on the side. Indeed, they are one of nature's unsung heroes of something called equilibrium or balance, for when an area has healthy colonies of paper wasps along with other carnivorous bug-eating animals, the landscape can stay lush and complete. The interconnections are, once again, unmistakable.

Paper wasps, at base, are the recycled tissues of caterpillars. Caterpillars are largely grazers on living plant tissues. When we think of a carnivore, typically a large animal comes to mind, such as a wolf or mountain lion. But the reality is that most carnivores are arthropods—centipedes, spiders, and many other kinds of insects. This fact alone says a lot about the manner in which the rich diversity of plant-grazing insects, by far this planet's largest slice of animal life, is kept in some semblance of balance.

I am not expecting you to become enamored with wasps by knowing something about their balancing role in the overall design of life. Nor do I expect you to applaud how they contribute to the processes in nature by which our forests, meadows, and gardens are not totally defoliated by the end of summer. But I do hope that when you encounter a paper wasp basking in the sun or stripping away slivers of wood pulp from your porch, you will give a moment of silent gratitude to this creature or share your insights about it with someone else. And when this creature inadvertently gets trapped inside your screen door or window, I hope that you opt to set it free out of doors, rather than giving it a swift death.

This is why I don't disturb the wasp nest on my window, and why I am glad to be with the wasp for another summer. When we begin to understand paper wasps and their rightful place in nature, we know that nothing is gained by destroying their nests, in most circumstances. In fact, much is lost, not just for the wasps, but for us. By observing wasps, whether at a nest on my window, on my deck as they shave off wood, or weaving through the weed patch in search of prey, I have come to respect these creatures and their role in the balance of nature. They are wonderful products of life's refined diversification. When I gaze out over the garden or hike through the field in summer, I remember nature's gift of carnivory:

thanks to insects like paper wasps, the land is lush and green, teeming with life. Messages of sentience course through the dense, sticky air of late summer. Everything is abuzz with the hurried antics of bees, wasps, and butterflies. There is no escaping this fact. I always relish these sounds and movements, knowing that in a few more months they will be gone. I also take solace in the summer night sounds of other creatures—crickets and katydids, the rustle of moths around electric lights, and distant signals of flashing light from silent fireflies zigzagging through the blackness. All of these signals of life, like those given by paper wasps, create the bigger picture, awesome in design and complexity, that defines the finer, exquisite interconnections among small creatures come late summer.

Firefly Magic

I am walking down a road in midsummer twilight toward an open space I call a "firefly meadow." With clear heavens above, there is little threat of a thunderstorm tonight, even though the night air smells humid, buttery even. In darkness, the embers of thought and enlightenment can ignite and burn late, so we need people with good intentions to sally forth into the night. Many creatures, from fireflies to whippoorwills, depend on darkness for survival. Coming here will put me in touch with them.

Even when there is no moon, I can still make out images in the dark, such as the outline and profile of the meadow up ahead. A truly dark summer night is a rare treat and not at all easy to find near a big city. Nighttime in and near the city is really one long artificial dusk extending from sunset to sunrise. Artificial lights now rule. Yet they have not yet vanquished the gutsy little firefly, whose light show I have come out to see.

The meadow already twinkles and glows with hundreds of moving lights, like the bright, crisp sparks of sputtering, damp cardboard matches—an age-old ritual of nature. I think of their muted flashes as conversation, simple and elusive, but powerfully complex and utterly necessary. And what a sight it is. From the lowest points of the brush to the tops of the trees, an electrified latticework emerges in the inky darkness. Except for the calls of crickets and cone-headed grasshoppers, ethereal silence reigns, adding greater intensity to the dancing flashes of light everywhere. The whole scene is a peppered blaze of tiny, burning flares shimmering quietly, without crackle, and mysteriously ignited without heat, fire, lightning, or lighter fluid. No one can convince me this is not magical.

In their glow this meadow takes an different personality. During the day there are few clues that fireflies live here. Occasionally I have found one clinging in slumber to the underside of a leaf. Now the air is filled

with them, and I find myself grateful that this meadow has been spared the fate of so many others that once hosted fireflies. In terms of absolute numbers and species, I really don't know how many fireflies are here tonight, but I do know that there are not many other fields and woodlots in this area that even come close to the sparkle of this place. It has been at least ten years since I have seen another field like this, especially this close to the city. In the daylight, this meadow resembles many others in the area, but most of them have few or no fireflies. Nowadays, it is mostly in rural areas that firefly meadows such as this one can still be found. This firefly meadow is a disappearing natural wonder, a display of life on the verge of extinction.

Much of what was once prime firefly habitat is now covered with shopping malls, farmlands, sprawling residential areas, and superhighways, places far different from damp forests and meadows. Farm pesticides too have killed off many of the tiny creatures on which firefly larvae feed. Unsurprisingly, fireflies have been in a broad pattern of decline for some time now. Some rare species have already disappeared. This loss is a real pity as a firefly meadow awakens a long-dormant childhood sense of wonder. I remember how I used to chase after fireflies long ago, holding them captive in jars filled with grass so that I could watch them up close. I tried again and again to keep my captives alive but by the next day, they were always dead or close to it, so I quickly learned that the best thing to do was to let them go right away. The light shows that fascinated me then, I've learned since, are really discrete signal flashes, a collective effort by male fireflies broadcasting "I am here," and females responding "yes" or "no." But this display of soft, blinking lights is by no means a harmonious, synchronous affair, a show of firefly unity. Competition is the game of the hour and the future of the species hangs on how well these blinking individuals manage that game.

Perhaps I should mention that fireflies, also called lightning bugs, are neither flies nor bugs, but beetles—harmless, soft-bodied, slow-flying ones called Lampyridae, a word derived from Greek and meaning "lamp-fire." Other lampyrids do not make light and are active in the daytime, but in North America alone, there are more than a hundred species that do, each with its own distinctive flash color and flash pattern. In a meadow such as this one, it would not be at all surprising to find two to four species belonging to two groups or genera called *Photinus* and *Photuris*. Each of these species has a somewhat distinctive life cycle, but they also have a lot in common when it comes to survival.

It is not always easy to know when you are dealing with beetles rather than other kinds of insects. Beetles, which belong to the order Coleoptera, comprise the biggest group of insects and animals known to us: there are a staggering approximately 350,000 described species. The name of their order has to do with the tough, leathery condition of a beetle's forewings, which typically cover up the membranous hind wings when the animal is at rest. Lampyrids are just one of 166 families of beetles worldwide. What contributes to the great diversification and success of the beetles has been their broad range of feeding habits and capacity to occupy many kinds of habitats. Unlike some groups of insects, such as the dragonflies, butterflies, moths, and grasshoppers, in which all or most species are either carnivorous or plant-eaters, the beetles employ both of these feeding styles and scavenging.

While all beetles have mouthparts for chewing, how they are used is often an important key to understanding the diversity of the group. In the plant-feeding group alone, we find the greatest number of beetle species. Physiologically, herbivorous beetles—who attack foliage, wood, flowers, seeds, fruits, and roots—have undergone a tremendous amount of diversified adaptation to the defensive systems of plants. Furthermore, beetles display a very wide range of body sizes, permitting them to occupy a generous spectrum of places in the environment. Whereas most insects are terrestrial, beetles are well represented by both terrestrial and aquatic forms. But like many other groups (such as flies, butterflies, and moths, bees, wasps and ants), beetles have a highly adaptive four-stage life cycle in which the immature stages often occupy a different resource base than the adults. The evolutionary and ecological prowess of beetles is truly impressive.

Still, this meadow is rife with many other creatures, including spiders and predatory bugs, which dine on easy targets like fireflies, so being a firefly can be a very risky affair. Each one has to pass through a sequence of gauntlets during its year-long life in order to survive long enough to reproduce. Each has only a slim chance of succeeding.

While we know some intriguing facts about fireflies, though, our knowledge of them, as is true for most insects, is still rudimentary. Some species have intriguing associations with other insects. One interesting group lives inside the nests of fungus-growing ants in Florida. The ants ignore the larvae, pupae, and adults of this firefly, even in the queen ant's fungal chamber. The wingless female flashes at night from the ant nest entrance, attracting winged males that flash in response. Somehow the ants and fireflies live in harmony, and we have only the vaguest notions of how or why they manage this. In most species, adult male fireflies don't eat at all and the female is carnivorous, but again we don't know why. There is much to learn beyond the basics.

When a female firefly is successfully mated on a summer night such as this one, a feat mediated by flashing signals between the sexes, she lays her eggs in moist soil or mulch, usually near the edge of a stream or permanent drainage ditch. The eggs hatch in a couple of weeks and the larvae, called glowworms, eat tiny insects, mites, even snails. Glowworms use a constant light signal to warn enemies such as field mice that they are not good to eat. A glowworm's flash comes from a pair of small spots near the end of the body. There are a few places on the edges of this meadow where the mushy cover of thatch glitters with glowworms. Some species also have wingless females known as glowworms.

By autumn a firefly larva is only partly grown and prepares for winter by finding shelter under a log, tree stump, or stone when it stays in a semi-active state. The following spring it completes its growth cycle, becoming an adult during summer. Much of its life is spent in the obscurity of mulch and soil. We easily spot a magnificent butterfly appearing in the garden, hear a katydid's raspy call in a tree, or marvel at the jewel-flecked metallic sheen of a basking dragonfly perched on a fence post. It is harder to see those who spend large parts of their lives hidden.

Many things threaten fireflies. A pregnant beetle falls prey to a spider; a snare of eggs molds over if there is too much wetness. Adults are picked off by marauding dragonflies and bats. During the daytime, some are plucked off tree bark and foliage by songbirds. Despite being armed with antifreeze, many overwintering larvae die from freezing. A mild winter followed by a warm, wet spring leads to massive hatches of insects come summer, including fireflies. But when it has been a very dry winter and spring, there are far fewer fireflies. A dry fall also spells disaster for the larvae since they need moist places to pass the long winter.

But when all goes well and it is a good year for fireflies, summer nights can be like this one: dotted with a light show that is a product of nature's own trash and the minutia of creatures it supports. The connections seem clear. Plant life provides the mulch that fireflies need for their life cycle, and the mulch is home for the creatures they eat. In turn, fireflies are recycled into other animal life. The whole system seems to be balanced and works well insofar as sufficient suitable firefly meadows remain intact and healthy.

What makes a meadow suitable for fireflies has much to do with its suitability for breeding. This particular meadow sits in a low marshy area surrounded by a woods and spring rains often flood its margins from a natural stream nearby, making it predictably wet much of the summer—an excellent situation for fireflies. Some of the most familiar ones breed in the soft mud debris accumulating every spring along the margins of natural streams, drainage ditches, and the mud-bottomed canals of storm areas. During the past few decades, though, long sections of natural streams, especially in urban and suburban areas, have been lined with concrete for storm sewers and flood control. As more and more culverts and drainage ditches are concreted, our woodlands and fields are becoming increasingly vacant of the insect life that needs these moist places to breed, including fireflies. And since this is the same insect life that feeds songbirds, the negative effects of our "need" for pavement simply expands outward exponentially. As I stand here, marveling at this light show, I wonder if we can afford our "needs" anymore.

So much in this meadow remains a mystery. Even the flashes of light testify to the diversity represented here. Close to the ground, through the tall grasses and goldenrod, some fireflies are creating a golden tracing, an almost seamless zigzagging maze of yellowish lines, from one species of *Photinus*. In the bushes the slower moving and blinking green lights expose a different *Photinus*. High in the tree tops at the meadow's edge a ribbon of larger orange dots weaving in steep undulating strokes scrolls the signature of a third species. It is not at all uncommon to find the hatches of different fireflies overlapping in a warm, moist meadow such as this one. But the mating-code light signal unique to each species is not only a matter of color, but also of time lapse between flashes, intensity of flashes, even the length of the flash pulse. This fine-tuning prevents interference among firefly species during courtship, and it is far from a trivial matter.

Firefly flashing is all about sex, males using their lights to signal females. In a firefly meadow males can outnumber females by fifty to one. But while the urge to mate is very keen among male fireflies, all is not frenzied and chaotic. There is, in fact, an excellent sense of order coursing through this quest for procreation. Some kinds of fireflies are only active for a brief time after sunset while others wait until it is very dark. Regardless of twilight or nighttime carousing, a male firefly's quest for a temporary bride is doggedly persistent, if not downright impressive. He will travel a good six-tenths of a mile, giving off close to 500 flashes in a single evening. Since it may take as long as a week for a male to find a mate, many die before this happens. Consider *Photinus* again. A male flashes two blips of light two seconds apart. If she is interested, the female answers with a flash one second later, and he flies to her. A male's flash pattern, therefore, is only half of the species-specific courting code; the other half is the female's response flash. The interval of time between the male's two flashes is critical. If a male flashes less than two seconds apart, the female does not respond. This precision in the system prevents females from responding to the signals of other species of fireflies in the area. The timing of the system, too, is controlled by air temperatures. At 76 degrees Fahrenheit a female *Photinus* waits three seconds before answering a male; at 55 degrees the pause expands to nine seconds.

Mating lasts less than six minutes, and the mated female quickly returns to her burrow or some other sheltered place. This is crucial. Each female only has about 150 eggs, low by insect standards, and if she dies before laying them, the loss can be sizable. This downsizing effect is magnified by interference to successful firefly matings from streetlights, backyard lights, and pollution. Together these factors severely imperil firefly populations.

The mating game itself can prove a deadly proposition. A female *Photuris,* a larger firefly than a *Photinus,* flashes a signal that mimics a female *Photinus.* A male *Photinus* logically rushes in, lured by the deceptive "come hither" cue, and is swiftly overpowered, captured, and eaten by the femme fatale. This merciless ploy gives another advantage to this female other than a meal. She picks up a precious defensive chemical from her victim's body that protects her from being eaten by other animals such as spiders, birds, and bats. Otherwise she lacks this prized, helpful substance. As one might expect, female *Photuris* use a very different flash signal to attract their rightful mates.

So this firefly meadow is not all about beauty and peace; it is one of nature's battlefields in which skirmishes among species have few winners and many losers. There is further pressure on the system. Adult fireflies only live a scant 24 hours to a couple of weeks, so the prudent use of time for mating is of the essence. And late in the firefly season, when virgin females are scarce, battles intensify among males. *Photinus* males go so far as to disrupt approaches of their fellow males toward flashing, receptive females, sometimes even displacing males on the verge of mating. But an important lesson of this ecological minefield is that some do win. So the reality of a firefly meadow, behind the calming allure of a twinkling façade, is an intense drama about competition, deception, and carnivory, all mediated by captivating bioluminescence. This last quality, the firefly's ability to make light, is perhaps its most fascinating.

The last three segments of a firefly's body is both the battery and the bulb of its light, and 100 percent of the energy produced here is given off as light, unlike an electric light bulb, which gives off only about 10 percent of its energy as light. Because of this extremely high efficiency, a firefly's flash is "cold light," since no heat is given off. A firefly makes light by combining three key substances in the light organ. Two of these, luciferin and luciferase, get their names from Lucifer, the "Bearer of Light." The third substance, ATP, energizes the very efficient union of luciferin and luciferase that results in the production of light. While this is the foundation of the firefly's light system, there are variations on the theme that encode species differences. Observable differences in firefly signal colors reflect the presence of slightly different luciferase molecules in different species, producing light at different wavelengths and, therefore, different colors. At the heart of the firefly's flash system is the stimulation of its tiny brain by flashes of light captured by the eyes, which then activate the light organ within a swift 200 milliseconds. A firefly's brain clocks time very well, acting as a pacemaker to control the pulse of light flashes from the light organ. Timing is everything in firefly courtship.

There are approximately 2,000 kinds of fireflies around the world and four large groupings of these species based upon distinctive features of their flash signal patterns. Studies based on observing dead firefly specimens alone, such as those found in museum collections, have sometimes resulted in serious errors: two or more distinct species of *Photinus* have sometimes been erroneously lumped as one. Not until a closer look was taken at their flash behaviors in the wild were these species distinguished. This is a sobering thought, given how rapidly we are killing off our fireflies. Once their flashes are gone, we will not be able to correct our errors.

This magical gentle little light show, then, is fragile and vulnerable to extinction. This is not a matter to be taken lightly. If we continue to exert pressure on nature's food chains, we will surely douse the lights of fireflies altogether and our own well-being as a species will become a bit more tattered, a lot less rich. What is also endangered is the unusual communication system of fireflies, something based in chemistry and not at all simple to understand. A loss of fireflies from our world thus holds a deeper message. Our world is accumulating a debt-load of more and more endangered wonders, not just species, but something even more serious, the unique processes and phenomena of life. As things stand now, not a single firefly is really expendable given the tenuous state of their species these days.

There is thus something very good to be said about old, dirty drainage ditches and creeks running through grassy meadows. Unfortunately, creatures like fireflies that depend upon ditch waters or the clogs of matted, wet plant debris just above the water line are in trouble. The great beauty of a summer night is born in the rot of these places, but it has to be pure rot, not the stuff of natural decay adulterated with the contaminating wastes of people. Compressing and poisoning natural areas surely douses the lights of a firefly evening, muffles the whispers of katydids and crickets, and does much more damage. Damage neither we nor the fireflies can afford.

The air is getting cooler now and the fireflies are slowing down. Those throngs of tiny flashes that drew me to this place tonight are bowing out, and soon only darkness will prevail. I feel a touch of melancholy, a sense of loss that our children are not growing up with the wonder of fireflies and may soon know this feisty little beetle only through stories. In the past when there were fewer electric street lights, more unpaved roads, and more people apt to be sitting on porches, there were many more fireflies. Crickets and katydids chirped more, fireflies were caught and held gently in awe; whippoorwills called and bats swooped low. There was no doubt that the land was healthier then than it is now. Even though we could not see these singing creatures of the night, there was still comfort in having their presence close by. Nature's summer night music flowed and melded with the shine of fireflies, creating a window in the inky blackness into the soul of all life. No human genius could ever copy such sensuality, much less reproduce it. Summer at night was an irreproducible composite moment of unadulterated magic. If we would only take a few elementary precautions—like considering the effects of our land-use practices on fireflies—we could ensure that it stays with us in the future. This harried time does not have to be nightfall for the fireflies.

The meadow is much darker now, with only an occasional flash, a lone blinking here and there. I sense, as I walk back to the house, a plea for enlightenment about nature. The magic of a firefly meadow can spark refreshing recognition of the great inspiration and joy that nature bestows upon our own existence and well-being. It has an aura of antiquity beyond antiquity, of the land speaking to us in a marvelous and textured way. The message of the fireflies is elegant and profound. On the surface it appears simple and minute. One prolonged glance at a meadow flashing argues the opposite. Beneath their dancing glows lies a deeply complex story woven into this landscape over eons of time.

The very pulses generated by excited nerve tissues coiled in our brain are akin to those triggering the flash of a firefly—a dormant bond between us and them. We have the best tools at hand for knowing and respecting this planet's vast citizenry of life, our own minds. In the firefly, we have the whole gamut of the human experience, unabashed appreciation of beauty to rigorous discovery, a continuum of understanding born on the quirky winds of time and chance, fate and effort. A firefly meadow on a summer night can remind us of our own mind's collective special light and encourage us to tend it while we have the chance.

The firefly's glow in the muggy thickness of a summer night is a beacon of enlightenment; it is a warm, alive ember of hope that we will look for the true wonder that fills our lives through the guise of small creatures. Their blinking lights testify still to the staggering richness of life on this planet. We neither created it nor contributed to it. Most of the time we're too busy or unaware to even notice it. But the gift persists. Fireflies, unseen moths, and flies crisscross the warm air above, seeking food and mates. Bats follow in hot pursuit. I will go to sleep tonight overwhelmed and humbled by what I saw in the darkened meadow—and hoping that those who come after me will have the opportunity to do the same thing eons into the future from this night.

Bat Plays

I am seated outside, wedged into one of the hard uncomfortable chairs at a summer theater waiting, along with 300 other people, for Shakespeare's *Romeo and Juliet* to begin. As the sky slips from ashen to ebony, a ring of stage lights snaps on, readying the stage for a different theatrical performance, one much older and more awesome than all the Elizabethan dramas put together.

This stifling summer night is already abuzz with an onslaught of blood-hungry mosquitoes. Our bodies are pumping out carbon dioxide, a prime mosquito lure. We are excellent mosquito bait, a collective feast held captive for the next couple of hours. We have paid top dollar to twist, squirm, and swat our way through a night of insectan wrath, and the sickly sweet small of repellent clings to us already. As the landscape darkens, the glare from the floodlights and stage lights intensifies, creating a bowl of brightness, drawing our attention to the human drama about to unfold on stage. Now erased from our view is a rim of forest bordering this little theater. In the inky night, we can no longer gaze out over a sweeping patchwork of forest and farms. This theater was carved from fallow farmland, which had replaced woodlands long ago. Erased too from our view, and thankfully so, is what lies beyond these hills: a mosaic of mega–shopping malls, sheets of asphalt, Astroturf playing fields, and millions of electric lights blotting out the heavens every night.

This is turning out to be a good summer for mosquitoes. A mild winter followed by a warm, wet spring shaped a bumper crop of them, a fraction of which is here tonight. As we revel in timeless human tragedy, the mosquitoes will surely descend on our space from that nearby strip of cooling forest trees where they have been waiting all day, clinging to foliage in deep shade and preparing to spring forth into open spaces in search of us once the sun left. But pesky mosquitos aren't the only hungry beasts here for the show.

As we wait for *Romeo and Juliet* to begin, the musical fanfare foretells both symmetry and discordance. There! The other theater, the one not crafted by Shakespeare, is starting up first, not on the lighted stage, but in the high dark spaces around it. I am speaking, of course, of bats. First just one, then several, swooping low, then high, in and out of the light-streaked night above where we sit. We're paying for the Shakespeare, but getting an even more magnificent natural performance for free. I like bats anyway, but tonight they might well be our saviors. As the costumed actors begin their bantering, the distant call of crickets and katydids evaporates into a faint din. We are drawn to Shakespeare tonight with an expectation of colorful clothing, intrigue, and complex characters, but nature's complexion is all of these things as well, only it nurtures a far more elaborate shifting set of sagas, cooperation, competition, bloody death scenes, and exquisite courtships.

When a bat suddenly swoops back and forth through the lights, the audience sees it as a swiftly moving shadow. A bat seems bigger than it really is, as if magnified in the split seconds when slicing through the beams of the stage lights. Its motion is broad and sweeping, guided by the throngs of flying insects drawn to the lights from the surrounding forest and fields. On just one night here one bat can eat 200 mosquitoes, so over the course of a single summer season, a few hundred bats living in a square mile of this landscape consume many millions of insects. Being warm-blooded, bats need a bounty of insects to fuel their highly tactical existence. It should come as no surprise that our night skies sometimes resemble a traffic maze, chock full of hungry bats zigzagging through clouds of light-hypnotized moths, beetles, and flies.

What seems at first to be several identical objects with fluttering wings is really a snapshot composite of more than one bat species. Here is one potential roster: little brown bat (*Myotis lucifugus*), big brown bat (*Eptesicus fuscus*), Indiana bat (*Myotis sodalis*), silver-haired bat (*Lasionycteris noctivagons*), hoary bat (*Lasiurus cinereus*), red bat (*Lasiurus borealis*) and pipistrelle bat (*Pipistrellus subflavus*). Most likely what I am seeing tonight is a mix of big brown bats and little brown bats, two of the four species that overwinter here.

Bats are skillful hunters with a strong sense of purpose and commitment to family, but they don't all hunt in the same way or for the same kinds of insects. Some bats swing very low and glean insects clinging to leaves and branches or skim water for the same purpose. Others use a system of echoes to find their targets in the dark. While some bats readily engage their prey around powerful electric lights lining streets, stadiums, and malls, others shy away from these places and hunt in the dark. When there are big hatches of insects, several kinds of bats may converge to feast

upon them all at once. Insectan exoskeletons are crushed in a bat's teeth, wings torn off and dropped, and muscles and fatty tissues extracted during digestion. By examining very closely bat feces or guano, we can reconstruct the diets of bats because of the distinctive nondigestible hard parts of insects found. And, come daylight, pieces of moth wings, beetle wing covers, and legs will litter the stage before us, the only telltale clue that bats live in the area and came here for dinner tonight.

Bats live up to 30 years, participate in social groups, and rear young. A mother bat suckles her babies pretty much the way humans do, and bats form extended families that can last for many years. Having excellent communication skills and good eyesight, their sonar is far better than the one we have invented to maneuver submarines. Unfortunately, few people ever get past the myths about bats long enough to appreciate them. Whenever I get half a chance, I offer a bit of advice: forget the myths. Bats do not get tangled up in people's hair. Bats are not this planet's primary carriers of rabies. And bats are far from being blind. Bats, however, do speak for the land, and it is exceptionally difficult to hear their message when cowering in a corner, squealing, or covering our heads.

The true story of the bat is rather ordinary. Like many other mammals, bats are essentially recycled insects and parts of plants, but they are also integral players in much of the design of life on earth and their ties to this land are glaringly evident. On the stage we applaud the creative genius of Shakespeare in bringing to the forefront that timeless struggle and foment of human emotions. We are reminded by *Romeo and Juliet* of the forces that cause tragic things to happen to people. The playwright ingeniously weaves together those quizzical facets of the frail human condition—love, achievement, power, and intellect outwitted at times by old grudges, jealousy, envy, and greed. However, in a bat's world, there is little room for such tragedy. What precipitates death in nature is an issue of survival, not pathos. A bat's gnashing of its teeth reflects the big story of this night, and the theme is clearly a matter of struggle and death, of hunter and quarry, but not tragedy.

I am not suggesting that nature is free of cheating, stealing, and deceit. Getting food, escaping death, and cuckolding fellow partners ripples through the natural world, but in nature, this tension among species is not tragic. Natural discordance and struggle endows nature with changeable balance and symmetry. Humans, though, tend to intensify discordance, generating chaos and disorder, eroding or destroying natural webs with little thought or concern. No wonder it is so easy for us to miss the significance of the ecological dramas unfolding about us: for example, we're often so busy being annoyed at mosquitos that we forget how valuable they are to this planet. And it's not uncommon for us to spend so much energy trying to get away from bats that we forget entirely they are here to dine on mosquitos.

Ecological theatrics are dynamic, yet balanced. The health of our wetlands, for example, depends in no small way upon healthy stocks of mosquitoes and other freshwater insect life. Mosquitoes support the fish populations and feed legions of our native species of dragonflies, bats, and songbirds. Bats, especially, kill and digest mosquitoes, beetles, and moths in order to mate, breed, rear their young and build up the fat reserves in their bodies that they need to survive the winter season. Good hunters stock up well for a long winter; what is happening over much of the landscape tonight will ensure the presence of bats here next year. Millions of insects are becoming bat tissues as I sit here. So the bats caught momentarily in the glare of stage lights cannot be viewed as a single act or monologue, but rather a tiny piece of a complex yet explainable portrait of nature. I consider it wise to respect bats and the many other creatures they depend on for their survival because these animals promote the survival of others.

Although humans regularly attempt to parse nature at whim, the refreshing shade of a wooded glen, the coolness of a lake, or the crystalline gurgle of a creek cannot really be lopped off from the interplay of insects, plants, and other animals. Just as the majesty of a tall old tree cannot be separated from what grows under and in it, neither can the healthiness of a tree's foliage be separated from the grazing prowess of bats. There is a wholeness to life, a complex networking of players and pieces, a masterpiece theater omnipresent yet elusive, and this is what drives our own engine of existence. No living thing is exempt from this pattern. I read this unwavering maxim aloud in my mind as I sit and watch this grand game between bats and insects in the night air. Its moral rings truer for me than any Shakespeare could have written: we must have all the characters in order for the show to go on.

So in a very real sense, the concerted theatrics of various animals, including bats and mosquitoes, define this summer landscape, and have done so for eons of time, long before our presence here. I am quietly enjoying the lesson tonight under the stars, out here in this notch between two hills. I do not mean to ignore Shakespeare, but the juxtaposition of these two theatrical performances is too uncanny to be ignored. In both performances, one made by human beings and the other by bats and insects, strife and death prevail, but to very different ends and with very different underlying causes.

Like any good tragedy, though, even nature's tale must be leavened by the unpredictable, the humorous, the clumsy even. There has to be a certain amount of sloppiness in the system in order for nature to work. The bats cannot be perfect in their lightning-speed strikes at mosquitoes or moths, and these targets must be clever enough to get away. In this teetering play of imperfections emerges the exquisite survival of nature. The aerial chases are a type of game. Most of life actually functions exactly like a game in which a roll of the dice may bring success or misfortune. Living itself assumes a statistical veneer. Who wins and who loses is not entirely clear after the fact, and point-blank cannot be predicted.

I do not wish to ascribe to bats or any other creature more than what they do for us and nature. But clearly one of the best things about this season is the drumming and pulse of life that is more difficult to detect at other seasons here. Very soon, what is right now a gloriously lush and alive landscape will change quickly with that brash sweep of death's chilling autumn paintbrush. Life here is necessarily skewered to a frantic pace, of bats stuffing themselves on as many insects as possible, of bees gathering pollen, of caterpillars gorging themselves before autumn toughens foliage. The soft melodies, tones, and feel of summer are fleeting; this is certain. In this inevitability I am reminded that forever is never really far off, but always close at hand, that all of life and living is exposed to an end, sneakingly tragic or otherwise expected, anticipated.

Romeo and Juliet is in its final act. The mosquitoes did not turn out to be the nuisance everyone expected them to be after all, thanks in large part to the bats and other animals who help create bug-free spaces all summer long for us. What must be protected and encouraged is an understanding and respect for the process. Perhaps we could take a leaf from Shakespeare's page: rather than behave as half of a pair of star-crossed lovers toward our wild siblings, why not learn from the tragedy and simply love them?

I marvel sometimes at the human machine, an intricate system capable of great literature, art, music, inquisitiveness, and discovery. And then there is the network of millions of species, a seemingly endless multiplicity of creatures all interconnected to make an exquisite tapestry. Perhaps it is not a matter at all of comparing these dramas; perhaps they are really one, a continuum. But the record of humanity cries a different chant, one of discontinuity. We have long been unnerved by wildness and sought to escape that feeling by controlling and reshaping wilderness to suit our needs. The human species is truly a living paradox. While we are capable of great and noble things, we tragically destroy ourselves and other beings with whom we share this world. We are wrecking the food chains that sustain our own species. We threaten bats and other beneficial creatures; we pave over more natural areas every day. In short, we behave like the hidebound, tradition-steeped, stubborn families so bent on carrying out Shakespeare's feud: we sacrifice what is best and brightest in ourselves—our ability to love and cherish the natural world on which we depend for our very breath—for a few moments more of thoughtless idiocy. It is a tragedy of mind-boggling proportions.

By contrast the bats circle and sweep in harmony with even their prey. Their existence flows from that of insect life. A brown bat's survival is traced in the blooming of dusk and nocturnal flying insects and the peaking of their numbers by late summer and early autumn. The lesson could not be clearer than the glimmer of those distant stars. That impressive biomass of fur, muscle, bones, and brains filling the summer night air is a matter of living insects being recycled into these highly efficient and agile insect-eaters. It is a matter of the hunters following the herd, not by vision but by radar. It is a matter too of winged locomotion. As is readily evident among the bats, the acquisition and evolution of wings in insects opened new ecological opportunities, of which the bat would take advantage many millions of years later by becoming the only mammal with true wings. With the exception of whippoorwills and nighthawks, in these parts bats have little competition in the aerial hunt for insects at night.

I am reminded again of how the parade of the seasons offers feast and stress for creatures, as it plainly does for ourselves as well. For when the summer nights are still warm and dripping, bats gather up the energy they need to sustain them in the months to come. When the night air turns cool and frost-tipped, flying insects for the most part drop out of this scene, their own work accomplished and their eggs now well hidden away to withstand winter. And so too these hills will cease for a full year to whisper with the games of carnivory, for the bats also must now acquiesce or move away. This is an age-old drama celebrating the slippage of summer into autumn and what is to come.

The stage lights are now turned off for another evening and blackness prevails. The bats will continue hunting long after we have fallen asleep. Some semblance of natural harmony will prevail. With the lights off, people drifting away, and the music of katydids and crickets again taking prominence, I sense a symmetry embossed on this land by its wild citizens. Nature is struggling to hold on here. Once again I find myself wishing for a torrid love affair between people and the rest of nature. What a good thing that would be. In the meantime, the commingled aerial dances of bats and insects will continue in the nights to come, and as long as it does a wisp of nature will flourish. I will come again for more Shakespeare—come to laugh and cry and smile at the absurdities of the human farce—but when I leave, my mind will always be on the bats.

Green Darners

As perverse as it sounds, I think a lot about carnivory, especially when strolling near dusk on summer evenings. But mind you, I am not thinking about hawks, wolves, snakes, or big cats: my subjects are significantly smaller in physical size, though not in importance. Big dragonflies skillfully swoop through the ashen sky, aiming for truly raw flesh. Sometimes there is only one, or perhaps two, resembling whirling sticks dancing through the fading sunlight. Their silent movements are punctuated by the sounds of their jaws crunching insects they have captured in midair, an aural testament to their status as carnivores.

With the exception of wasps and birds, I place dragonflies and bats highest on my list of favorite insect-eating animals. Their antics at thinning out the myriad small flying insects in my backyard have brought me great pleasure near twilight for many summers. These little flesh-eaters are very good at aerial bug hunting. One of the most impressive is the green darner, *Anax junius,* one of the biggest dragonflies in North America.

Of all of the 5,000 known species of dragonflies worldwide, my favorite has always been the green darner. Together with other dragonfly species across this continent, it has a long history of being a "devil's darning needle," the mythological creature capable of sewing together the lips of an errant child. The real historical character, of course, is neither capable of such treachery nor all that interested in disciplining human children. Such tales, unfortunately, have made children fear dragonflies rather than learn to give these exquisitely engineered and clever creatures the love and respect they truly deserve. That is a shame because the green darner is truly an intriguing beast, often called the "Lord of June," and well worth getting to know. A single green darner can eat hundreds of mosquitoes and gnats in one dusk period, using its lightning-fast aerial gyrations to whiplash clouds of these insects, thinning their number in less than 30

102

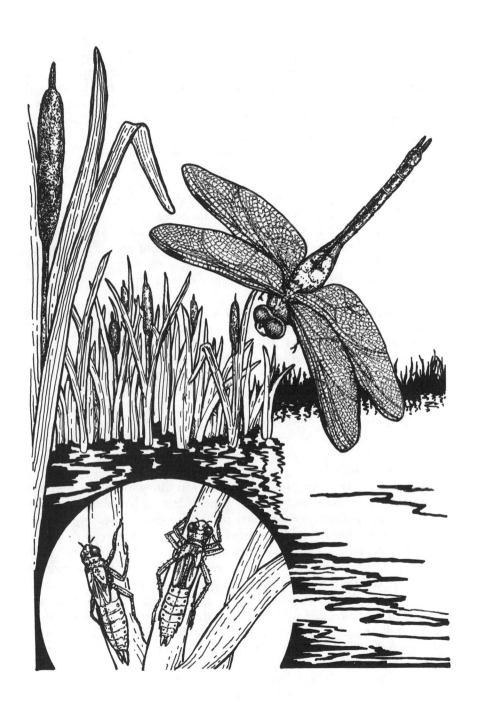

minutes. Their naiads, too, in grazing herds of midge and mosquito wrigglers in ponds and swampy backwaters, are equally voracious.

Many years ago, while at college in New York, I had a summer job as a laboratory technician in the Kitchewan Research Laboratory of the Brooklyn Botanical Garden in Westchester. During lunch breaks, I would take a path through the forest surrounding the facility to a large elbow-shaped pond at the edge of a rolling tall-grass meadow. This is where I first became acquainted with the green darner and several other kinds of dragonflies. From these intermittent forays to the pond at noon, I quickly learned that even when everything else is thickly stilled by the heat of August, laid flushed and satiated against a background of whining cicadas, the dragonflies moved swiftly about, flashes of blue, crimson, powdery white, and green zigzagging above the water. They seemed to have endless strength packed into their four-inch bodies and six-inch wingspans. Such dimensions pale in contrast to fossils of ancient dragonflies dating back to the Carboniferous, of course, some of which reportedly had two-foot wingspans, but they look big and impressive by today's standards.

Examining a dragonfly up close always gives me a strange sense of something very ancient, almost as if I am staring at a being that lived many millions of years ago, which in fact, it did. No one knows for sure why modern insects don't reach the mammoth dimensions attained by some of their relic counterparts millions of years ago. But size is really not the issue, is it? That dragonflies and other insects have survived all of this time is what is of utmost significance. Perhaps intense competition from small vertebrate animals made it wise for insects to go small in an evolutionary context. No matter, the modern dragonfly is a wonderful example of the inherent survivability of the ancient winged-insect design, and by any standards the green darner is a stunning beast.

Thirty-seven years ago, I would walk slowly along the entire shoreline of the pond, counting and observing green darners. All the ones I saw doing regular patrols over the water turned out to be males. Male green darners have a bluish abdomen, green thorax, and huge reddish-brown eyes. Females have the same eye coloring but the rest of the body is mostly green. Both sexes have flecks of dark markings on their bodies, but the males are clearly recognizable from a distance owing to the distinctive blue color of the abdomen. Over time I discovered that each male appeared to have a regular flight beat over the water, and sometimes, when the patrolling routes of two dragonflies would intersect, there would be a noisy aerial clash and disengagement. These frequent collisions were accompanied by soft rustling sounds from their clattering wings. Only once in a while did I see a female at the pond, and when she appeared, she was either copulating with a male or laying eggs.

I found this curious, but over the ensuing years learned that female green darners are never as numerous as males at ponds. The female comes to water only to mate and lay eggs, and when done, she leaves. She spends most of her time away from water, hunting for insects in fields when not laying eggs, and she needs to mate just once to fertilize her full load of eggs. A male green darner lives a very different life. He tends to be around water much more often because he can mate not just with one female, but with several, essentially surfing the course of the breeding season. In fact, male green darners become downright competitive when it comes to sex and wooing females. Supposedly a female chooses her mate based upon some recognizable features of his territorial space, such as whether it contains suitable places to lay eggs. Emergent reed stalks and piles of partly submerged plant debris are signs of good egg-laying sites, and the male who has some of this stuff within his territory is lucky. For even though a male dragonfly appears to be defending a space above the water, what he is really guarding is a potentially good place for a female to lay her eggs in the water.

When green darners are mating, the joined couple stays near the edge of the water and alights on reeds. Sometimes they move further out into the meadow where they are less likely to be pestered by mate-seeking males at the pond. Then, when a mated female later begins to lay eggs, the male appears to guard over her as she dips her abdomen into the water. If another male attempts to approach the busy mother, the guarding male chases it away or enters into a brief skirmish with the intruder.

The events of those summers piqued my interest in the green darner and I went on to learn more about this somewhat mysterious dragonfly. While in graduate school at the University of Chicago a few years later, I found myself fascinated by a seemingly trivial matter. I began making sketches of the color patterns of male green darners netted along the edges of a small lake near the campus. Naturally, the patterns were never identical. There were slight to large variations in the arrangement and sizes of the dark flecks on the sides of the abdomens from different males sampled from the same population. Of course, from a distance, all of the males looked the same. It was only when examining them up close that I could spot the difference. I wondered at the time if such differences in color patterns reflected other differences among the males, traits that could eventually distinguish them in the eyes of female conspecifics looking for a mate. After all, dragonflies rank high among the insects having the best vision. For that matter, they rank high in other abilities as well.

A dragonfly basically consists of a very powerful set of jaws, wings, and legs, very large eyes, and a brain sophisticated enough to endow it with abilities for intricate aerial maneuvering along with complicated courtship and breeding. Its keen vision is enhanced by an ability to rotate its entire head almost 360 degrees. Wings and legs are attached to a compact muscle-packed, box-like thorax, and in flight a green darner can hold its spiny legs in a cup-like position and use it literally to scoop small insects such as mosquitoes from the air as it flies. Some dragonflies not only take prey on the wing, but actually land on tree trunks or branches and snatch resting insects such as butterflies, moths, beetles, ants, and even foul-smelling coreid bugs.

Within the vast evolutionary scheme of the insects, dragonflies, together with damselflies, comprise the order of Odonata. The odonates are one of the earliest known groups of flying insects. The name of this order means "toothed ones," an appropriate label for these live flying machines outfitted with flesh-crushing mandibles. Dragonflies on the wing snare, bite, and grind up mosquitoes, earning them the moniker "mosquito hawks." And they have been doing this a long, long time, essentially acting as sentinels to earth's history since millions of years before even the time of the dinosaurs, some 70 million years ago. As a result, odonates have incredible staying powers when it comes to complex behaviors associated with courtship, egg-laying, and feeding.

With the exception of the brief period just after the final molt from nymph to adult dragonfly, dragonflies keep their wings spread out horizontally rather then flexing them back at rest. This condition has something to do with dragonflies being among the first insects to have wings. Other kinds of flying insects, those which evolved later, such as butterflies and beetles, have the option of being able to fold their wings when resting. There is great advantage in being able to do this, since the feature allows butterflies and other insects to conceal themselves more effectively. Because dragonflies rank high on the list of our oldest insects, I consider them to be successful anachronisms of long passed eras as well as modern stories of ecological success. But studying them is easier said than done.

In particular, snaring a dragonfly in a net, let alone snaring a swift, powerful green darner, is tough to do. Not only are dragonflies some of our fastest flying insects (having been clocked at speeds exceeding 25 miles an hour) but they also outmaneuver the gyrations of hovercrafts. Flight muscles comprise some 30 percent of a dragonfly's body mass. Armed with sturdy wings that glisten in the sun like brittle panels of cellophane but that are well endowed with a network of cross-bracing veins that give them incredible bending capabilities, dragonflies can stop in midair and suddenly reverse the direction of flight in an instant.

Scientists and students of natural history have always been enthralled with dragonflies. I believe this has a lot to do with their behavior and their overt physicality. The sexual dimorphism in body color, found in the green darner, for example, also occurs in many other kinds of dragonflies. In some species, the males sport bright red bodies compared to a drab brown for females. Because of their incredible visual acuity, there is little doubt that much of their courtship is initiated by a recognition of their opposite by body-color differences, which can be seen from a considerable distance. Highly flexible motor abilities coupled with excellent vision allows a male not just to recognize a potential mate but also to learn landmarks around a body of water and stake out a territorial space. Having a well-developed sense of space and dealing successfully with nearest neighbors that also have similar spaces appears to be a hallmark trait for dragonfly success. I know how difficult it is for people to accept the sophistication of an insect's brain. But the dragonflies compel us all to believe. They are just too good at what they do for us not to accept their ingenuity and guile.

Like most insects, dragonflies have large compound eyes, which in their case comprise a major portion of the head. These huge eyes, containing up to 30,000 individual lenses in each, allow them to detect the slightest of movements of a prey insect from several feet away. Imagine a series of separate images of the same subject moving across a wide field of vision. What the dragonfly sees is a set of overlapping yet distinct images. Because they and other insects also see in the ultraviolet range of the light spectrum, they are very keen at distinguishing different images from the environment, ones not perceived by the human visual apparatus. Dragonflies, again, like other insects, also have simple, single-lens eyes in the middle of the head called ocelli. Unlike compound eyes which are the organs of visual image perception, the ocelli register polarized light and colors. Between the two kinds of eyes, dragonflies are well equipped to receive the kinds of sensory input they need in order to carry out the incredible aerial maneuvers they do so well. It has been estimated that close to 80 percent of the insect's brain is devoted to processing visual and light intensities.

Courtship provides an excellent example of how visual acuity helps dragonflies. This act is not an ordinary matter by any means. When I see copulating green darners, as with other species of this group, I am amazed at their contortions. A female green darner recognizes a mate-seeking male at a pond first by the blue color of his abdomen and then by his flight patterns. Some level of assessment of this male, a potential mate, is made by the unmated female. If she chooses to copulate, the challenge to join up begins. The male's sperm is produced and stored in an organ located on the underside of the ninth abdominal segment, near the very rear of the dragonfly's long body, but his penis, which must be inserted into the female to deliver the sperm, is located far forward, on the second abdominal segment. In order to copulate, the male therefore has to literally double up, curling the abdomen under himself in order to transfer seminal fluid into a special pocket behind the penis. The male seizes the receptive female by the back of her head using his claspers at the tip of his abdomen. She curls her abdomen so that her genital opening on the ninth segment lines up with the penis. In this wheel position, the two dragonflies are oriented tail to head and belly to tail and sperm is transferred to the female, fertilizing her eggs. When the two partners separate, the male will remain with her, guarding her during egg-laying and thus ensuring that his offspring are given a chance at survival. All of this behavior is made possible by a combination of excellent vision and intricate motor skills. Lacking either or both would render the dragonfly helpless in the watery environs it inhabits.

It is, of course, the egg and naiad (nymph) stages of the dragonfly life cycle that depend upon water and the other life it holds. Dragonflies have split personalities in this regard, and it is not easy to understand them, but I am intrigued by this dual life. In some way, I see a bond between dragonflies, insects whose lives are split between water and land, and cicadas, whose lives are divided between underground and above ground. In both groups, the immatures are hidden away from us and we know little about their lives. Dragonfly naiads, of course, are more readily accessible than cicada nymphs tunneling through thick earth. To take a lesson here from the human experience, these situations bear a touch of Victor Hugo. For dragonflies and cicadas are creatures, unlike most insects, that exist first in great darkness in the murky depths of water or soil, by human standards a difficult existence. And then, all of a sudden, following a great clock guided in no small way by celestial events, they transform into creatures of the land and air, aficionados of the sun for a brief, tenuous moment. If they manage to live long enough to mate and lay eggs, they will have succeeded in perpetuating their kind.

A pregnant green darner helps ensure that the success of the individual will benefit the species: it works to spread its many eggs out over a network of permanent bodies of freshwater rather than placing all of the eggs in one pond. Green darners, then, depend upon multiple bodies of water for their survival as a species. In fact, one of the things I admire most about the green darner is its ability to thrive in a sizable range of different bodies of permanent water as a nymph. This is not at all the case for many other kinds of dragonflies. Some species need very specific freshwater conditions in which to breed successfully. Others only dwell as nymphs in rivers and streams. Still others are specialists of deep, shaded woods while others prefer open marshes and swamps. But not the green darner. It seems almost ubiquitous—equally at home in city and country as long as a body of water is available. Unsurprisingly, it is one of the most widespread dragonfly species across much of the continent.

Of the more than 100 species of odonates known from this region, the

green darner is one of the best at adapting to different habitats. But its ability to breed in a fairly broad range of habitats should not remove a concern for its long-term survival. Dragonflies have been around for a very long time and have done well for the most part, but recently even they have had to contend with massive, widespread pollution caused by people. Even green darners, as adaptable as they are, may not be able to cope with swampy backwaters becoming waste dumps for human trash and chemicals. Then too, the green darner does have some very real limitations on where it breeds. Because it is large, its nymphs need habitats with plenty of prey on which to feed. So, muddy pond bottoms, lakes, and the backwaters of big rivers, with their prolific populations of water-breeding flies and other insects, are ideal for this species. Freshwater habitats with plentiful small fish, tadpoles, crayfish, and insects are also relished hunting grounds for green darner nymphs and adults. Since it sometimes requires two years to complete nymphal development in some regions, the green darner requires permanent water that does not intermittently dry up.

Being a dragonfly nymph cannot be an easy existence by any stretch of the imagination. The more time it takes to reach maturity and become a winged adult flying off into the relative safety of the sunshine, the more likely it is that an individual naiad will not make it at all. Because dragonfly nymphs live underwater, we do not know very much about their lives, and most of what we do know comes from observing them in captivity. The challenge to survive begins the moment a mother green darner slips her eggs under the water, placing them on a pile of debris in shallow areas. The innocuous eggs can be quickly gobbled up along with plant debris and other small creatures by bottom-feeding fish and scavenging insects. If an egg survives to hatch in a matter of weeks, the baby naiad runs the same risks. Being a newly hatched tiny naiad on the bottom of a pond is like walking through an ecological minefield—for 12 months. The most hazardous part of such an existence is being hunted and eaten by the variety of fishes, crayfish, diving beetles, ducks, and loons for whom insect larvae serve as delectable sources of protein. In this sense, dragonflies are pivotal elements in the chain of life in a pond, lake, or stream.

I enjoy going out to a pond with students and running a net along the bottom, bringing up treasure troves of scurrying animals, including naiads. Dragonfly naiads are quite strange-looking little animals. Each kind looks a bit different too. Some turn out to be flattish and thick, while others, like those of the green darner, are elongated and streamlined. They all have bulbous eyes and filament gills at the tip of the abdomen used for breathing underwater. The gills, resembling small flat blades, are filled with a meshwork of very fine capillary-like extensions of the insect's tracheal system. The tracheal system itself is a network of tubes extending throughout the insect's body. Insect blood is not designed to transport oxygen to tissues and to receive carbon dioxide from them in exchange. This crucial cycle is undertaken instead by the tracheal system. The naiad's capillary gill net absorbs oxygen from the water and allows the insect to breathe underwater. Adult dragonflies, of course, do not have these gill-like structures and must gather air through the line of tiny openings called spiracles along each side of the body.

In another fascinating adaptation, naiads can collect water in the body through the anus and then expel it rapidly, giving these creatures their own personal jet propulsion system that pushes them forward at an incredible speed. The speed can be adjusted by the amount of water drawn into the body and expelled, and by the insect's locomotoring skills. Additionally, the dragonfly naiad also has strong legs enabling it to stalk prey and strike swiftly at it. Close examination of the muddy-brown naiad, a creature almost invisible in its near-perfect match to the pond bottom and debris, reveals tiny wing pads coming off the sides of the thorax and held flat against the sides of the abdomen. The naiad, of course, has no use for wings in its watery existence, which, in the case of the green darner at least, is quite long relative to most dragonflies.

The naiad spends its life looking for food and escaping danger. Naiads of most dragonflies develop during one summer season, staying active all the time. Under some circumstances, green darner naiads require not one but two summers to complete their growth cycle. It is not too difficult to imagine why it takes this long for the cycle to be completed. Like the adult, the dragonfly nymph is a carnivore, eating many kinds of aquatic insects and crustaceans it stalks on the muddy bottom of its home. When it is very large, a green darner nymph will even attack tadpoles and small fish as prey. Dragonfly nymphs have a remarkable lower lip that unfolds at lightning speed to help capture a prey. Like the adult, the nymph has a keen sense of vision and detects even the slightest movements of its victims. However, because of its large size, in order for the green darner nymph to produce an adult, it needs two growing seasons in which to mature. It also needs bodies of water that support large enough populations of the animal life it consumes. Other kinds of dragonflies, including their close cousins, the damselflies, being smaller in size, do not need two years to complete the life cycle.

Many times in the past I would poke through the reeds and brush along the edge of ponds on warm sunny days looking for the telltale evidence of dragonfly breeding. My quarry was not the adult dragonflies dive-bombing and crisscrossing my path as I knelt in the damp mats of brush. I was looking for the cast skins or cuticles of their naiads. While my primary game were the casts of green darners, I found several other kinds of dragonfly cast skins on most of these forays. Like the living naiad beneath the water, the cast skins are perfect replicas of their body features, making it almost possible to identify individual species. Sometimes the cast skins were caked with mud, giving them an eerie appearance; others were smooth and clean. But each one told a unique story, one of survival beneath the water out of our view.

I always found this feature of insect life cycles—that is, the evidence of their hidden lives thrust upon us in the form of cast skins—very captivating. In some ways at least, looking for dragonfly cast skins among the reeds was the aquatic counterpart of my equally fun hunts for the bulbous cast skins of cicadas around the bottoms of big trees in my backyard, a seamlessly familiar, yet different experience. Quite simply, I am drawn to the idea of a creature crawling out of its skin or cuticle and leaving it behind as real evidence of once having lived in this place. Seeing a cast skin of a dragonfly or cicada clinging to a branch or reed affirms in my mind that wondrous move from an earthen or watery darkness to air and sunlight.

These hunts became somewhat addictive at times, for I did not want to stop once started, and I still find something very enjoyable in gathering up these lifeless clues of insect existence, looking at them closely, measuring their locations, and tracking the times of the year when they seem to peak at a particular pond. The green darner's large cast skins are readily distinguished from those of other smaller dragonflies breeding in the same ponds, which always makes me wonder at how these various species coexist on the bottom of a pond as naiads presumably seeking the same kinds of food.

By going back to the same pond over the course of a summer, and going back again the following summer and thereby collecting naiad cast skins over and over, I discovered that it is possible to sketch out a time-sensitive portrait of a dragonfly species' existence, and that its life cycle meshes with that of the season. This seasonal portrait is not the same for all areas where I observed green darners over the years. Here, near the western edge of this great lake, for example, green darners peak in hatching anywhere from late June through August, the middle of our summer, but those in other areas come earlier or later. I discovered other things about the tenuous life of green darners in transition between water and land too. While searching for cast skins early in the day, I sometimes found catbirds stalking silently through the brush in search of a splendid feast of sitting, soft, newly eclosed (shed) adults. I also learned that even fully hardened green darners in flight are not without enemies. At certain times in the summer when large numbers of them are present at ponds, birds such as robins catch them to feed to their nestlings. Although robins usually feed their nestlings other kinds of food, it might be opportunistic for them to plunder gatherings of dragonflies when they are available near nesting sites.

In my limited experience, green darners and other dragonflies transformed from full-grown naiad to the adult in the early morning hours. If you have ever had the good fortune to watch a cicada nymph, clinging to a tree trunk, in the act of splitting open its cuticle down the back and a soft new cicada pushing outwards, you get a ready sense of just how intense this struggle to be free can be. It is not a fast process. Consider the physical dynamics involved. A fully grown green darner naiad, like the cicada, senses when it is time to make the final molt and positions itself carefully to do so. By now, the naiad has molted many times underwater, each time shedding a tight cuticle and walking away from it as the new one hardened into a fully protective new coat. Since insects and other arthropods have their supporting skeletons on the outside, growth can only be accomplished by periodic shedding of this exoskeletal layer of tough material. But for every molt there is a new exoskeleton formed beneath the old one, sized larger to accommodate a period of further body growth.

A green darner's final molt, which takes place out of the water, can require up to an hour, perhaps longer, to complete. The newly eclosed adult dragonfly, its wings very soft and easily damaged at this point, crawls up the reed or stem and rests there for a while. At this stage the insect is called teneral, meaning that its exoskeleton and wings are still very soft and the creature is incapable of flight. When the dragonfly is finally ready to take wing, it is still teneral, but not as much as before. Freshly teneral dragonflies, like the naiads emerging from the water, are sitting targets for the sharp eyes of waterfowl. Imagine what a prize catch the big green darner would be to a bird. When capable of flight, the first order of business for the dragonfly is to head off into a meadow to feed. At full body strength, a new green darner is ready to fly over large areas of habitat and terrain. They probably move around considerably more than do most other dragonflies, a consequence of their large body size and powerful wings and the amount of fuel they must consume to function.

Sometimes I have come across hundreds of green darners in a field or along the edge of a forest. In this area, it is not unusual to encounter small pockets of them swarming near the shoreline of the lake in early autumn. These groupings apparently coalesce at some point into larger groups that move south en masse. Researchers are discovering that green darners migrate over great distances in autumn, heading for warmer regions. And if any dragonfly could migrate, the green darner is surely one of our best candidates given its size and strength. Being very strong fliers, they can move rapidly over long distances, leaving here as teneral adults in late summer and becoming fully mature en route to their overwintering grounds in the southern United States and Mexico, perhaps even into northern Central America.

Migrating green darners, which include both sexes, tend to exhibit a more directed flight than the crisscrossing of female-luring males over a pond or the swooping of both males and females over a meadow or yard hunting insects at dusk. Furthermore, the migrations have many more individuals packed into small spaces than would normally gather at a pond or in a meadow. We don't know all of the details of their migrations, but there are some good clues and facts available. It appears that autumn migrant green darners breed when they arrive at their final destination in late fall and early winter. Green darners have been seen in places such as the Yucatán and Belize during October and November, apparently migrants arriving from as far north as here in Wisconsin. Copulating pairs and egg-laying females are also seen in these far south areas at this time.

Some researchers have suggested that it is the offspring of these autumn migrants that fully develop into a new generation of adults by early spring season in the north. They apparently are spring migrants heading north from their southern birthplaces. Strong southerly winds behind warm fronts in spring push influxes of them into the northern latitudes. Unlike the fall migration, in which the aggregations and swarms of green darners can be prodigious, perhaps reflective of larger dragonfly populations building up by late summer due to peaking prey numbers at these times, the spring move north is more scattered and of lower density. It is not known if green darners in the northward migration breed along the way as monarch butterflies do on their migration north.

The spring migration of the green darner is strikingly similar to that of the monarch, diffuse and spread out. But unlike the monarch, it is likely that a different generation of dragonflies initiates the spring movement rather than the ones that survived the arduous fall migration. But still, there may be another similarity with monarchs. The monarchs arriving here by late spring or early summer represent one or more new generations that developed in the south during spring and then continued moving north: they were not the same butterflies that made the last fall migration. Such a condition might also be true for green darners arriving here. We simply do not know for sure at this point.

What we do know from studies of green darners at high northern latitudes is that a breeding population in any given summer apparently consists of two distinct sub-groups representing different life-cycle strategies associated with the cycle of seasons. There is a resident group and a migratory group. The resident green darners pass the winter as half-grown naiads and need about eleven months to complete their development. This span of time is from when eggs were laid in the water in late July or early August in the first summer until the adults from this brood emerge in late June or early July of the following summer. This prolonged naiad stage is deliberate, ensuring that a local breeding population exists here every summer, and it is the phase of the green darner most adapted to the northern cycle of seasons. Migratory-phase green darner naiads, by contrast, need only about three months to develop, even though they coexist in the same ponds with resident-phase naiads taking almost a year to do the same. In the migratory phase, eggs laid in June by spring migrants from the south produce a crop of new adults in September of the same year. It is these adults that become fall migrants.

We do not know why it is that the magnificent green darner has a breeding system in which there are two different groups, one residential and the other migratory, embedded in the same population occupying the same breeding sites at the high latitudes. We know even less about what happens to them between north and south. One thing is clear: the green darner approaches the monarch butterfly in its strength as a species. And even the monarch doesn't employ both residential and migratory patterns in its northern range for survival. All of our monarchs across the entire continent, as far as we know, are migratory; none are residents. We have to venture very far south into Central America and the Caribbean archipelago to find residential monarchs.

The green darner is obviously a very tenacious and adaptable dragonfly. It seems to be found almost anywhere, despite how much humans have despoiled wetlands and river systems over the last two centuries. These changes have unquestionably imperiled some species of our dragonflies, but the green darner seems to be doing well for the time being. It is safe to say, though, that between 30 and 40 percent of our region's dragonfly fauna near the edge of this great lake are now imperiled, and it would be foolish to believe for a moment that this loss of life will stop there. Dragonflies everywhere are threatened. For the time being, those species with versatile habits such as the green darner will stay off the imperiled list. Its ability to move great distances and to breed in a variety of permanent bodies of water have given this dragonfly a bit of an edge in the game of survival. This is a good thing, because the green darner, along with other dragonflies, helps keep a balance of life in both land and aquatic food chains.

But all dragonflies need clean water and clean air if they are to continue upholding a very ancient legacy on this planet. We need the green darner and other dragonflies. They are a part of our summer's legacy of life. I for one hope to enjoy many more summer dusks with them, flies, and other insects stirring to life in the sweet dusk air. I relish catching glimpses of them, slowed by the coolness of autumn's approach, readying themselves for the long journey south. This helps to define for me the slippage of summer into autumn.

While there is still time during this season of harvest, just before summer's simmering cools on approaching autumn breezes, before the air in my backyard is lightened of its water and cleansed of its clinging mist of dusk swarms of minute insects, I will take a snapshot of green darners in my mind's eye for one last time. For when this air and space is chilled, these aerial theatrics of summer's rhythms will be gone, and so too the green darners for almost another year. Sealed beneath the cold waters, even under ice in a few months hence, their feisty naiads will thrive, while the season's last hatch of adults wings south. Both phases of this species hold the promise that there will be green darners with us next summer. When autumn chills fill the night air, then, I can sit by the fire and reflect on dragonfly dramas I hope will usher in another summer near the edge of this great lake.

Autumn

Less than a month ago I sat out here on the deck in the backyard with the morning summer air steaming with the pulse of life. I remember spotting, just for a moment, a striking pair of cardinals flitting through the thick brambles at the rear of the yard. Bumblebees noisily plundered rich payloads of russet and yellow pollen from that tall patch of purple coneflowers and black-eyed Susans bordering the garage. Small heaps of shavings from walnut shells piled up on the fence posts, the persistent handiwork of squirrels, caught my attention. As dawn evaporated away into high noon like the disappearing dew, the big silver maple in the middle of the yard sprang to life with the whine of unseen cicadas clinging to its drooping branches. And of course, tenacious yellowjackets tried to chase me off the deck and, on occasion, almost succeeded. Life from the deck by late summer was a richly textured scene, more so than in some other recent summers. I could feel the drumming of life's bigger design in the drone of bees, buzz of cicadas, splashes of butterfly colors, and soft nighttime melodies of snowy tree crickets. For a place close to the city, this yard was well blessed with full cast of characters.

I'd like to think this condition had something to do with my refusal to keep a fastidious, tidy yard. For by summer's close, the borders were fuzzy and frazzled with bent weeds of many kinds, great breeding grounds for insects and spiders. All of this I did not mind and, in fact, had hoped would be the end product of my unabashed lack of attention. I view my backyard as a natural experiment of sorts—a place where I freely encourage the struggle between traditional yard care and letting things be. In short, I urge my yard to act as my summer entertainment. Indeed, by summer's end this year, my backyard was a grand success, delightfully messy.

This kind of untidiness says something very good about the land. No matter if it is a backyard or field or patch of forest. This was a great summer, with just the right mix of warm temperatures and rainfall to shape bumper crops of plants and insects. It was a good season too for my little vegetable garden. Now, on the verge of a cold snap, there are a few green tomatoes left on the vines, but over the past two months we gorged ourselves over and over on fresh salads using those tomatoes. The corn this year did its usual thing. What few tender ears there were went quickly to the squirrels. Nevertheless we enjoyed planting the garden and making the earth produce. And anyway, I don't mind not eating all of the harvest from the garden. I get great pleasure from seeing things sprout out of the dark earth, reach toward the sky, and bear fruit. My garden serves all that live in the yard and all that pass through it. No mind that my vegetable patch was invaded by creeping Charlie and other weeds, native and exotic. Again, ecological messiness, no matter the players and game plan, does not bother me. In the backyard as everywhere else, nature is messy.

Nor is there any such thing as pristine, since every place is a mix of native species and outside invaders. These situations, of course, engender awesome distress in preservationists, but it should be less of an issue for ecologists and conservationists. All of the land is one big experiment. The rules and steps change all of the time, as do the players. I like to think of my yard, at the end of the growing season and when autumn begins to show its personality, as part of this messiness. This welcome untidiness in the yard marches along with the turn of the season. Great celestial events, unfolding with the elegance of an immense timepiece, have changed the complexion of the backyard. The grass and weed patches are littered with golden dead leaves cascading from the silver maple as the cooling breezes of autumn push off the dense, steamy air of summer's last hurrah. By this time, it is almost impossible to find, upon close inspection, a single leaf still on a tree or bush that is not riddled with holes made by legions of beetles, grasshoppers, and caterpillars. Stems and leaves are now tough and pithy, a far cry from their soft tenderness in spring and early summer. My garden tools are stored away in the garage already, and soon the push mower will follow them. Change rings through the air as skies leaden by day become crystalline clear at night with a crisp light show of a million stars. Now when I go for a walk in the neighborhood, it is downright cold and feels raw to the bone on some nights.

Leaving the deck for a nearby meadow, I see unmistakable evidence that what I observed in the yard was but a sliver of the full drama that the heavenly move from summer into autumn brings to insects and other creatures. Here too are signs of summer's closure and the doomed path that those who have survived this far will surely follow. I push through reedy, dying brush dripping with thick liquid, something between dew

118

and true frost. On the tall yellow crests of goldenrod, life is stilled in some sort of suspended animation. The place is a freeze frame portrait of that which was once very animated but now stands numbed by night's chill. I see wild bees, including bumblebees, clinging to the goldenrod florets. I could pick them off. They seem lifeless but they are not. When the air warms up later in the morning, the bees will stir from their slumber and crawl slowly over the flowers and attempt to fly. But now they are at the mercy of the cold and me. I try to avoid knocking them off as I move through the fields. Further down the stems, red-legged grasshoppers sit stoically. How different they seem than when I walked here in late August and they flew off in endless directions by the hundreds as I parted the brush. Now nothing darts away at my approach.

Yet even now, on the eve of frost and more cold, this meadow remains a testimonial to the fertility of summer. The clues are everywhere. Summer's smoldering, steamy dog days nursed lush waving crests of stately Queen Anne's lace, thistles, milkweeds, Joe-Pye weed, goldenrods, and, of course, roadside legions of the unmistakable chicory. This floral exuberance was laden with throngs of beetles, flies, wasps, and butterflies frantically stuffing themselves on this season's last treasure chests of pollen and nectar. Spiders and ambush bugs lurking in these flowers gorged themselves on nectar-seeking insects. These scenarios, each a microcosm of a bigger portrait, that of a landscape once gloriously clothed but now clad in a faded and tired verdancy, exposes the soul of a timepiece uniting all creatures. The challenge is to force summer's shutdown for another year. When nature's cycle of birth, growth, death, and continuance marches into autumn, cool winds and frosted nights signal that death is kicking in.

Back on the deck in the yard, I relish the signs of summer's demise from dawn to dusk, and well into the night. Much can be learned by watching carefully from the vantage point of a deck at different times of the day. Dragonflies would appear as the cicadas ceased to sing at dusk, when the setting sun sent stiletto rays through the branches and foliage, creating a spatter of tiny floodlights speckling the darkening yard. The dragonflies flew swiftly back and forth, up and down, dodging and weaving through this sparkling air, no doubt snaring hoards of tiny gnats and mosquitoes cued into action as the air cooled and light dimmed.

But much of this is fading now. Several nights of frost will soon muffle and still the yard. There will be no calls of cicadas, no rustle of birds. The monarch butterflies I saw on the milkweed plants in the garden weeks ago are only a memory now. The calls of crickets and katydids are slowed. Now all I hear is the rattle of dried foliage on the bushes and trees, and the snapping of twigs whipped by autumn's stinging winds. Nights are beginning to be downright chilly and the heavens sparkle without the veil of thunderstorm clouds. Heavy frost, that dusting of ice that knocks down life, is not far off now. The hustle and rush of symphony is being swept aside. Winter is closing in.

But the cold mornings of light frost have not stopped me from sitting on the deck at dawn, even though everything now is parched, browned, and withered. What leaves still remain on the bushes and the grass are crusted in a trace of white icing. They resemble large frosted cereal flakes. The view is clear, clean, and crisp, not the soft blurred mosaic of summer's impressionist portrait that filled this place the past several months. But the mode and tempo of this cleansing of the landscape does not always follow a definitive rhythm one year to the next. A first killing frost of the season always sneaks up on me. I really don't know when it will come, only that it surely will. In fact, in these parts, there can be as much as a 30-day variance in the first killing frost date from one year to the next. This presents a tricky, teasing dilemma for many creatures.

The arriving cold of autumn is good in a special way. With summer's ebullient finale behind, I must look hard and with great patience into the fields, woods, gardens, and parks to sense autumn's message. Born of the sun's glow and captured by the remarkable food-making chemistry of plants in months past are the waning stragglers left over from a crop of insects. Field crickets, often heard but seldom seen sentinels in a Lilliputian world where time is measured by clocks genetically blueprinted in creatures, chirp with a slowed beat from hidden lairs beneath old rock piles, logs, and rock gardens. The season silences the blasts of summertime rock concerts and loud human music that robbed the night air of its soft chants of katydids, crickets, and frogs. Even we quiet down in the fall.

I must struggle now to hear the faint, melodic purrings of the snowy tree cricket, an ethereal, pale-green creature haunting garden bushes, above the remaining noises of society's technological overkill. Senescing, sunburst tufts of tall grasses in fields at night hold only an occasional "zip-zip-zip" dirge of a cone-headed grasshopper, not the full symphony that ringed the air here before. Wooded lots proliferate autumn's batches of tiny moths, a smorgasbord of diverse, intricately patterned wing-color designs, a virtual multitude of little understood species clinging to cold, lighted window screens.

For some, there is confusion about when summer ends and autumn begins. But true autumn is always abundantly clear to me. The signs of that season reign supreme. When true autumn sweeps across the land, its cooling brush repaints the canvas of foliage from greens to bright colors at the other end of the light spectrum. The process is irreversible, even if temperatures rise again. The fields turn reedy and brittle and their once ebullient insects and spiders fall away, burying themselves in the dense thatch or dying off. This is true autumn. It is a season, however, of be-

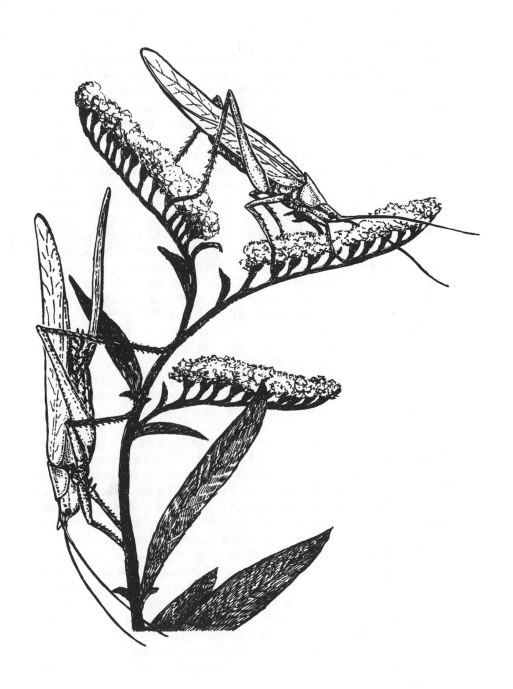

trayal. Life does not go away quickly. The march is clearly into deathly cold and programmed senescence.

But dying is always an individual matter, or should be. Some grasshoppers die off more quickly than others in the same field. When the weather turns cold, I look to the sun-drenched spots in the yard or field near noon to find clues that life struggles to hold on, even though it is doomed. Insects and their close relatives among the arthropods, such as spiders, remember, are generally unable to maintain a warm internal body temperature at a level allowing them to stay active. When it gets cold, the solution is to move into warm spots and out of the shade to warm up. This is what these creatures do all of the time, no matter the season. But in autumn, the behavior takes on special meaning as life winds down. Call it a last-ditch effort, one that gives a final, passing glimpse of life that will not grace the land until next summer.

Autumn seasons nowadays do not necessarily have the same feel to them they had many years ago. Burning leaves along the roadsides, whether one agrees with the practice or not, gave the air a special incense seeping through the cold. Shifting eddies of breeze fanned the stacked and packed embers of the pile's core, casting a warm orange glow as the sun disappeared. Red-hot, wind-whipped ashes crackled, giving those late Saturday afternoons in October a ritualistic feel that seemed as ancient as druid celebrations. In some manner, this was a neighborhood happening, playing out against the descending frost. Somehow that practice added a patina of finality to the end of warmth and the promise of much colder days and weeks ahead. That event is mostly gone now; yet the debut of autumn, with its persistent chill, still comes to mark the exodus of summer.

Now and then, there are occasional warm days wedged into the descending curtain of cold. On days like this, I am out on the deck or taking a walk, sensing that life struggles to hold on, to get in one last hurrah before hard frost and, after that, winter will shut it down. When airspaces are still golden and warm, life suddenly reappears, if ever so briefly, in the middle of autumn. An occasional magnificent, immense green and blue dragonfly now flies slowly over the garden. Just a few months ago, many fattened themselves on thousands of mosquitoes, gnats, and flies. Ornery, high-strung yellowjackets, their ranks now well thinned by frosts, frantically search for the sweets of mashed apples on the driveway. Near the fence line at the rear of the yard, a few hardy workers of thatching ants are roaming across the high mound of their nest. But not all insect life surges back for another moment in the sun. I can no longer find metallic green beetles skirting a sandy path down to the lake. Indeed, all that is left now are remnants of the breeding populations that flourished in summer.

We are now in the season of a few loose ends, but for the most part, the lines are sharper on the landscape, the air less dense, and autumn's message is to the point, clean and definite. Features of the land, once hidden by foliage, now become boldly obvious. When the weather conditions are right, very few, if any, sojourns along a wooded path compare to the inspirational magnificence and celebratory mood of autumn colors. The seemingly simple beauty of these trees uplifts the spirit in spite of summer's passing and energizes you to walk briskly on. Living close to a city makes the "nature" experience even more treasured. These are the best days for gazing at the portrait autumn has splashed on nature's canvas. Sunlight cascades down through the branches or brightens a distant slope of forest with a vibrancy that is impossible to describe. Being in the woods on such days cleanses the spirit and mind, bringing joy and a welcome respite from life's ups and downs.

The botanical basis of autumn colors alone is fascinating. We know quite a lot about how leaves go from green to reds and yellows, but we understand much less of the adaptive role, if any, of these metamorphoses. What we do know is that plants at this latitude are governed by a seasonal clock. With shorter days and cooler weather in autumn, tree growth slows and shuts down. The green pigment in foliage, chlorophyll, mediates the production of food that allows plants to grow, especially in spring and summer. But conditions in late summer and autumn change the tissues in the petioles of leaves, causing them to dry out and shutting off their photosynthetic activities.

The whole process is triggered by a lowering of the chlorophyll content in response to changes in day length and air temperatures. As chlorophyll ceases, the land's palette is cleaned of verdancy, exposing the other pigments present in leaves. What had been masked by chlorophyll in warm weeks and months comes out in full force and glamour. One such pigment, carotene, generously endows the foliage of trees such as aspen, birch, and hickory with vivid yellows. It is the same pigment that colors corn, carrots, and even egg yolks. But the yellow hues of an autumn landscape are no more effective than are the deep reds and maroons so pronounced and splendid in sumac and sugar maples. This pigment is anthocyanin, made from sugars stored in foliage, which makes its full debut as the curtain of chlorophyll dissipates in the season's veil of coolness and eventual frost. Neither pigment alone could produce excellent autumn colors.

A lot depends upon the balance between alkaline and acidic conditions embedded in the physiology of the particular species of tree or shrub. Red maples, with their more acidic chemistry, expose the effect of anthocyanin as vivid reds, while the more alkaline conditions of other trees, such as ash, portray this same pigment as more purplish rather than red. Clearly, there is great complexity in the colors gracing autumn near the western rim of this great lake. They only appear from an elegant interplay of weather, plant physiology, and the concentrations of pigments in foliage. It is far from a simple matter.

Perhaps the most intriguing question to ponder about the colors of an autumn landscape have less to do with how it comes about, and more with why it occurs at all. We do not understand how much energy it takes a tree to turn its foliage at the end of the growing season. Perhaps the value of the process has more to do with a cleansing of the tree of foliage that is basically tired and damaged by insects. Getting rid of old foliage paves the way for new foliage to appear when the conditions are right in spring. Old leaves only add useless clutter to the life cycle of the tree. One thing we know for sure is that the leaves begin a new life once they leave the tree. The feel of crunchy, dry fallen leaves underfoot is a testament to this process. Fallen leaves are a lifeline of the forest, providing a rotting carpet of debris that eventually feeds the plant life of this ecosystem. Decomposing leaves, the gift of autumn to the earth, release substances such as nitrogen and carbon that trees absorb through their roots during the following spring and summer.

Not only do leaves nourish the forest in death, but they also add a nutrient base to streams, lakes, and ponds. Here they support a diverse assemblage of aquatic insects and crustaceans, including isopods, caddis fly larvae, stone fly nymphs, and mayfly nymphs. On land, the forest floor's carpet of leaves is filled with legions of mice, ants, millipedes, insect larvae, isopods, and other small creatures that, together with bacteria and fungi, break down dead foliage, twigs, fruits, and seeds into substances that feed both plants and animals. In both situations, in water and on land, small creatures rip and shred decaying leaves, changing their structure, chemistry, and exposure to the elements. In so doing, these animals digest the rotting leaf tissues, commonly with the aid of specialized bacteria and fungi housed inside their digestive systems. Like wood, rotting leaves are not the easiest tissues of life to digest. Yet even in their decaying state, fallen leaves contain valuable nutrients that are exploited by other creatures and broken down to feed the forest.

These are intricate food chains in which nothing that is digestible in one form or another is wasted. Viewing autumn this way suggests that it is a time of life, not an ending or death. Imagine too the mice, salamanders, woodland frogs, snakes, and birds that poke and prod leaf litter in search of arthropodan foods. A thick, spongy layer of rotting leaves is a virtual treasure chest of small animals that support other life in the forest. Stream arthropods, dependent upon accumulating and decaying foliage for shelter and food, support fish populations, which in turn provide food for other animals that live in water or come into the water from the land.

These are excellent reasons to give thanks to autumn as a season that unlocks food for both the more obvious and the not so obvious players of forest and stream.

Autumn, then, sets the stage. Tonnages of leaves and twigs may drop to the ground during this season, but many arthropods and other creatures that dwell among the matted leaves, underneath them or on top of them, become inactive in the growing coldness. The more obvious action does not move into full swing until spring and summer. During winter, snow and ice form a blanket above the leaves, and during a spring thaw, this moisture hastens the rotting process.

As already stated, the real handiwork that autumn sets into play occurs in warm weather when largely innocuous assemblages of small creatures, which in concert with microbes and fungi form a loose group called the Cryptozoa, awaken and process mulch. Walking through the woods, it is easy to miss this crucial drama. But when you poke through the litter and reach the soil line, it begins to reveal itself. Closest to the ground, the leaves are broken and decayed into little pieces. Tiny creatures scurry away. Near the top of the pile, the situation appears more inert and dead. The leaves, though, even as they are processed at the soil line are being absorbed into the earth as a natural fertilizer. This organic matter percolates through the soil by the actions of soil creatures including earthworms, ants, and others. Dirt beneath a thick layer of fallen forest leaves is thus a truly wonderful thing.

Autumn, therefore, is intimately connected to the other seasons in a seamless, blended way. The shedding of dead or dying senesced leaves brings the gift of both new life and the sustenance of the old as well. Warmth promotes the proliferation of the intriguing and little understood cryptozoans of our woodlands, whose actions release the energy needed to maintain the trees and shrubs. Trees and shrubs support insects, birds, spiders, and squirrels. Looking at the forest or woodland stream like this makes the seemingly disparate seasons readable as connected chapters in the elusive storybook of life defining existence at this latitude.

Perhaps this story is best appreciated on days like this one. In the vivid colors of a crisp, near-perfect autumn day, I sense winter, spring, and summer as I meander through the woods. Even if in some years the edges of the season are dulled by too much dry weather, too much rain, or early freezes subduing the leaf colors, I still find it hopeful to go out into the woods and fields and seek the pulse of change. No matter how alive or subdued one autumn season is relative to ones that came before it or that will follow, I will continue to go into the woods and gaze at the colors.

Like spring, autumn can be a time to sharpen listening skills, for even on the cusp of winter's door, the land still speaks to us. Not all autumns speak in the same way, but they all speak. This is the beauty of our nature.

125

Metamorphosing foliage is very noisy and chatty in breezes and biting gusts of cold wind. But it does not mask the clatter of a squirrel churning up fallen leaves in its search for acorns. Nor does the rustle of dry leaves always drown out the cold-slowed chirp of a lone field cricket lucky enough to be sitting in an old rock wall heated up for a brief while by the sun. There even can be autumns in which the spring peeper sings, though this tiny frog usually choruses in spring, not fall. The season can betray them, dupe them with spring-like weather, compelling them to court at a time of the year when it is pointless, even deadly foolish, to do so. Life still drums away in an autumn forest.

Sometimes when walking in the woods in autumn, I catch myself philosophizing about the games of survival that confront animals at this time of the year. The lesson has overtones for human existence. A squirrel clambers to get that last acorn for its winter cache. The weakened cricket pours out, as best it can, its last song. There is an urge to increase the odds of survival, to push the envelope on the biggest wager, to stay alive, healthy. But there is another side to this two-faced strategy of existence. It is that of conservancy, of leaving little to chance, of already having taken the steps necessary to expend as little energy as possible. Well before autumn's center, creatures have stored away their goods for the year. They have placed their eggs and young in safe places. They have done all these things and more well in advance of the cruel, harsh cold. And so it is for me too. It is always wise to plan ahead, to anticipate disaster, to account for possible troubled times. But it is equally essential to push the envelope a bit. This is a little like cutting back on expenses and doing more to bring in more resources at the same time. Autumn, it seems, is nature's time of bet hedging. Imagine getting all of this from a walk in the woods!

Every year I do things in my backyard that, as a side benefit, occasionally help create an opportunity for animals to cope better as autumn becomes winter. Halloween happens to be one of my favorite annual celebrations. I take great joy in going for a ride with a friend to find a pumpkin stand or patch to choose two or three big pumpkins. I enjoy carving them, but more of late, I simply place them whole on the deck in the backyard. Pumpkins symbolize for me the harvest on the one hand but the womb of new life as well. I admire this thick-walled fruit filled with lots of seeds swathed and suspended in stringy pulp. While I know that pumpkins have been selectively bred to be what they are, I nonetheless find great insight and pleasure in them. It has something to do with squirrels.

I let my pumpkins stay put well beyond Halloween. In fact, I do not throw them out. They stay on the deck. Naturally when it is freezing, they keep erect and full. But when it warms up later, they soften and fold over. No matter. By December or January, the squirrels are plundering them,

gnawing through the rinds and eating the seeds. By March, all that is left on the deck are piles of chiseled flakes and pieces of old pumpkin, minus most of the seeds. Sometimes the seeds are there too, each one skillfully opened along one edge and its meat taken out. I have watched the squirrels do this, and I take great pleasure in knowing that my Halloween pumpkins have been recycled in the middle of winter into squirrel food.

This is a one-shot arrangement at my house. While I have nothing against people putting out seed-filled bird feeders, I am not prone to this kind of supplemental feeding of animals. For me it is more a matter of using up in a limited manner the remains of pumpkins. I have no intent of helping out squirrels in winter. They have been around long enough without my assistance. I just cannot see throwing away pumpkins, and I do enjoy watching the squirrels gouging a hole to get inside the fruit: I admire their bent toward opportunism, their determination to get at the nourishing seeds buried inside. Seeing this carries autumn into winter for me. And winter into spring.

Consider thinking of this cycle of seasons the following way. In spring, life sprouts from the eggs and seeds sown last summer, well before the first frost and autumn's descent over the land. In summer, life reaches a full bloom, not just among plants but among animals too. Then in autumn, life literally falls off its pedestal of prolific glory. But while autumn may feel and behave as an ending, it is really a new beginning. For all that we enjoyed in the yard or meadow this summer has its living fate now sealed away beneath the leaf mulch, in the soil below the frost line, even in the middle of rotting logs in the forest. Life has gone underground only to be saved from winter's wrath and to bloom once again to great heights next summer. In autumn, the drama of life switches for most creatures from branches, leaves, and stems to the mulch below, and in winter to the deep recesses of pond-bottom mud and sand. Life flourishes but it is temporarily more subdued than exuberant. It is also put to the ultimate test of its versatility and fortitude, challenging some numbers of each species, be it arthropod or plant, to survive the rigors of winter seasons at the western edge of this great lake.

Life is very seasoned at sowing its eggs and seeds well in advance of the hard frost. Reedy stems in the meadow bear the bulbous galls of flies and an occasional egg case of a praying mantis. A new generation of some 40 species of this region's wild bees are sealed away as pupae in earthen cells. Those that survive will hatch in spring to be the new season's first wave of pollinators that will allow many of our native species of plants to propagate. Grasshoppers are hunkered down under the tall grass thatch of the meadow. And very soon, all of those colors and sounds of summer will be but memories for another year. Things are fading out fast. But I can still see in my mind those puffs of yellow butterflies swirling around a roadside mud puddle on a steamy afternoon after a thunderstorm.

The woods now going threadbare shows us the forest's inner strength. We see the strong profile of the trees, blurred and softened over summer by dense foliage and the pleasantly distracting rustle of small animals, often heard but not seen. As the leaves turn and fall, the woods takes on a new personality, exposing its core. Time is tilting, branches are creaky, and squirrels scamper through the undergrowth. Here and there an evergreen still stands as a reminder of what was, but this is the time when deciduousness paints the land with new tones and messages.

But for sure, as I sit on the deck in the cool air or stroll through the woods nearby, autumn exudes an illusion, one of completeness and finality. Life is unquestionably present, just wisely concealed. Butterflies are chrysalises sheltered from the wind or partly grown caterpillars wrapped in silken sheaths and plant debris. Crickets, grasshoppers, and katydids are knots of eggs in the earth and twigs. Moths are tough cocoons and sticky masses on branches. Dragonflies, diving beetles, and tadpoles are nestled in mud. Squirrels and chipmunks are holing up with hoards of nuts and seeds. Mated, fattened queen wasps are wedged in tight crevices in log and rocks, ready to build new colonies next summer. When the dried leaves of autumn crunch beneath our feet, all is not dead, but rather transformed into a different state to cope with winter's impending wrath.

So we must not let autumn fool us into believing that life, so aptly expressed in many different creatures big and small, drab and gaudy, is on the verge of being snuffed out by its frosts. Look to the gaudy colors of autumn leaves to signal the eventual presence of renewed life. In autumn's vibrant colors there are reminders of summer's fullness of life, of winter's impending bleakness, and the prospect of spring not far beyond. Autumn compels us to think about life's transience and continuity all in one. What perishes come the descending cold and frosty nights are the leftovers, the tired individuals that have passed their breeding cycle and fulfilled their roles or those caught off guard by the cold. But for the most part, other members of these species are well ensconced by this time for winter.

Take as an example that huge spherical gray object suspended from a thick branch high up in the red maple tree at the rear of my yard. There's a lesson here about preparedness for winter and the expandability of some numbers of a species. Only now, as the trees are thinned of their leaves, can I see this intimidating yet beautiful nest of the bald-faced hornet. How many times did I push my old hand mower under the shadow of this spot where the wasp nest hangs 15 feet from the ground? Although I did not know it at the time, this nest surely flourished all summer, swelling to this immense size by the end of the season. Judging from what little I know about paper wasps, this colony must have been just shy of a thousand inhabitants when it peaked in late summer. I am sure that the nest has brood yet to hatch too, though they won't be able to because of the cold.

How could it be that such a big wasp nest could go unnoticed all summer? I believe it is a matter of perspective. I feel comfortable in my backyard, knowing its borders and all that grows in it. But then I come up short by autumn. When the leaves fall, other clues to the drama of life reveal themselves. Suddenly I am confronted with the evidence of the paper wasp's work for the past several months: how easy it would have been to miss their whole story.

Judging from the large size of the nest, this was a good summer for wasps. A bald-faced hornet's success, measured by nest size, is linked closely to other life. I speak again here of interconnections, clues of which I have seen and heard from this very deck. Wasps are at the heart of the matter. Because many caterpillars succumb to bald-faced hornets, wasps are beneficial to the garden and shade trees. Without them, trees and shrubs would be stripped of their welcome foliage and shade. As I gaze out at the yard and that maple tree with its wasp nest rattling in the breeze above it, the hard frost coating the ground, I am both pulled back to summer past and pushed ahead to what mysteries of nature will again unfold next spring. But for now, I sit back and praise the labor of the bald-faced hornet, a fierce and fearsome creature. The empty wasp nest is a testimonial to the several hundred now-dead wasps that built and occupied the nest in summer, and to the caterpillars and nectars that nourished the wasps. Within a few months winter storms will batter the nest to pieces. In this I sense a balance, a diverse yet interconnected web of life, with all creatures being equal players so that one participant does not outshadow or dominate the others. This is the portrait of nature that I continue to paint in my mind out here on the deck, no matter the season.

I know that the killing frost is close at hand. The land still simmers with the final ebbing of summer's harvests, but soon it will be over. When I sense these transitions, from warmth to cold, from insects abounding everywhere to their crescendo and exit, I am pulled up short by the realization that very soon hard frost will clear the landscape of insect sounds and colors for another year. But life is not gone. Life is never gone. An optimistic, strong message prevails.

Beyond the killer ice and later the bitter winds and deep snows, life flourishes. As with the bald-faced hornet, all creatures prepare for survival through frost and winter well before the frost sets in. Beneath the ice and snow, the hardened soil holds the numbed but living capsules of new life. The soil is a tomb now of spores, seeds, and roots—not a dead, but a living tomb—that will sprout a fresh, new verdancy when spring softens and warms the earth and all it holds. When the mornings are much colder and the view from the deck is one of silence and snowy whiteness, I will think about the cricket's eggs in the soil, the butterfly chrysalises and moth cocoons in the brambles, the dragonfly nymphs ensconced in mud beneath the ice of the pond.

So, in the hard frost I sense that is not far off now, there will be not just the cleansing of the landscape of mosquitoes, flies, and yellowjackets, but a reinscription of the promise of life yet to be. I am sure that out there, in the now brittle and naked brush, under a rock or log, lies a living new mother bald-faced hornet. I would be honored if she would appear in my yard next year, but this is unlikely. Nature is that way, a shifting, whimsical cacophony of changing scenes and players, a guarantee that nothing stays the same one year to the next.

In the meantime, I will pay close attention to the sentinels of this season. There is still time to celebrate what summer has given, simple yet complex and exquisite living graces, high in the treetops or close to the ground. As the weather turns and the nights become frosty rather than steamy, life still clings to the branches above my head as I walk along, and as more and more falling leaves create an amazing portrait of colors on grass, pavement, and forest floor. Life struggles to hold on, to give us those now fading, weakening sounds—acoustical shadows of summer— as the cold closes in.

True Katydids

In late autumn, on a star-studded night such as this one, there is crystal clear anticipation of a first hard frost. I walk along on this street lined with big maples and oaks to bear witness to the season's finale, a whisper of song slicing through the crisp chill. Autumn's tangy smell and mounting mantle of cold has all but erased summer into a faint distant smudge, cleansing the landscape's palette for winter's entrance.

There it is again, that slight rhythmic sound poking through the rustling leaves of an old maple a few feet away. It is the cold-slowed call of a weakened northern true katydid, struggling to sing out a few last chords of what weeks before was part of a magnificent, purposeful effort by many, and now is only a seemingly pointless lament of one. But even these frail and tired notes have something to say, a broader message for this season.

I try to remember what it was like to walk through this area during early summer. The night air was silent. Then, all of a sudden, it awakened with a cacophony of melodies as if some mysterious and wonderful alarm clock had gone off and jostled everyone awake at once. For many weeks the night noises grew and grew, encouraged by mugginess and heat. But this symphony was doomed to die, and it is doing so now, slowly. First the days and nights cooled down and the katydid music began to slip away. There was a big drop in the serenades, but some singers held on. Soon all will be silent again, similar to what it was like here in early summer but different too. Now the trees contain katydid eggs; then they contained katydid hatchlings. This is a life cycle that makes good sense.

I feel no rush to get back to the house. True, this is a good night to build a fire, but I'd rather walk farther, pondering katydids and their destiny, of which we are a part. It's a night of stragglers, one last northern true katydid and me. Come late autumn, a katydid's life is measured in days and hours. For those who like the outdoors, katydids and crickets

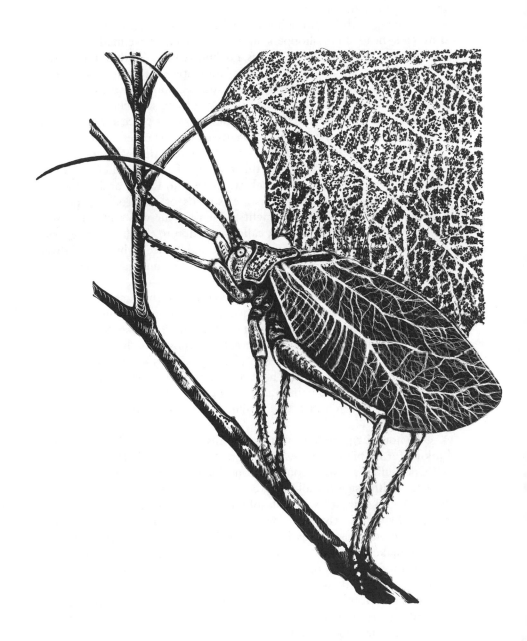

are good signs. But of all the singing insects, it is the northern true katydid that dominates the autumn.

By staying with us through the fall, long after the cicadas, bush katydids, cone-headed grasshoppers, and some crickets have made their exodus, the northern true katydid gives a definitive time-depth to the passage of our seasons and the history of this landscape. The creature's presence says a lot about the history of our trees and deciduous hardwood forests. Its unmistakable call chronicles the passage of late summer into autumn, ushering autumn into winter. The katydid knows its place and time in the design of the landscape, and its existence cannot be taken lightly.

Through its presence, in fact, I can reconstruct the events of summer and autumn that brought me to this evening. The mindful cry of a lone katydid forecasts the passage of all creatures into winter and beyond. In some ways those blended yet distinct sounds of crickets and katydids heard on many early autumn nights, when the air was still warm with only a very slight blush of chill, called attention to this land's staggering ecological harvest of small creatures, that major slice of biological diversity largely hidden, little understood, and certainly underappreciated. But now things are very different.

The katydids have been quickly bowing out for the past several weeks now, a staccato of procrastinative curtain calls, as autumn quickens. And katydids in treetops are not alone in confronting the season's sneaky ambushes of frost that snuff out aged creatures, those who have served their purpose in nature's overall scheme. Nature prepares its legions to bridge one growing season with the next and coping with winter in between. This is a portrait worth painting, of taking a small piece, a starting point, and building a sketch of life's movement from warmth into brutal cold and escape.

On a hot muggy night some two months ago I strolled down this street looking for fireflies. There was insect racket all around. The air titillated with deafening katydid conversations high in these great maples and oaks, a healthy sign for all, but I could not find or see a single musician even though I searched with a flashlight. There I stood, being teased from all sides by that unstoppable, maddening treetop noise. There must have been hundreds of katydids in these few blocks, enough arboreal musicians to make several big city symphony orchestras. Yet I went the whole night without seeing a one.

The true katydid, like other Orthoptera, the group to which it belongs, eats foliage. However, some are also opportunistic meat-eaters. In the Central American tropics, I have watched certain rainforest katydids dining on other insects drawn to electric lights at night. They are well equipped for the task. All katydids have powerful, sharp mandibles capable of giving even a person a good smarting bite, one that draws blood.

With these tools they slice easily through tough foliage, seeds, and even the thick cuticles of beetles. Other orthopterans, such as roaches, mantids, walking sticks, crickets, and grasshoppers, may be more familiar. Within this scheme of insectan life and order, katydids are closely akin to bona fide "grasshoppers," having extra-long hind legs for jumping. The Orthoptera comprise one of the oldest insect orders, dating back to the Carboniferous together with the Odonata (dragonflies). Both groups have been called "primitively winged insects," and have a three-stage life cycle as compared to the more evolutionarily advanced conditions of a four-part life cycle found in true flies, butterflies, hymenopterans (ants, bees, wasps), and beetles.

This particular beast goes by the scientific name of *Pterophylla camellifolia,* the species for which the name "katydid" was derived, in part from an early paraphrasing of its call in eighteenth-century colonial North America. It has even been suggested that the Pilgrims, within a year after landing at Plymouth in late 1620, were the first to name this creature the true katydid. The call of this insect became a symbol of the approach of the harvest season, and the moniker "katydid" was later applied to some other singing orthopterans as well.

Of the more than 200 species of singing insects east of the Rockies, the northern true katydid is one of the most fascinating. It is the only member species of a larger group of true katydids found well south of the U.S. border that has made it this far north. We do not know how the species got here, but we do know it has a spotty occurrence over much of North America east of the Rockies.

In four decades of working daily with insects, I have only seen a couple of living individuals of the northern true katydid. Searching for other kinds is a much easier task. Many different species live in low bushes rather than in tall trees and are collectively called "bush katydids" as a result. But some species, like the elusive true katydid, hang out high up in the tops of big trees; they seem especially fond of oaks and maples. Usually the only time one is collected is when it falls to the ground, numbed by cold or weakened otherwise and near death.

The katydid's personality, aptly expressed by its song, is symbolic of the innate spirituality of nature—best sensed, I believe, as a melody in the dark center of night. As August slipped into September, those unmistakable two-part and three-part harmonies in the treetops went back and forth almost every night. "Rack-rack" from one tree, and then "rack-rack" from another close by. A conversation of deep, simple beauty. True, its rather plain pulse rhythm bears little semblance to the works of art given to this world by a Mozart or Beethoven. But the real beauty of the katydid song resides more in its context than in its design. This seemingly simplistic insectan call reflects nature's awesome complexity.

Nature's face is now a chilly senescence spreading across the landscape. Two weeks ago the nearby field still bobbed with some vibrant heads of New England aster, thistle, and the ebbed milkweed. But, for the most part anyway, what had been a place bristling with a colorful kaleidoscope of life was turning brittle and tweedy. Bumblebees were more lethargic, clinging like dummies to waning flowers, struggling to warm up and shake off the cold. And although this summer produced a bumper crop of the regal monarch butterflies, most had already left the area, heading south to Mexico well before cold pushed aside summer's sultry complexion. Straggler yellowjackets and bald-faced hornets were ornerier than ever, sensing in some instinctive way, perhaps, their own doom. The land was speaking. Tonight, hearing the sluggish dirge of a sole katydid on an almost frost-dusted street closes the door on summer and braces all for winter.

Even up to two weeks ago the katydids on this block were still singing, perhaps not as frenetic as a month ago, but still a hearty effort, a good show. But then the nights turned much cooler, daytime skies more slate gray than shiny blue, and wind gusts more insistent. Autumn began its full sweep and this weakening band of katydids struggled to stay here, as if nagging us not to forget summer and to keep a watchful eye out for winter. From one night to the next, their symphony strained more and more, as death claimed and quieted them one by one.

And then there was almost complete stoic silence, no more insectan sonnets wafting through the night air. Wind grating through the dying foliage replaced katydid concerts for another year. All seems dead, the trees now stripped clean of their myriad small creatures. But that is not all bad. Throngs of corpses, most shorter than a paper clip, will accumulate in the mulch and soil, dying yes, but enriching and enhancing the growth of new life later.

The northern true katydid's call, then, is really a celebration of continuance. Katydids, like the rest of nature at this latitude, wisely sow their seeds well ahead of winter's debut. Since the arrival date of this area's first hard killing frost can vary as much as 30 days from one year to another, katydids, whose ability to move is at the mercy of the air temperature, do their best to sow seeds always on the early side of the shift. So even though the broken melody I am hearing tonight is a loose end, an endpiece to a magnificent seamless epic played out year after year, it hints at the bigger saga. By autumn, all creatures have sowed their seeds and otherwise prepared themselves for winter. True katydids are no exception. Their story is fascinating, complex, and ultimately as elusive as they are.

The true katydid's remarkable leaf appearance comes from the large bowed wing covers concealing much of its body. Both sexes of the insect, about the length of a man's thumb, manage to avoid being eaten to some degree just by looking like a green leaf. By staying immobile and silent during the day and blending with foliage, katydids increase their chances of not being spotted by watchful birds, and other enemies—even katydid collectors.

Night brings forth other dangers. Singing katydids are prized targets for bats, uncanny carnivores with excellent hearing. Hatching in late spring from overwintered eggs and growing as nymphs through summer, katydids also fall victim to spiders, ants, wasps, and birds. Katydids are even stalked by cats. You see, because the true katydid is a native species, it has many natural enemies. Having been a part of our deciduous hardwood forests for a very long time, its rhythm, as with the rest of this land's native species, is in tune, intertwined with the lives of many other species. And even as leaf-like and clever as they are, katydids are not stripping our trees. They live *in* them. True katydids are well-designed to do this. Consider, for example, how they produce their songs.

Where the wing covers meet and overlap on top, the male katydid has a rasp and file device that functions like a musical instrument. The wing covers open and close, producing the "rack-rack" call. The convex shape of the wing covers creates an enclosed airspace in which the call is greatly amplified, allowing it to be heard over a considerable distance. On warm muggy nights, the katydid's call is more easily made, but when the insect is subdued and weakened by cold it is more difficult. Each kind of katydid has a distinct call, minimizing conjugal confusion in trees and bushes.

True katydids, being big heavy insects with a laterally compressed body profile with the wings held tightly alongside the abdomen, are extremely skilled at hiding in the foliage. I know their cleverness at hiding very well. Once, many years ago, I climbed into a maple tree late at night to capture a singing male. At first I thought I had a good idea where he was located in the tree, but soon found myself going off in different directions after him. It was quite an ordeal in the dark. Even though I tried very hard not to jar the branches, my movements in the tree caused the katydid to stop singing periodically. I would stay motionless until he would start up again. This went on for several very long minutes, and I almost missed him completely until I finally caught a glimpse of him clinging to the underside of a leaf. It was his slight movement, caught in the beams of my light, that gave him away. I lunged and scooped him up in my hand while keeping my balance in the branches.

I kept this katydid in a large clear-plastic bag fitted with fresh sprigs of maple twigs and foliage in my house for several weeks. Pet katydids have a long history dating back many centuries, but I do not know if anyone has kept a true katydid in the house. In captivity, it took several days before the insect would sing. Unlike its soft melodic pulse in the wild, though, my captive belted out a continued monotone of rapid-fire short pulses, as if in protest. He did this for many nights, at the end of which I set him free in a maple tree in front of the house. While I had him, I noticed a curious pattern to the way he ate maple leaves. On several occasions, he chewed out the central vein areas of a leaf and only a little of the surrounding tissues. On other occasions, he nibbled large holes into the edges of leaves. I had no idea why he opted to make many leaves veinless in this manner. In spite of spraying water mist on his leaves daily, I surmised at the time that perhaps there was greater moisture present in the primary veins than in the rest of the leaf and that he was thirsty. But this, of course, is only conjecture. All in all, I found this male true katydid a delightful and beautiful guest in my house.

I would be remiss in not commenting upon katydid courtship and the manner in which they communicate among themselves. Only male true katydids sing, and they undoubtedly use their song to establish a special pattern in a clump of trees or forest; singing is not necessarily a matter of male rivalry. Listening is a basic rule of katydid conduct and manners, and allows males to position themselves in an amicable manner in the treetops. Each male stays put in the same spot in a tree for the season and uses his distinctive loud call to attract females for mating. Having too many male katydids in one tree or in a few adjoining trees could create interference in the mating game, so a true katydid modulates its singing in response to how close other katydids are, and whether or not they are male or female. The end result, of course, is courtship and breeding. This creature's call is genetically ingrained, and because there are no overlapping generations with a new crop of adults being produced every summer and autumn, no learning of the call is involved at all.

Katydids have a pair of ears on each of their forelegs. The ears occur at the base of the tibia, the second section of the leg above the bottommost segment, the tarsus. This ear is called a tympanum and is basically a thin membrane of cuticle stretched and secured over an air sac. The air sac is an extension of the insect's breathing system, which is a network of tubes that carry air into the body through openings on the sides called spiracles. The tympana vibrate when sound hits them, sending a message to the katydid's brain.

Female katydids recognize the specific sounds made by males of their own species. The male, as mentioned before, produces a characteristic song by vibrating the sturdy wing covers, which are fashioned into a ridge-and-file overlapping design at the top. Each species of katydid has its own signature song, a feature that cuts down on any confusion that could result from cross-signaling between different species occupying the same habitat.

Females respond favorably to the call if they have not been mated, while mated females stay away from concerts altogether. The receptive female katydid moves toward the singing male, guided by his song, which modulates her approach. When close, their antennae touch while he continues to sing. This mutual stroking results in the two katydids turning so that their bodies are now end-to-end rather than facing head-on. While grasping a twig or leaf, the male spreads his rear legs and holds the female's body with his cerci, a pair of appendages at the rear of his abdomen. The female clings to the male while he pulls her forward and under his body. He produces a package of jelly and sperm called a spermatophore which he passes to the female. She inserts the spermatophore into her genital opening just forward of the blade-like ovipositor at the end of her abdomen.

Over a day or so the eggs get fertilized as she nibbles away on the jelly, a protein snack, by bending herself under her thorax. From this mating, the female's entire batch of eggs gets fertilized. By late summer and early autumn a future generation of true katydids is sealed high above in the trees long before the leaves fall and the snow flies. The timing is exquisite. A mother true katydid is very clever, and with good reason. She uses her ovipositor to artfully gouge out a slit in bark. She then carefully places her eggs in the fibrous pouch. Depending upon how many eggs she has, the mother moves on and repeats the process. Preference is given to thick branches less likely to snap off during winter storms. Next season's supply of beautiful musicians hinges upon the katydid skills employed during the season before.

But by tonight these arboreal antics are long over. I am quite sure that I am walking right now beneath branches holding katydid eggs, endowed to survive subzero temperatures, blizzards, and deathly wind chills. These babies are destined to survive long after their parents have succumbed. Such a system is not foolproof, however, for there is little doubt that some katydid eggs die before spring. Nature's strategy, again, is a game of odds, and what is learned from the true katydid indeed mirrors all of nature for that matter. If a true katydid egg manages to make it through the winter, it hatches by early summer into a tiny ant-like nymph, crawls to a leaf, and begins to nibble its first meal. A baby katydid looks pretty much like the adult form minus wings. As it feeds, foliage becomes new katydid tissue, and the nymph molts several times along the way. With the final molt, its wings appear and the musical theatrics begin. Katydid music means one thing: now is the time to prepare for winter.

The true katydid singing above my head tonight sneaks in a few last calls, having little or nothing to do by this time with preparing for winter. Its leafy green apparel no doubt now looks like some anticlimactic trace of summer's suit, well out of context amidst the colorful russet foliage so characteristic of maples and oaks come autumn. Perhaps even now this katydid is easy prey for a bird or squirrel. But this is a matter of small importance because this year's crop of katydids have completed their work and sealed the destiny of new life ahead. They have perished, and he will too, but the work they did will endure.

There is a wisdom here I did not always appreciate or understand. Back in my childhood days with insects, I went through a period in which I tried to keep creatures alive well beyond their programmed cycles. I enjoyed looking for the field cricket, for example, and bringing the chirping males of this species into the house during autumn. The field cricket is a good-sized, respectable insect. Its large black, shiny body, about three-fourths of an inch long, distinguishes it quickly from anything else scurrying about when you dismantle a pile of rocks looking for it. When I was ten, I captured two or three male field crickets in the fall, naively thinking that I could keep them alive by rescuing them from winter's cold. I shredded newspaper and filled a cigar box with it and fed them small pieces of bread dipped in milk, which they seemed to relish. Intent on keeping them warm, I put the cricket den next to a radiator in my bedroom. Their chirping filled the little room. But eventually, in a matter of weeks at most, they died. Old age and natural senescence took its toll.

Yet I was pleased to have kept the crickets alive for a while, perhaps a bit longer than they would have survived outdoors. From my *Golden Guide to Insects,* I learned that the field cricket lays its eggs in the ground before winter and a new generation of crickets begins the following spring. I admired the seemingly tireless persistence of male field crickets to keep on singing, even if slowed, until the weather really turned cold. What the true katydid came to represent to me as a fading balladeer of our tree tops at the end of summer, the field cricket gave me on the ground: a sense of closure to autumn and a herald of winter.

Something else I have learned about katydids and crickets over the years is that the size of the population from one season to the next depends a lot upon weather. In some years, generous rain and plenty of warm weather in early summer yields an ebullience of foliage, a succulent salad which allows a lot of insect life to proliferate profusely by late summer and autumn. Dry cool weather dampens this exuberance. As with many animals, there are good katydid years, so-so years, and not so good years. But as long as we keep old trees in neighborhoods and deciduous hardwood forests, year-to-year ups and downs in katydids need not concern us. The big trees are essential to their existence.

The powerful forces that have been kneading and churning this landscape over eons have much to do with why the northern true katydid is found where it is today. Consider the Midwest's glaciers, moving masses of ice. I can only surmise that creatures like the northern true katydid, having been around at that time and even much earlier, thrived in the expansive, preglacial deciduous hardwood forests. More than likely, at

140

that time they were active fliers moving around over vast territories of very palatable foliage. When glaciers moved through the Midwest, these forests were pushed aside in some places but spared in others. What might very well have been a large population of the northern true katydid was splintered off as isolated colonies in scattered pockets of remaining forest. With time, these colonies, separated by as much as a hundred miles or more, changed into different local forms recognizable by slightly different calls.

It seems to be an axiom of nature that some winged insects, when confined to small pieces of isolated forest for a long time, will adopt a flightless existence. This has been the case for the northern true katydid. It is no coincidence that there are many neighborhoods in this city where the true katydid is absent every year. While it uses its elegant wing covers to facilitate ardor and perpetuate the species, the animal today is largely flightless. Its wings are capable of flight, but this katydid seldom flies, preferring instead to glide or walk from one branch to another. Because of their sedentary habit and colonial living arrangement, a whole group of katydids and their descendants tend to stay in the same place for many years, so long as trees are not destroyed. So a mated female tends to stay in the same tree in which she herself was born and in which she and her partner grew up. It can take 20 or more years for the northern true katydid to appear in a new area and establish a breeding colony. Today, then, this enigmatic katydid, save for having moved in stepping-stone fashion into shade trees planted by people long ago, is mostly confined to relic pieces of old forest.

A katydid's presence is not a simple gift; it is a profound life blessing. That is why I stand here shivering, keeping company with the season's last dying katydid. Doesn't his cold-stunned message tell us something that is good for people too? Isn't it also true that people need to engage in more conversations with the land as it changes from one seasonal coat to the next?

In summer and early autumn, the land speaks to us quite easily. Nature's citizens, even some small creatures like butterflies, give us ready clues to the bigger picture, defining the personality of the landscape. But as autumn moves toward winter, the challenge to converse with nature is greater, because nature is more subdued in many ways. But it is the very subtlety of the season that delivers a message defining winter's essence. Again, consider this lone katydid tonight. As I listen to him sing in the face of his own death, I think too about the faces of death and the possibility that death really means continuance and not absolute finality. Autumn appears to be the premier season for an expected and well-timed end to life. Big trees and their katydids tell us that there is more to the story.

141

Each creature dies an efficient, purposeful death that recycles a summer's harvest of energy stored in living tissues, and releases this treasure which nourishes the earth. It is part of a collective death preceded by seeding the landscape in order to ensure that life will continue. Death in nature is seldom guided by choice; rather, it is an efficient departure contingent upon assurances that life continues. The kinds of death humans wreak on the planet—deliberate or accidental erasures of life with little thought or concern for the future—are what worry me. Our species seems hellbent on cutting down trees, draining wetlands, and polluting wild areas no matter what the cost.

Thinking out loud about these issues can be good for the land. When we begin to understand even the sketchiest pieces of an elusive katydid's existence, we gain a refreshed sense of perspective. The katydid's life is balanced by all that impinges it and its very existence adds balance to other lives as well. Balance in our own attitudes about nature and the land is a good thing too, but it is a choice we must willfully make. Isn't nature itself here a matter of morphing, of blended balanced theatrics and players guided by the passage of seemingly distinctive seasons blending into one another? Can we not figure out how to morph and live within the scene too?

I for one, welcome the season's first hard frost. I do not sense an ending to katydids and other life when it arrives—only a beginning. Perhaps as the nights get colder I will hear again the faint, slowed rasp of a katydid or a field cricket ensconced in the woodpile. But when these sounds cease altogether for this season, I will celebrate the payloads of katydid and cricket eggs tucked away in safe places for the winter. Let the cold descend and add its white edging to all that grows from the land. This cleansing is good, healthy, and rooted in natural history. The only real tragedy here is how difficult people have made it for wild creatures to find the places they need to survive the winter. That is all the more reason to admire the presence of katydids dying in the tree tops this time of the year: they survived even *us*.

Many wild creatures, like katydids, really need big trees. They aren't optional pieces of furniture. Big, old trees like maples and oaks, aside from their key roles in shaping a deciduous hardwood forest, add quality to a neighborhood, a city. Their presence and the life they support reseeds our own sense of what the natural landscape here was once like, back before settlers and modern sprawl. Who can imagine feeling the essence of the autumn season without the rustling of trees drenched in deep yellows, oranges, and russets? Who does not enjoy the crunch of freshly fallen leaves underfoot?

Nature is not poetic beauty. There is no glaze, no soft sell, on the advent of hard frost, even a first snowfall. Autumn is a challenge to all of life, as is winter. Autumn is nature's purgatory. I let the dying ember of a lone katydid pull at me, enticing me to have such thoughts about trees, neighborhoods, relic woodlands, and people. A faint, fading message spun on the chilly autumn air, with its starts and stops and pending disappearances, speaks of nature's creative use of death, forever changing over eons. I am grateful for this walk through this hard night, accepting what is and what will be, and forsaking the warmth of a good fire for now in exchange for relearning a lesson for all time.

Hard Frost

By making a special effort to get up at first light this morning, I can encounter something that still holds me in awe after many years of living near this great lake. I speak of "hard frost." It is a familiar yearly event in this region: dawn's thick crusty coating of ice crystals, a deathly latticework blanketing the fields and knocking down many living things quite literally for at least one more year. Hard frost truly defines the end of the growing season. Before it comes, nature is a whiplash of sputtering stops and starts, a staccato medley of autumn's false alarms of morning's dew becoming a teasing "light frost." But with the arrival of a hard frost, a sharp, crisp sense of finality is emblazoned across the land, stamping life into silence and heralding the start of winter.

It is true, of course, that hard frost mornings can be followed by a welcomed, bug-free streak of warm days that we call Indian Summer. But by then, much of nature's ebullience has made its final curtain call for the year. That is why, on mornings like this, I struggle out of my warm bed and head outdoors. I can never guarantee what I might see on such a bone-chilling foray into the little meadow across the way. But I do know what I will feel and sense here about the cycle of the seasons in the glorious northern realm of this continent. Bands of wispy mist spiral up from the water near the lakeshore. On the horizon to the east, the sun appears at this awakening hour as a deep orange wafer, tinged with a red flare and punching through a ribbon of low, layered magenta clouds. Where this solar vibrancy meets the sullen pall of autumn's leaden clouds, I sense a dramatic transition in nature's ancient game plan.

I decide to walk back from the lake's high bluff into the meadow and woods behind it. Just a month ago when I came through this exact spot at high noon one sunny day, things were very different. The tall goldenrods blushed with thickened pollen, creating a frenzy among beetles, flies, and wasps to consume as much as they could of the season's last harvest. That patch of flowering Canadian thistles crowned with burr-like purple heads was hosting many monarch butterflies intent on gathering strength and nourishment from its nectar for their long journey south to Mexico. Much later that day, near dark, as I lingered here, I could not believe the hordes of dragonflies of at least three varieties that dive-bombed the meadow, catching all manner of gnats. The nearby trees throbbed with the deafening screams of this summer's bulging crop of cicadas. In short, and in no small measure either, this field drummed away with the pulsing of life, a late summer mosaic of insect sights and sounds. I noticed only a small fraction of it.

This morning the landscape still bears a few weakening signs of summer's fading beauty. A brownish veil has descended over much of the meadow with only the vivid lavender of asters adding a sense of the life that abounded here weeks before. There is a deafening silence among the fading crests of wildflowers and the yellowed, frost-stained leaves of milkweeds. Not even a faint chirp from a distant field cricket can be heard now. Life has slowed to a dying ember. My feet make crunching noises as I cross the meadow and turn into the woods. Even inside the forest the fallen leaves are now coated with frost, as if a sea of giant dusted flakes has settled beneath the aspens and birches. Yet this landscape, with its skeletal network of trees stripped bare of their foliage, is anything but dead. Nature is a genius at ensuring its own survival, albeit not without requiring hard struggles.

This log, for example, is well coated with heavy frost. Within a couple of hours, the frost will be gone, but its handiwork will endure. Anything on top of the log is now surely dead, whatever is inside or beneath may well not be. There beneath it, lying belly up and exposed, is a mother bald-faced hornet in a little cubicle it carved in the softened, rotting wood when the air still breathed summer. She lies in perfect numbed slumber and will stay so until spring. With the exception of a few sisters that mated a month ago like she did, the rest of her nestmates—a colony of several hundred wasps churning in a large paper nest suspended from a tree branch somewhere else in these woods—have all succumbed to the hard frost. Resting in this one tiny survivor, this black-and-white beast curled up in a crevice, is part of next summer's legacy of paper wasps. How vulnerable and passive the queen wasp is at this moment! I gently return the log to its original slot in the leaf mulch and move along.

Had I probed farther into the log, I would no doubt have seen centipedes, sowbugs, beetle grubs, and ants all hunkered down for winter—wizened little escapees from both the frost and the coming snow. Beneath my feet the thick, matted mulch seals legions of microbes, insect eggs, and other minute life forms, all endowed with a natural resistance to cold. Less hardy creatures have long since burrowed deeper into the soil be-

neath the mulch and frost line. Loosened sheaths of bark on tree trunks give similar shelter to overwintering angle-wing butterflies like the familiar mourning cloak, one of the last butterflies spotted in autumn and the first to appear in spring. Squirrel nests, leafy boughs, and branches high above my head harbor ants, flies, and much more. Every opportunity to survive is exploited in this forest, even now. A hard frost such as the one this morning drops leaves very quickly, save on the more tenacious old oaks scattered about these woods which take a bit longer to shed their leaves. But once the leaves are gone, it is easier to spot nature's signs of winter preparedness. Along one edge of the woods, where trees thin out and low scrub meets an old railroad bed, scrubby wild cherry and swamp willow are good places to find large silken cocoons of giant silk moths like Cecropia and Promethea. All of the signs of life still here beseech us to appreciate the interconnections that exist among all living creatures. The beauty of hard frost is that it is an anticlimactic curtain call, snuffing out only stragglers, long after most members of each species have prepared themselves for winter. There is much to marvel and contemplate about life's tenacity while wading through a frosty meadow and a companion woods.

Nature's elegance in the north resides in its capacity to cope with the mercilessness of cold and ice. Everything is about 90 percent water, a blessing and a curse at the same time. Water in its fluid state is intrinsically friendly to life, for life on this planet originally developed in water. But in its frozen state, water kills. From a one-celled speck of pond scum to the billions of cells in a newborn human, no living tissues can survive being busted apart by ice. Yet nature copes.

Queen wasps, katydid eggs, butterfly chrysalises, silk moth pupae, and maggots in plant galls are exquisitely endowed with an inborn antifreeze that keeps their watery tissues sluggishly fluid but not frozen. These small creatures and many others drop the freezing points of their tissues to well below that of water in order to pass winter in one life stage or another. Plant seeds, roots, and tubers do much the same thing. How does this neat adaptation spring into action? How creatures survive both a hard frost, the gateway to winter, and winter's even more deathly grasp on life, requires an appreciation of how the cycle of the northern seasons, so evident along the western edge of this great lake, is intertwined with the lives of creatures.

In late summer, day length gradually tightens its reign on nature. Days become shorter and, at some point, organisms cross a physiological threshold, one that signals summer's end and the advent of winter. The lesson is brutally simple and direct. Whatever creatures must do to survive winter, they must do well before the first hard frost. Otherwise all would perish and there would be no spring awakening, no ensuing summer of songbirds, wildflowers, butterflies, and cricket serenades. There would be no flicker of fireflies among the garden brush. Nature's clock would wind down. But the celestial timepiece, the tilt of earth on its imaginary axis while continuing its journey through the heavens, sounds a warning every year of the necessity to escape, in one form or another, from the coming season of cold death.

Spring and early summer generations or phases of eggs and caterpillars grow up quickly, not impeded by harsh challenges of survival. Their chemistry is quite different from that of late-summer bloomers. A quickening collapse of daytime light triggers chemical changes in many creatures, compelling them instinctively to alter their state of being and what they are doing. In short, ordering them to prepare for winter. Wasp nests turn out fresh young queens that swiftly mate with a handful of males and then search out safe nooks under logs and rocks or in an attic. Caterpillars quickly metamorphose into chrysalises or spin cocoons, shutting down much of their growth to wait out winter. Some caterpillars, only partly grown, like that of the great spangled fritillary, burrow deep into leaf mulch in August. Cicadas and katydids, our late summer daytime and nighttime balladeers and residents of the tallest oaks and maples, place rafts of flat eggs into carefully carved crevices in tree branches from August into October. Fastidious dragonfly mothers drop their eggs into ponds as precious payloads that settle in the bottom muck and slime to be stirred into action next spring. Songbirds migrate south, not able to withstand the northern winter's brutal cold. Bat colonies move deeper into caves or abandoned mine shafts before yielding to winter's stupor.

Many kinds of seeds, with their rich supplies of fats and oils, withstand freezing temperatures while strewn in leaf mulch or hoarded in ground squirrel caches in the ground. Autumn and winter winds scatter all manner of seed across the landscape, a plant's way of hedging its bets for survival, ensuring that a fraction of its offspring will wind up enjoying the proper circumstances to sprout next season. Without seeds and a means of scattering them about, there would be no replenishing of the fields and forests, no food supplies for insects, and no insects to feed our songbirds and other larger creatures. I marvel at nature's investment plan in the north. It is a simple, yet almost unbelievably complex system.

From one year to the next, hard frosts can be early or late; there can even be as much as a full month's difference in the first appearance of hard frost between years. The relationship between the change of seasons and earth's northern creatures is not a perfect system, but one fraught with this sort of unpredictability. But nature invariably errs, it seems, on the conservative side, wrapping up much of its business well before the debut of a hard frost.

As I complete my walk this day, the frost has melted away, burned off by the sun, but its effect is lasting. Hard frosts and the winter snows that follow cleanse the visual landscape of a lot of life. But they leave an awful lot behind as well. The billowing clouds, streaked with bands of sheer gold sunlight, surely warn that winter is on its way. Even if today turns out to be unseasonably warm, and tomorrow too, life's stirring after this hard frost will be minimal. The creatures of this meadow and woods are safely ensconced for winter. And by this day's end, when this place chills again and the silence is broken only by the wind rattling branches and stirring up fallen leaves, I will still be rejoicing that life goes on here. In what will soon become a frozen oasis of winter, my joy rides hard on the heels of last night's hard frost.

A Withered Patch
of Wildflowers

I t is just a little past dawn and I am looking out the window at the
handiwork of a heavy first snowfall from last night. I am almost
dazed by what is before me. The yard is now an ethereal, deafeningly
quiet landscape. From where I stand, my face separated from winter's art-
istry by only a pane of glass, ribbons of sunlight are cascading down
through a distant line of threadbare high brambles. The effect is stunning.
Thick blue lines grace the virgin snow, creating some sort of surrealistic
painting against the crystalline blanket. Closer in, maybe 20 feet from the
window and directly in front of me, even deeper etchings of shadows, cast
by a patch of tall, tweedy stalks adorned with curled dry leaves and seed
heads, slice through the puffy snow.

I find it very helpful to identify with icons on the landscape come winter. I need this bond with the land and nature. The wildflower patch is
one of my favorites. And, even though I have stared out this window every
morning as autumn slips into winter, only a heavy snowfall could really
stir this icon to life in my psyche. The small wildflower patch outside my
window, now magnified by the freshly fallen snow, is really a temple of
life, a temple fashioned from bended and broken sticks, the plant corpses
of last season's garden.

Looking across the way at the crisscrossed thatch, it is hard to believe
that just four months ago, it was a majestic array of tall, stately wildflowers brimming with life. Purple coneflower, black-eyed Susan, New England aster, milkweed, obedient plant, goldenrod, and others gave this
weedy patch a beauty that embodied much of what is a midwestern bountiful autumn. But despite appearances, all that is not lost, not at all. That
tangle of reeds and dry stems is drumming with life even now, and I am

drawn to this decrepit, broken, and withered weed patch by the memory of what I witnessed here just last summer. This patch was a wellspring then, an ecological hotbed of thriving insects and plants. Each day brought a new discovery of some insect visiting the flowers or another chewing on a leaf; always new varieties, seldom the same players from one day to the next. Yet some bonds between the flowers and insects remained steadfast over the weeks, lasting well into the cusp of autumn. Consider native bees and the purple coneflower. On shimmering hot mornings in August and September, the fresh, long-lasting blooms of purple cone-flower lured a parade of thick, stout bumblebees who toiled at the flowers all day long, taking precious payloads of nectar and pollen to their nest in the ground alongside the house. Before the coneflowers bloomed I had noticed only a few bees, earlier in the season, flying off to parts unknown. In and out they would go, winding their way down through the thick brush into the nest in the ground. When the coneflowers and black-eyed Susans blossomed, the bees turned their attention to them.

What I see before me now on this early winter morning is a skeleton of the life that pulsed and buzzed through the wildflowers last summer, but I am confident that the bees will be back come next summer. Bumble-bees are good to have around. They pollinate a variety of plants and, un-like the domestic honeybee, a transplant from Europe dating back to the 1600s, bumblebees are native kindred. Because of this, they are efficient pollinators of wildflowers, not to mention fodder crops such as red clover, the primary food of dairy cattle. Bumblebees thus give life to the land. Acts of pollination create seeds, and those that survive establish new plants. It is gratifying in winter to reflect on the events of summer in the garden, of bees fecundating wildflowers, of the same bees sleeping in the ground close by, scattered new queen bees and plants protected together under a blanket of fresh snow.

The northern winter season, especially after heavy snows, is an excel-lent opportunity to appreciate life underground rather than above. In winter the skeletized landscape does not offer a lot of distraction. The real action is beneath the snow and ice. The weed patch seems lifeless above the ground, but it is very much alive, especially in the mulch and soil. True, all living things go through the cycle of life and death, but life regularly persists through winter, the toughest, most demanding of seasons. It is a matter of adapting, coping, and waiting. What at first seems to be a down time is really a window of preparation. Debris in the yard helps a lot. Mulch and topsoil, catching winter's cascade of fallen tree debris, is life's potting bed for continuance when the spring thaw arrives.

I look always for bridges in nature, the partnerships and interconnec-tions that weave the paths of interdependency and build a natural system

good for all living creatures. Bridges and icons, not surprisingly, often stand together, fused as one. Bumblebees give back to the land new waves of wildflowers, and wildflowers guarantee that there will be more pollinators in future seasons. Such things are as bold and real as the forlorn outlines of the pile of dead stalks in front of me. Deep inside this message is yet another. The bumblebee's existence is tied not only to flowers, but to the earth and its users. Bumblebees need vacated animal burrows, for example. An animal, perhaps a chipmunk, made the burrow but vacated it long before the queen bumblebee came upon it last spring, so one creature's abandoned home becomes a palace for a colony of another. In order for the bumblebee to be able to visit my wildflower patch, it has to have been able to establish that homesite. All living creatures are tightly interconnected in very practical ways with all others.

Therefore, I do not read dismal doom in this frozen landscape; rather I sense the reality of life: continuance. Winter is an opportune season in which nature's legions have time to ready themselves for a new debut come spring and beyond. It is one thing to sit here, hot coffee in hand, and gaze out at this weed patch to see some erstwhile dark oasis bathed in a desert of bleached sand; it is something else entirely to sense the real warmth, the drumming life only temporarily muffled, that waits beneath the frozen surface. The living root systems lying dormant in the ground right now ensure that these interconnections will be set into motion again next spring, summer, and autumn.

But the patch also gives life right now, even in the cold. During the past few weeks I have seen a variety of small birds, including finches, sparrows, and chickadees passing through the patch, clinging to the button heads of the coneflowers and taking out seeds still lodged in them. So clearly, it is helpful to wildlife for us to resist clipping off dead wildflower stalks in autumn. I am not one to follow readily the gardener's creed and gospel. Instead I believe in leaving undisturbed the dead remnants, the tweedy mish-mash of brittle reeds and stems that transforms the yard every autumn. They will fall on their own as winter advances. This is, after all, the way things worked long before people came to the land and imposed their will upon it. Dead stalks and the fragments of life still clinging to them in winter, be they insect eggs, seed pods, a spider's egg sac, gall, or cocoon, play their part in ensuring that life will return in its full glory next summer.

Up against the fresh snow, the dead thatch is indeed a stoic temple, a place of life and worship, perhaps more so this time of the year than summer. The old purple coneflower stalks, almost five feet tall themselves, rise up sharply towards the sky. They refuse to bow or snap, in spite of the heavy caps of wet snow covering their seed crowns. Yet they, like the rest of the dead thatch around them, are breaking down even now.

Everything in nature dissolves at some point, enriching the chance for new life to spring up in its place, even in a small pocket of wildflowers like this one.

Understanding this larger story of connections, though, is a matter of knowing events and of taking note of them year-round. The garden is a disorganized mix of hardy perennials whose lifestyle and habits have been etched across the Great Plains and the Midwest over many millennia. Such is also the case for the many insects evolving along with it. On several days last summer I noticed a monarch butterfly or two and at least one tiger swallowtail visiting the coneflowers. At least one monarch laid eggs on the milkweed plants in the patch, although none of the caterpillars survived for very long. I suspect they were attacked by ants or predatory bugs wandering over the leaves in search of prey. A red admiral butterfly used one of the tallest coneflowers as its surveillance point, perching on its apex and darting out swiftly to chase off any intruders into its air space. And I cannot begin to count how many hover flies sneaked between the bees to take their own share of the energy-rich pollen. Most likely, though, the bumblebees got most of the food, for both themselves and to make a mash to feed their growing brood in the nest.

By sunset on a hot humid day in late August, when the ebbing sun was just right, the tall flowers in the patch were encased in a cloud of tiny insects, gnats, and other dusk visitors. The air was filled with the pulse of their life, the underpinnings, if you will, of whole wetlands, forests, and meadows. Dragonflies appeared on some evenings too, lured into the frenzied maze of whirling gnats, claiming their own rightful feast in the design of life. And a golden orb weaver spider set up its sturdy web in the patch. This large black-and-yellow fellow sat motionless in its sticky yellow web much of the time on hot days, but moved at a lightning speed to wrap up in silk any fly or bee that landed in its snare. The mulch beneath the flowers was also home to at least four species of ants and sowbugs, ground beetles, and millipedes. A respectable layer of mulch had built up in the patch over several years and these small arthropods, together with myriad fungi and bacteria, distilled the essence of dead stalks, leaves, and flowers into a fertilizer that would be reclaimed into the earth's bloodstream, nourishing the sap-filled collective arterial network coursing through the newly sprouted, quickly growing fresh stalks come spring.

In September I discovered three kinds of moth caterpillars grazing on the coneflower foliage. Red-legged grasshoppers, as if appearing out of nowhere, passed through the patch, leaving their telltale gnaw marks in the succulent foliage. On more than one occasion, an intimidating worker bald-faced hornet wove its way through the thickening foliage beneath the flowers like a menacing attack helicopter preparing for a skirmish. I spotted these wasps in the yard many times over last summer, residents, I suspect, of the large gray nest exposed by early November in a maple tree located half a block away. No one had noticed the nest all summer.

These are only a few of the many kinds of creatures who came through this now ragged flower patch last summer and fall. The place literally teemed with life. While I knew that my modest flower patch could not compare to the ecological exquisiteness of a whole meadow or prairie, I still felt humbled by the intricacy of what I had seen so close at hand. There is an unspeakable beauty in the movement of life through my patch's corridors, shadow-riddled passageways, over the tops of its flowers, through its deep dark mulch, crunching through its stems, leaves, and roots that fascinates me. Yet unspeakable, perhaps even invisible, beauty of this kind does not equate to physical beauty, pleasure, and space. Nature is a matter of conflict, of fierce competition, eat or be eaten. Every living creature, big or small, plant or animal, is sculptured by the same genetic blueprint, pushed this way and that, kneaded and molded in many millions of ways by the capricious roller coaster of earth's ever-changing challenges. This is what the weed patch outside the window is all about. There remains much to learn from it and about it.

My weed patch, like any forest or meadow, exists because its pieces— the network of minute creatures living in it or passing through it—are indivisible. They function as a marvelous whole, a whole much bigger than the mere sum of the parts. The patch began small. A bare section of earth was opened in the yard when a strip of sod was peeled away many years ago. Seeds were introduced into the exposed soil, itself a rich clay byproduct of this region's geology. This is not a soil particularly good for plants, but it would do. The soil was nourished by the dead leaves and twigs falling off a mighty elm tree and two young maples nearby. Little was done to clean away this accumulating mulch, itself a good thing for wild plants. While some seeds were deliberately sown, other plants sprang up by themselves, a succession of species, an unruly crowd that attracted insects and other animals. No doubt strong winds, birds, and other animals dropped some of these seeds in the fresh bed. What had once been bare earth became a low canopy, already changing the personality of this little place. With the growth of tall plants, the canopy rose up to a dramatic five feet, as if some tiny forest. Maple and other tree seedlings appeared and then disappeared. And now, several years later, this patch of wildflowers shows every sign of holding on, perhaps changing one year to the next, but still here.

I will never know precisely how many citizens occupy my patch. My hunch tells me there are at least a couple dozen insect species and an equal number or more of other arthropods, most dependent in one way or another upon the vegetation, dead or alive. And I surely have not encountered even a fraction of the creatures here. You see, this weedy patch is an ecological chessboard, each space of which attracts a unique set of insects and other creatures. Such an arrangement in turn helps promote other diversity, even small insect-eating and seed-eating birds. Generous snowfalls are very good for the patch. A snow cover insulates its mulch and roots, protecting that which is alive and guaranteeing a full show come next summer. Beneath the thick snow, mulch provides a refuge for thousands of spores, insect eggs, and minute life forms, the collective engine that fuels the cycles of life that endow the landscape with vegetation and the larger animal life it supports.

In spring, this spot is mostly a lush green, with a hint here and there of white and purple splashes, violets deep down. It is really not until late summer and early autumn that the patch puts on its full colors. Long after the bees have gone, the katydids and field crickets have finally hushed, and the monarchs have left for Mexico, the patch still retains its vibrant hues. But with a succession of hard frosts, the sturdy coneflowers wither, leaving behind buttons of seeds from which new seedlings will grow.

Existence, though, is always a chancy thing. From the act of pollination through the making of seeds, seed sprouting, and maturity, a purple coneflower passes through many gates of challenge, as do all living creatures. Some fraction of the hundreds of seeds set in a single coneflower button will perish, devoured by insects in autumn or winter-hungry birds. A coneflower seed must be blown away or dislodged by the feathers of a bird or some other animal in order to land in a place suitable for germination. It can take a long time for the seed to find its place in the mulch and sprout into a seedling, but seeds dislodged before the first heavy snow of the season are protected under this blanket, pressing down into the mulch. Seedlings are prime fodder for rabbits come spring and summer, cropping the supply of the wildflowers even further. And grazing does not end with rabbits. As they grow, the plants are attacked by a variety of moth and beetle caterpillars and other insects, all of which, in turn, are usually kept in check by some natural means, usually their own enemies.

When wildness is allowed to reclaim small areas of the land, a natural sense of order is established among the wild species native to our region and this continent. I am not speaking about irascible exotics such as garlic mustard, buckhorn, loosestrife, and others. Nor do I speak of artificially bred ornamental plants. When I see that wildflower patch outside the window on a winter's day, I am reminded of a natural system, a place where a sense of natural control prevails to some degree. And when natural controls are operating there is little worry about pestilence problems. The whole system works, especially when people leave it be. Nature itself distills itself, editing anew the notes and chords of its symphony each summer.

Weedy patches of wild species breed a real hope, a refreshed optimism as crystal clear and bright as a sun-drenched crust of new snow, that people will respect our natural heritage, our biological diversity. This is the exact opposite from the ecological holocaust occurring across the world today. As more and more land is cleared of its wild things, nature tends to be replaced with a barrenness rife with pests and exotic weeds. But the wildflower patch argues that hardy exotics need not ascend to pitiful dominance, and homogeneity of the landscape need not prevail. A small patch of withered wildflowers in a suburban yard near a great lake in winter can teach us a lot about stewardship and conservation of all natural systems.

In summer, it is easy to take for granted the sights and sounds of nature. Thick foliage, the drone of bees, chirps of crickets, the scurrying of squirrels, and the flitting of butterflies all gild our senses with strong awareness of nature. But in winter, the challenge is to see beyond the cold and bleak, to find life in the withering pieces of last summer's harvests. My small temple in winter, this icon of life near my window, beseeches me to celebrate the life of all seasons.

There is thus something almost sacred about a snow-encrusted wildflower patch. In its shabby, mossy lines, angles, and surfaces, the tangle of its dying stalks, I see much worthy of awe, reverence even. An intricate lacework of living interconnections rests at its heart. The thought alone is enough to pull me out from behind this window. Leaving the warmth and security of the house, I go forth into the cold and snow to listen for life's drumming, that invisible, awesome beauty that defines the very nature of this place. My face gets stung by the icy wind and the blowing snow. But at such a moment, I am also taken back to warmer days when this same place howled with the music of life. Now most of it is silenced, muffled, though still breathing in the ground beneath the snow. And even now some music survives. Every seed, twig, flap of loosened bark, and leaf all add their voices to the subtle melodies of winter.

Branches and twigs will be blown down into the weed patch more and more often as the season advances. This is what winter does. Nature's garbage gets tossed and turned upside down, then buried in the snow. Snow is a helpful cushion, softening the crush of this natural debris, readying it for the spring thaw, adding a tonic to the mulch that feeds wildflowers and more. There is no need to despair about this icy havoc; nature is only taking its course. Loving all of this, all of winter's seemingly brutal crash course on life, is a lot like loving another person. It is a slow process, one cemented with respect, devotion, and commitment. No one can become a true fan of a broken-down weed patch in winter overnight. One must simply take the plunge, brace for the cold, and begin. The icons of nature await. That ultimately is the promise of the withered wildflower patch.

Winter

The bone-chilling fierce wind near the wooded edge of this frozen lake brings to mind an executioner's song. The blowing bands of snow whipping my face make it difficult to see where the lake meets the woods. Nature is a fuzzy, shifting network of interconnections.

In winter, walking across a frozen lake, I can focus on the totality of nature, its collective pool of species, and their interrelationships. The northern winter especially, with its seemingly endless days of cold and grayness, gives a compelling sense of place and time. A tiny milkweed seed, a mere speck of reddish brown plastered to the crystalline snow and almost crushed underfoot, argues that indeed nature replenishes itself with the passage of winter.

The bitter winter wind is a whimsical, symphonic melody, unpredictable from one minute to the next and from one spot along the ice to another a few more feet up the shoreline. In this mantle of now motionless water, earthen hues peek through the ice here and there where the snow has been scoured away by the wind. It is easy to be fooled by the monotony of the snow and ice, the sheer nakedness of this scene, but this frozen oasis is rich with life sleeping in its belly, well beneath the ice cover. Both the lake and its citizens have been around for thousands of years, since the last retreat of the great glacier.

Off in the distance, porcelain-like trunks of birches are strewn along the shoreline, a summer's legacy of beavers. They share this lake with a pair of loons, an occasional blue heron, and a multitude of fishes, frogs, dragonflies, beetles, and many other creatures. Much of the lake's wildlife feeds the beaver colony, so beavers need both lake and forest to survive. The beavers are still here, close by even, as I walk on the ice and the brutal cold stings my flesh. The loons, herons, and eagles have left these woods, heading south to open waters. They will return with spring. But the beavers are safely nestled together in a deep sleep in their lair of piled, criss-

crossed branches, above the water line. Their bodies live off a winter's layer of brown fat, ensuring their survival until spring, when once again, in the great thaws that sweep across this land, they will glide through these sparkling, crystal waters in search of crayfish, mussels, and shoots. The beaver is an agent of natural change in this lake, slicing off trees along the water's edge all summer long, endowing the lake itself with an ever-shifting personality.

This beaver lair has been here for several years, but its size and shape keep changing. As the nest sloughs off sticks every year into the lake, new ones are added. Settling on the lake's bottom, these sticks rot away with time and become part of the organic matter that fuels other life in the lake. This is not at all a trivial fact. Nature's decay is the cornerstone of new life, of whole food chains. Every year thousands of leaves and branches fall into the lake, and dying animals here add to this mix of life's broth.

Walking along, through the blinding snow, it is easy to be distracted from the web of life, well muffled, like nature itself, beneath this sheet of deathly ice. The future of life in and around this body of water, to a great extent, lies on its bottom, home to many species, the vast majority of which are small and easily dismissed. Arthropods and microorganisms, in particular, contribute immensely to the ecological foundation upon which all life depends, and in this system, each species is equally significant in the lake's functioning and natural well-being. In the years to come, each new generation of frogs, fishes, loons, beavers, and other more readily acknowledged creatures is already being molded from the seminal clay of the lake, from the legions of tiny creatures dwelling there right now.

So, once again, even in the apparent death of this cruel cold, a carpet of life stirs in the darkened mud and sand of this lake. The glory and wonder that is the loon's call at a summer sunrise, the shimmering gossamer wings of the huge green darner dragonfly in its helicoptering gyrations above the gnat-clouded waters near dusk, or the staccato nocturnal chirps of a frog all exist because of that food-rich scum coating the bottom. By moving to a spot where the ice is not as thick, but sturdy enough to hold my weight, kneeling down, brushing away the snow, and pressing my face against the ice—if the sunlight is just right, that is—I can catch a glimpse of the greenish fluff that teems with tiny creatures: insect larvae, crustaceans, worms, and protists—not randomly arranged throngs, but an intricate, highly organized orchestration, the food chain of the lake.

Stunned now by cold, in summer the lake springs back, its engine of life awakened and cranked up by the sun's warmth. Lilliputian carnivores such as dragonfly nymphs gobble up smaller creatures, even baby fish, and become food themselves for frogs, fish, and water birds such as the loon. The story is complex, with many parts, each one a species embedded in life's ancient prose and honed by nature's forces of adaptation. This story shines with the creatures we often see and take for granted, be they frogs, muskies, or ospreys. The challenge is to sense the bigger picture, the interconnections. Pondering those ties among this frozen lake's creatures, the relation of these creatures to the lake's capacity to stay healthy for life, and the lake's connection to the surrounding landscape, allows the picture to take shape.

Standing upright again, bracing against the wind and pushing on, I head for another side of the lake where there are other interconnections to appreciate. When the swirling snow momentarily clears, the border of wispy aspens becomes discernible, a curtain of gray columns and threadbare crowns. One tree stands out from the others as I approach land from the ice.

A large, oblong gray object is suspended from an aspen branch slung low over the lake's edge. It is the now empty nest of the bald-faced hornet, that fierce black-and-white wasp whose carnivorous habits in summer winnows the populations of plant-feeding insects in the surrounding woodlands. By now most of the nest's occupants have long since succumbed to last autumn's killing frosts, but not before producing a handful of new queen wasps that quickly mated, left the doomed nest, and are now surviving the winter by hiding in logs and under rocks until spring.

This nest is little more than a featherweight paper shell rattling in the wind—nothing like the heavy nursery it was last summer when it bulged with hundreds of wasps and their brood. Come spring, the nest will be shredded and torn beyond recognition, but I can almost guarantee that new nests will appear again along the edge of this lake. Next summer, those queens that make it through this killing cold will begin the cycle all over again—the world's first true papermakers hard at work once more, stripping away slivers of worn wood and mixing it with body juices to make paper and to sculpt their nests—ensuring future broods of paper wasps.

The straggler mother wasp will awaken in spring, energize her winter-worn body on the sugary sap flows of the old birch trees near the lake, and begin to build a paper nest. Her body already contains all of the eggs needed to make a full colony of worker wasps, the labor force that will take over nest construction and brood care by season's end. In the northern spring, there are few bugs around on which she can feed, so she will take advantage of the feverish handiwork of woodpeckers that live in these woods and gouge holes in tree trunks to hunt for grubs. Woodland butterflies overwintering as adults under loosened tree bark, such as the Compton's tortoise shell and the mourning cloak, will also feed off that sap as it ages and becomes a vintage wine. As the new nest swells in size and numbers and summer proceeds, workers will scour the countryside in search of caterpillars to pulverize with their powerful jaws, making balls of mushy flesh to feed their brood. The wasp cannot ultimately be separated from any other living thing: the connections of creature to creature and creature to place are simply too integral, too absolutely crucial to the continuance of life. Even in winter's deathly grasp these ever so important interconnections in nature's design are evident. On a brief walk across the ice, one encounters only a handful of reminders of nature's complex tapestry, but enough, I think, to engender respect for nature's fabric.

We do not understand fully the natural history of a midwestern lake and its ecological ties with the surrounding woods, fields, and farms. Yet, in spite of this lack of knowledge, a more threatening form of ignorance casts its long shadow across the lake, even in winter. It is a set of human attitudes that judge the beaver as being bad for local property values; view wasps as a menace; and figure that it's okay to push aside the woodlands and drain marshes. Because of this, nature's integrity in the lake and elsewhere may not always be safe.

These unfortunate attitudes generate real doom and unnatural death. Winter's brutal force challenges wild things to be cunning and adapt to an endless chain of events and circumstances that include death as a natural consequence of winter's wrath. But for each species, some creatures do survive, and therefore, so does the species. The real executioner's song here is not one of winter's northern winds and deathly cold, for in this mantle of ice, snow, and wind, nature survives, blooming again in spring seasons yet to be. Human ignorance of things wild and of the interconnections among species, along with our almost instinctively judgmental stances on what is "good" and what is "bad" in the landscape, spells collective death to many species, perhaps even our own one day soon. We not only play the executioner's song: we conduct the execution. What are truly endangered, therefore, are the ecological interconnections among creatures in the lake, and the interconnections of the lake to the woods along its edges. Who is to say that the drab dragonfly nymph burrowing through the lake's muddy bottom under winter's ice is any less significant to nature's well-being than the eagle soaring high above the same place on a summer's day?

It is close to the dusk hour now. The sky is leadening quickly, and a sense of gloom settles over the frozen lake. The cold seems even more brutal, cutting to the bone as nightfall beckons. Winter's wind sounds off the fragility, vulnerability, and subjugation of nature not only to the cold but to the follies of humankind. I must hurry now to get off the lake and back to the warmth of the fireplace. But I cannot leave the ice and wind without a rekindled sense of awe and respect for the wonder that is life itself, in all its many elegant manifestations, and the myriad connections of one creature to the next one. There is much to be thankful for when it comes to nature. In the ice and cold of this day on the lake and in the woodlands hugging its shores, there is much reason to rejoice over the vast theater of life that will blossom here next spring and summer, just as it has for millennia. We haven't yet managed to destroy it all. Nature's legacy still breathes beneath the frozen ice, in the snow-draped boughs of the pines, in the snapping of aspen branches in the wind, in the beavers' life-filled lair, and in that abandoned wasp nest. It will remain and continue as long as we respect it and leave it alone.

Between Cornfield and Forest

A walk on a winter day near high noon, when it is near freezing, is a memorable experience. When it is this cold, a simple walk can be downright painful. Even when I am wearing proper clothing, my feet ache and my breath comes up hesitantly. The key is to keep moving. Despite the physical difficulties, I wouldn't forego these walks at this time of year for anything.

Very early in the season, fresh snowfalls and even bitter cold are welcomed sisters. But quickly they become tiresome, like even the best-loved siblings can with too much exposure. Winter begins to drag along, one gray day bleeding into the next. The human body's engine slows, its fluids feel sluggish, cool and detached as embalmer's fluid. The pulse of life becomes faint, the embers of vitality strain to glow against adversity.

In this time of bland resignation, I go outside to seek icons with which to jump-start my psyche; an excellent place to do this is at a boundary. The borderlines between farmland and forests, between streams and wetlands, or at a ribbon of a brook slicing across an old field, sharpen the dull edges of this season and my mind. It is a good time to look for the overlooked stories nature holds in such places. Even the most seemingly insignificant things, such as a dried, dangling seedpod on a milkweed stalk, tell an exquisite story.

Although I dread the cold winter months ahead, I know that we really do need the deep cold and snow. The clear, ungodly cold winter nights that carve our flesh with their cutting sweeps of arctic air, unwelcomed as they are, prepare the land for life to be. Trudging across this rolling cornfield to that distant line of trees, even slogging through knee-high wind-whipped snow in some spots, isn't really all that bad right now. The icy gusts that usually blast across these hills have eased off. There is little rustle of dead cornstalks, no whistling and crackling branches, only a dead silence. This is a good day to be out here. I already feel a surge of

inner warmth, a refreshing of my spirit, a tinge of spirituality even. An eerie mist, vapors of frozen fog, softens and blurs the sprawling patchwork of cornfields and woods. Winter has spun a checkerboard quilt here; its squares of shattered falling cornstalks glazed in ice alternating with intermittent dark fragments of forest. Consider the striking polarity of this scene, the abruptness of the land's incipient personality at this spot. At first glance, its arrangement is neat, clean, and tidy, almost as if some master builder sewed together the patchwork squares and rectangles of farmland and forest.

I'm trying to follow a winding path I know from summer across the withered, broken corn; I can tell its contour by the zigzag line of dried milkweed stalks jutting above the snowline. This is the time of the year when the now wholly split milkweed pods are untethering their silken seeds, allowing them to be blown far and wide by winter's winds. Through this cold, the little brown seeds are very much alive; those that survive will sprout years later, becoming new milkweed plants that sustain future generations of monarch butterflies and other milkweed insects. Nestled in the snow between cornfield and forest is a suicidal advance line of seedlings and saplings too, including red osier dogwoods and willows. The forest is trying to re-stake its claim, little by little, beyond itself. It is a doomed effort; each year the line is pruned back, pushed aside, and tidied up for replanting corn. But if ever left to its own ingenuity and guile, the forest would creep out into the corn. So this boundary is not at all a natural one.

A natural boundary, of course, is much more irregular, weaving back and forth, to and fro, loaded with the natural tension that flourishes when colonist species step foot into the cornfield and the front line advances. Viewed this way, boundaries are fascinating windows of discovery into nature's proclivity for expansionism, a rightful attempt to reclaim lost land. The plant and animal species that do this form a toughened infantry expecting great casualties but sometimes making small gains, bit by bit, year by year.

This scene, a sullen composite of leaden sky and frozen hills, seems at first glance to be utter wasteland, and true enough, there is death here, but no despair, for life continues muffled and cold-slowed all about. Mosquitoes and butterflies are sleeping in crevices of loosened tree bark, under logs, and in the mulch. So, even in its threadbare state, the forest speaks of life. Its square quarter mile is studded with birches, oaks, maples, aspens, even a few beeches. Along one side, a band of cottonwoods stands out tall and bold, even now. The blown snow has begun to pile up along an old stone wall that separates one side of the forest from the cornfield. And along this wall line, oaks and an occasional shagbark hickory have sprouted and matured, perhaps more than half a century ago. I

167

feel as if I'm standing on hallowed ground. Near the wall, perhaps 30 feet away, a humped, brown shape lies in the snow. It is the frozen carcass of a deer who died a natural death. The carcass is rock-hard, like the stones next to it. But both frozen carcasses and even big stones in a wall eventually breathe new life into these hills.

A loud knocking suddenly ricochets through the woods. A dark silhouette is shuffling through the trees, some 30 feet above my head. It is a downy woodpecker moving swiftly through the old birches that have their tops missing, blown off in an ice storm or lightning strike years ago. This creature is both a skilled artisan and hunter. It chisels holes in dead or dying trees with uncanny instinct, choosing trunks most likely to contain wood-boring beetle grubs and ants who, in turn, process dead wood for their own nourishment and shelter, breaking down dead trees into food for living trees.

Woodpeckers are very crafty at getting their quarry. One spring afternoon not long ago my attention was drawn to an incessant rapping noise coming from a wooden telephone pole. Just below the top of the pole, I spotted a woodpecker tapping furiously, but intermittently. Between bouts, the bird moved to the top of the pole where I could tell, even from a distance, that it was picking up insects flushed out of the cut end of the pole. It did this several times before flying away. This woodpecker today stays here all winter, crisscrossing this landscape, stepping from one island of forest to others, back and forth, seeking food and tree cavities for shelter and coping with winter's deathly challenge to hold on, to survive.

A woodpecker is largely recycled wood-boring insects, and wood-boring insects are recycled dead wood. Dead wood is the skeleton of living trees, and living trees are recycled mulch, carcasses, sunlight, and water. The principle has no end. Songbirds, squirrels, beetles, moths, cicadas, katydids, bats, crickets, and everything else are all recycled and reshaped plant tissues. Life and death are close partners in the design and persistence of a forest. The woodpecker does not need the vast tracts of hilly cornfields fading off in the snow and mist, but it surely needs a forest and its trees, even small parcels of it. In the breeding season, this creature makes its nest in tree cavities and hunts for wood-inhabiting insects to feed its young. The woodpecker's food supply thus depends upon the natural cycle of birth, growth, and death that establishes a healthy woodland.

Other impressive creatures also live here. Last summer I saw a red fox skipping along the boundary. Deep inside the forest a little stand of pine trees with its ground cover of dense needles holds a treasure of animal middens, owl pellets filled with the packed fragments of bone, feather, and fur. Owls, of course, are recycled field mice, snakes, feral kittens, barn swallows, and more. A colony of beavers lives in the distant flowage that skirts a neighboring forest. Beavers can be good for the land. By

chewing through birch, aspen, and other trees, they create opportunities for other life, including birds, rodents, dragonflies, and paper wasps. Off in the distance, the beaver family den is still visible, a steepled latticework of gnawed-off tree trunks jutting up from the blackened ice of the coffee-hued flowage, now crusted and iced with snow, entombing life beneath the ice. A beaver den snags and encourages a lot of life; some stream fish set up lairs within this submerged tangle of packed branches. By stifling the flow of water, beavers create breeding opportunities for other creatures too. Slowing down the water dampens the proliferation of some mosquitoes while encouraging other less intimidating gnats to blossom, which in turn helps sustain the three or four species of dragonflies that depend on the flowage in summer.

The rerouting of the water also encourages frog life, including that of the spring peeper, whose tadpoles are growing in the belly of this flowage well beneath its canopy of ice. Come April, the ribbon of forest bordering the flowage will ring with the calls of these tiny tree frogs. Dragonfly nymphs will eat tadpoles and water insects, even tiny crayfish. Nature's message may be muted in winter, but it still speaks strongly: in both forest and stream, under ice and snow, inside muck and mulch, even in arboreal cracks and cavities, life is waiting for spring and summer, holding on through the brutal cold and pounding storms. Life will return.

The deer carcass will thaw, its flesh becoming a breeding ground for throngs of blowflies, carrion beetles, and other creatures. This heap of frozen meat will be spared from vultures that have moved south of here by now, but it may be gnawed by a passing feral cat, dog, or hungry skunk. Yet its full fate truly awaits spring, as is the case with much of life here. Burying beetles, creatures that live and breed in decaying animal carcasses will show up, as will carrion-breeding flies, to expedite the decay cycle, together with bacteria and scores of other minute organisms. Out of death life will emerge.

People have always been fascinated with death, but less palatable processes like defecation are just as intriguing. Seeing the deer carcass reminds me how often it left feces scattered about in fields and forests. In both death and defecation, unwanted and sometimes repulsive waste matter accumulates in the environment and is eventually recycled through the ecosystem. In the wild, especially, feces, scat, and dung are the inevitable result of animals feeding, and they hold fascinating clues to unraveling the habits and territories of elusive creatures. The size, shape, color, and odor of dung provides clues to the animals living in a place, even when you seldom can find them. Some scientists (sometimes known as fecophiles) spend their whole careers picking through feces, extracting insect fragments, bones, hair, feathers, and plant parts—items that can be useful in reconstructing the diets of animals. Others go even further, studying fossilized feces called coprolites, which have a lot to say about the habits of ancient life in past geological ages. This is all very fascinating work.

I am especially fond of dung and the creatures that use it. Certain beetles, called "dung beetles," deliberately stockpile dung as balls or ovoid accumulations in order to breed. Dung beetles were immortalized by the ancient Egyptians in their art and religion as the epitome of hard, vigorous workers. While there are many species of these industrious insects, they are not easily seen or encountered. They gather and roll dung to eat, and when ready to reproduce they lay their eggs in the dung, burying it in special chambers in soil. By placing egg-laden balls of dung in the ground and covering them up, parent beetles ensure the survival of the grubs, one to a ball, that will grow by eating the buried dung in which they hatch.

Dung beetles tend to be more prevalent in areas of the world where there are large grazing animals—creatures that sprinkle the landscape with considerable payloads of the precious commodity. In these places dung beetles play a key role in maintaining the grazing habitat. Collecting, rolling, and then burying dung by the beetles enriches the soil, fertilizes it, aerates it, and assists in the needed percolation of rain water. However, we have a generous variety of small dung beetles here too. Some of ours roll the dung of animals such as deer, raccoon, and other forest mammals. Certain of these beetles are often quite specific as to the type of dung they will utilize as food and for breeding. Their role in the overall system is easily brought to mind when spotting the frozen carcass of a deer near the edge of a woods on a winter day.

What is happening right now in these woods ensures this new life. Fallen, broken logs, whether the work of ice storms, lightning strikes, or beavers, are snug chambers for overwintering queen paper wasps mated last autumn. I am optimistic that next summer there will be at least one paper nest of the bald-faced hornets suspended in a tree near a border of these woods by the season's end. Within and under every log is a refuge for many small creatures, ones that help keep the balance of life intact in the woods. Logs hold big stories about life.

Darkness is approaching quickly now and I must head back, leaving behind the silence of these hills, the stillness of the forest, but taking with me the memory of the woodpecker's chiseling and the dead deer's legacy. The grand illusion of this season is crystal clear; only on the surface does winter appear to be a down time. Life is waiting, preparing itself. Winter is good for nature. The landscape skillfully purges its elders on its own terms, completing a necessary passage; the propagules of replacement are already seeded, the gate through death's broadly sweeping door sets our feet on the path toward renewal.

Whenever I return from a walk to sit by my fireplace, I always feel a bit different from when I started out into the cold; something feels changed. Perhaps it is me. Learning another lesson about boundaries helps me open my mind further. Living on earth is a privilege, an honor, one I cannot afford to take lightly or for granted. Such enlightenment grows when I spend time searching along a boundary between cornfield and forest during the crisp hours of a maturing winter. Back in the house, bathed in the fire's glow, I am separated from the cold; I have crossed another boundary, forsaking the frigid outdoors to press up close against the hearth. Here I realize what just happened on my walk across the cornfield to the edge of the forest: I stepped momentarily across another kind of boundary, a spiritual warmth burning a hole through the cold and mist and saw there a confirmation that life goes on through winter.

Cocooning

On this sunny Thanksgiving morning, with the landscape covered by a new snowfall, I'm bundling up for a walk. It is always good to get the body moving before the big feast.

This is no ordinary walk down the street. This is a hunt. Some people venture out into the woods, fields, and thickets to hunt and kill pheasant, deer, and grouse. I go—as I have been doing since I was ten years old—walking the marshes and railroad tracks in the cold, searching the brush high and low for wild silk moth cocoons. Usually by this date every year our landscape has turned, adopting its first drapings of winter's suit. This is the start of the cocooning season.

All too often when people think of moths, images of clothes moths, gypsy moths, and pesty tent caterpillars come to mind. But the moths I love to see are much bigger, less intrusive, and of absolutely no threat to human existence. In fact, they add a patina of astonishing beauty to our lives. In these parts the most familiar species are Cecropia, Polyphemus, Promethea, and Luna—all well named after legends and gods of Greek mythology. A fifth is the very elusive Io. Although I tend to bond with this handful of species, Wisconsin alone is home, in fact, to 16 species of these gracious creatures. It is a big group worldwide, showing the greatest diversity in the tropics. Altogether, with this many different species around, I have a good chance of finding some.

Many people enjoy cocooning; it is by no means limited to scientists. I even know a stock broker in his late 70s who has been cocooning most of his life. Some make a living by cocooning. There is a large market for wild silk moths from all over the world, including right here near the edge of this great lake. People have learned how to raise some moth species in captivity, building up large stores of cocoons that they sell to collectors through the mail. I neither sell nor buy them. Occasionally I do find and keep them until they hatch in the spring, but then I always set the moths free. Though I personally do not collect cocoons and then kill the moths for a collection, I do see great value in the work of natural history museums where samples of this planet's vast array of life are collected, inventoried, and identified.

I also see great value in keeping cocoons and allowing people, especially children and school classes, to witness the birth of a splendid Cecropia. Our silk moths are very elusive in their dusk or nocturnal habits, so the chance of finding them in the wild is pretty remote unless you hatch one from a captive cocoon. But the most important part of this lesson is to free the moth into the wild.

Whenever I see one of these moths freshly emerged from its tough silken cocoon in early summer, or even a faded pinned specimen in a museum collection, I am unfailingly impressed by the creature's mammoth size and colorful beauty. Of course, most moths, which along with butterflies make up most of the insect group Lepidoptera, are much smaller and less noticeable. Moths, however, collectively comprise a major ecological presence on a planetary scale. In fact, moths and butterflies together comprise the second largest and most diverse group of animals on the planet. They are tremendously pivotal in the design of terrestrial nature, crucial players and antagonists in the food chains and links with other animals and plants. Cocooning is about engaging a key player.

I am walking toward a distant row of pencil-thin threadbare shrubbery. The low bushes form a straight line as they follow an abandoned side spur of the railroad. This sort of place can be great for finding silk moth cocoons. The land slopes downward into a marshy area, now crisp and hard, well drenched in whiskers of wind-pushed snow. Otherwise all is very quiet, yet the land still speaks. The air crackles with the crunch of my boots in the powdery snow, ruffled thumps of sound against the humming of branches at the mercy of the low winds.

It is important not to confuse wild silk moths with the creature that provides commercial silk for the clothing industry and other uses. The Chinese discovered thousands of years ago that one particular moth could be cultivated for its silk. The caterpillar of this particular small, grayish white moth spins a flimsy cocoon in which the entire structure is made of one continuous, unbroken strand of silk. When the cocoon is treated with heat and chemicals, the glue dissolves, leaving one long thread of silk. Yet, of earth's many thousands of moth species, only one has been useful in the silk trade. Wild silk moths do things differently. Their caterpillars build their cocoons by crisscrossing snippets of cut silk threads, making cocoons useless for commercial silk production.

What I am looking for are grayish or brown objects that somehow appear slightly different from the dead, dry leaves still clinging to some of the shrubs. There's a nearby pocket of wild cherry trees, good hunting

174

grounds for Promethea and Cecropia. Cocoons are often attached to branches and tree trunks where the caterpillars who made them fed last summer. But this is not always the case. Sometimes I have to be very persistent in this quest, covering a lot of ground before hitting pay dirt.

There is one curled leaf on the wild cherry tree that seems more compact than the others near it. The little stem where the leaf is attached to the twig is swathed in a tightly wound coating of silvery silk glistening in the sunlight. This dead leaf is wrapped around an oblong sturdy cocoon, about the thickness of a man's little finger and almost as long. How easy it would be to overlook this Promethea cocoon, since from a distance it blends in beautifully with the withered winter face of the cherry tree and its rattling dead leaves. I can remember times long ago when I'd discover one of the trees filled with a dozen or more of the dangling cocoons. Today the Promethea and our other native wild silk moths are in decline throughout much of North America, though no one knows why.

Finding these cocoons in the wild is a matter of acquired skill honed with time and perseverance. From a comfortable distance, a Promethea cocoon dangling from the bared branch of a wild cherry or ash tree looks like nothing more than a dead leaf, a last holdout against winter's storms when all of the others have long blown to the ground, buried beneath the snow. Novice cocoon hunters usually have to get up close before discovering its true identity, while skilled hunters can sometimes see from a distance that shiny band of whitish silk tethering the dry leaf to the branch. Nature is filled with these distance-related deceptions. A row of thorns on a stem in summer suddenly begins to move, giving away the presence of tree hoppers. Much of nature viewed from a distance is meant to resemble something that would not appeal to a predator or catch its eye. This is the way it is with wild silk moth cocoons, butterfly chrysalises, and insect egg masses on twigs. Like any shrewd predator, cocoon hunters must learn the subtle images of their quarry.

When I searched for cocoons in my youth in the northern suburbs of New York City, my bounty was modest but reliable. A couple of decades later I found many Cecropia moth cocoons in shrubs and trees near downtown Chicago. Cecropia, it seemed, was well adapted to the urban setting, but I simply cannot find such numbers of cocoons now and I am at a loss to explain why. While these moths have been sought by fervent hobbyists for many decades, I doubt that their numbers have dwindled from overzealous collecting. Since butterflies and moths are excellent indicators of environmental quality, I would expect that the answer is undoubtedly complex and daunting, but surely linked in some way to changes in the overall health of their habitats.

I have now found several Promethea cocoons this morning, a good catch. I will collect one or two in a paper bag and put them in the garage for winter in order to see the moths when they emerge next summer. The others I will leave undisturbed. I shake one cocoon in my hand and feel its heavy thump. This means the pupa inside is alive and well. A cocoon is a cradle, a magical bed of chemistry, of caterpillar tissues being dissolved and changed in the confines of the shell, and of the building of a new moth in all its regality. Another has a thin, tinny rattle. The pupa is dead, a shrunken mummy from which no moth will hatch.

Sometimes I find last year's cocoons still firmly attached to twigs, open at the valve at one end where the moth made its exit last spring or summer. Wild silk moth cocoons are so tough and durable that they can last for more than a season, long after their occupants have left. With Promethea especially, I have found fresh cocoons mixed in with older, hatched-out ones on the same bush.

This seemingly dead thing, the pupa—little more than a finely sculpted, oval-shaped, dark-brown vessel—is the bridge between caterpillar and moth or butterfly. Unlike what came before it and what follows if all goes well, the hapless pupa cannot walk or fly away from danger. It has to sit tight no matter what comes. A covering of some sort concealing the pupa adds some insurance, and the cocoon itself camouflages the tasty and juicy pupa, making it less of a sitting duck. Silk moth cocoons look like little more than dead leaves and blend into the hues of winter remarkably well, so even if I were a skilled cocoon hunter, it would be very foolish of me to claim that I had found more than a modest fraction of all that were around this morning.

If I head down the slope on the other side of the tracks I will be in what is a swampy area in summer. Bright red stems of red osier dogwood and thickets of swamp willow stand out boldly above the now flattened mats of dead grasses. This is good hunting ground for Cecropia cocoons. Cecropias lay their eggs on the leaves of many different plants, but some of their favorites here are willows and dogwoods. Cecropia moth caterpillars, fully grown by late summer, build sturdy brownish cocoons much larger than those of Promethea and attach them lengthwise to a branch, trunk, or stem. But like Promethea and others, their cocoons are really two envelopes, one inside the other.

A Cecropia moth cocoon thus provides a complex, durable house for its pupa. It takes days for a caterpillar to make this cocoon. The behavior itself is triggered in the newly matured caterpillars by cues from the climate. The waning length of days in late summer encourages the caterpillar to stop eating and begin spinning. What will become sturdy strands of silk begin as liquids in the caterpillar's plump body. Silk is basically a complex sugar attached to a few other ingredients. When the fluids are squeezed to the outside through a pair of tiny tubes near the mouth called spinnerets, the substance hardens, becoming a thread of silk that the cat-

177

erpillar positions by waving its head and guiding its motions with its front legs. The caterpillar literally draws the silk out, not unlike unraveling thread from a spool. Building a cocoon is instinctive. The cocoons of the wild silk moths are as beautiful and intricate as any of the engineering marvels evident in an orb spider's web.

Depending on the species, the cocoon assumes a characteristic size and shape, often incorporating leaves and twigs on the outer surfaces. The Cecropia moth attaches its big cocoon sturdily to a branch. First the caterpillar lays down a silken mat on the twig covering the length that the cocoon will be once it is completed. Then, waving its head and anterior portion of its body in wide arches, up and down and side to side and often snaring nearby leaves in the process, the creature works. The profile and size of the papery outer envelope takes shape within a few hours of continuous spinning. Since the silk is sticky, the accumulating threads become woven together. As more silk is deposited, the outer envelope becomes thick and multilayered, eventually sealing in the caterpillar and obliterating a view of it as the creature continues building the cocoon inside. The caterpillar knows instinctively when the outer envelope of its cocoon is completed and it can move on to other tasks.

In Cecropia, there are two types of cocoons, defined by the appearance of the outer envelope, "baggy" and "compact." I have no idea why some of them are big and baggy while others are compressed and compact. We do tend to find baggy cocoons nestled low to the ground near the base of a tree or shrub, sometimes even buried in snow, while compact cocoons are more frequently found up high, so perhaps the design of the cocoon is a matter of location and circumstances. On a thick sturdy branch, a tight, compact architecture might be best; but in a thicket of closely packed thin stems, multiple anchorage points and the baggy style might be best. Who knows the secrets of survival and design encoded in a caterpillar's brain? What we do know is that wild silk moths, like all of nature, instinctively do things that give them a slight edge on survival. In baggy cocoons, there is considerable space between the puffy outer envelope and the inner envelope encasing the pupa. In compact cocoons, this space is almost nonexistent, with both envelopes positioned against one another. In the baggy cocoons, a loose webbing of silk fills the space between the two envelopes. These strands are less noticeable but nonetheless present in the more compact cocoons. The caterpillar weaves the inner envelope tightly about itself and, when completed, impregnates it with a sealing fluid. The several hour period needed for the caterpillar to build its cocoon is soon followed by a pupation, the final molt which produces the ovoid dark brown pupa. At one end of both envelopes, the caterpillar has fashioned a weakened arc called a valve—the escape route of the future moth. This valve is noticeable when examining a Cecropia cocoon up close. It is always facing skyward or upward on the cocoon's near vertical or subvertical position on a tree or shrub. This valve is also noticeable in the pendant cocoons of the Promethea silk moth but not in the cocoons of Luna and Polyphemus.

Despite all the effort involved in building its cocoon, the caterpillar still might die inside. When conditions warm up again in spring and summer, what might emerge from a silk moth cocoon is not a beautiful moth but a handful of parasitic wasps. Parasitic insects, called "parasitoids," lay their eggs on silk moth caterpillars or on the foliage they eat. The parasitoid larvae burrow into the host caterpillar and eat its tissues from inside. Sometimes the parasitoid life cycle is not completed before spinning, and a weakened caterpillar, still able to spin its cocoon and pupate, becomes a new clutch of wasps instead of a moth. I have told school children, truly disappointed when the cocoon they have been caring for and watching all winter and spring produces wasps and not a moth, that this event too is something beautiful to behold, since this is nature's way of thinning its herds, part of the natural balance of life. Yet even I must admit that there are few things in nature that can rival in magnificence the emergence of a regal Cecropia moth from its brownish, seemingly inert cocoon, or the hatching of a butterfly, such as a monarch, from its chrysalis.

Cocoons are especially helpful when trying to illustrate nature's cycles and timepieces. At a vulnerable stage in the life cycle, moth pupae are swathed in silk and hidden in plain sight. In the Midwest, silk moths usually have already done this by mid-August, well in advance of winter's often unpredictable arrival date. Caterpillars, with their light-intensity-reading eyes, called ocelli, sense when the days are growing shorter, and their bodies produce a hormone that regulates the making of the pupa rather than another caterpillar shell at the next molt. It is a profoundly simple, yet complicated adaptation that keeps wild silk moths in step with the seasons.

Cocoons are fairly nondescript objects that do not easily stand out in nature. A butterfly chrysalis, however, is usually naked, hanging out there, so to speak, and is most often quite ornate, with a distinctive shape—very different from the smooth, roundish moth pupa. Yet, paradoxically, it is this very ornate appearance of the chrysalis that conceals it in the wild from enemies. It blends in beautifully with meadow or garden flora, as does a moth cocoon—in its very different way. Concealment from enemies in moths and butterflies during the stationary pupa stage is a matter of being either clothed or naked. Skippers, placed somewhere between moths and butterflies, often do something in between. Their caterpillars tether leaves with silk or tether a cut flap of leaf tissue, folding it over, to conceal both the caterpillar and, later, the moth-like pupa. This might very well be a matter of evolutionary status, cocoon or chrysalis, moth or butterfly. As a group, moths are much more diverse and numerous than butterflies, which may be partly explained by their having been on the earth for the past 175 million years, with butterflies as their younger cousins being here only about 40 million years. Cocoon building appears to be a more ancient protective strategy, with the exquisite deployment of silk a carry-over from another related, and even more primitive, group, the caddisflies. Adult caddisflies are moth-like and their aquatic larvae build silk-lined tube shelters covered with bottom debris such as pebbles and twigs. When I think about such matters, I am humbled and awed by the ingenuity of insects in meeting the challenges of survival.

If I am lucky, I will find a couple baggy Cecropia cocoons in this small area of the swamp with its patchwork of blazing red osier stems. I have been out here in other winters when I peeled away a thick layer of snow and found baggy life-encasing cocoons, but I've also found many that were dry rattles already or torn open, with the pupa missing—the handi-work of field mice, squirrels, or chipmunks. Meanwhile, woodpeckers, sapsuckers, and other hungry winter birds poke holes into lofty compact Cecropia and Promethea cocoons and suck out the contents of the pupa nestled snugly inside that inner envelope. Wild silk moths are unquestion-ably part of the food chain.

I remember very well the first time I saw a fresh new Cecropia moth clinging to its cocoon. That was over 40 years ago and the image is still as crisp now as it was then. I had checked that captive cocoon for days and weeks on end when the weather began to turn, spring moving into summer, but nothing had happened. The cocoon just sat in its shoe box. But then one day I opened the box and there it was! Breaking out of the cocoon is clearly no easy task. Each moth must produce a liquid that helps soften the silk, easing its access to the outside world through the little valve-like tuft at one end of the cocoon. The newly hatched moth was a stunning chocolate brown decorated in red, white, and yellow markings. As I sat watching, it rested quietly, moving its wings slowly up and down. The rule for all wild silk moths is if the feathery antennae are pencil thin, it is surely a female; if broad and conspicuous, the creature is surely male. Mine was a male.

A male silk moth uses its larger antennae as a radar screen to snare scent molecules emitted by an unmated female. When more and more of the female's love scent hits the screen, the male flies in her direction for mating. As he gets closer to the target, the wafting potion gets stronger and stronger. Mating takes place after dusk so coupling by perfume rather than sight makes better sense. And here is the kicker. *A male silk moth can often find a mate five miles away!* It takes only a couple of scent molecules to excite the male and start the mating game.

I don't expect to probe deeply into these exquisite details of the lives of our wild silk moths out here today. Turkey dinner, after all, is waiting back at the house. But I cannot avoid considering what I find out here right now either. Discovery of a silken, glistening Cecropia cocoon compels me to think back to last summer and forward to spring. Perhaps last June a mated mother Cecropia scattered some eggs over the red osiers here. She placed her eggs carefully on the tender new foliage, a tender salad for baby caterpillars. After broadcasting perhaps a few hundred fertile eggs over a large area of this marshy place, the exhausted moth died. Since wild silk moths do not have working mouth parts, all of their energy to mate, sustain flight, and lay eggs is born of the energy made by the caterpillar the summer before: foliage transformed into moth flesh. Probably the moth that sprinkled her babies in this marsh last summer was one of perhaps several hundred eggs and caterpillars that started life in this place two summers ago. Less than 5 percent of them would have survived to be in the cocoon stage by last fall.

With these figures, it's obvious that finding a healthy cocoon is very slim in many situations. The summer season for a growing Cecropia caterpillar is a treacherous battlefield, and death continues to hound the pupa inside the cocoon. Most caterpillars die before even having had a chance to spin a cocoon by summer's end. They are fair game for a variety of parasitic flies and wasps that use them as hosts to rear their own young. And there are many other enemies too, such as yellowjackets, predatory bugs, and, of course, songbirds. Put this way, it is nothing short of a miracle that some wild silk moth caterpillars ever make it to the point of spinning a cocoon.

I follow the line of the tracks toward a wooded area where there is a small stand of young birches in a clearing. This could be a good place to find a cocoon of the Polyphemus moth. Unlike Cecropia, Polyphemus is a tan moth with a very prominent bluish eyespot on each hindwing. People usually find this moth fluttering around powerful electric lights on summer nights. Finding a Polyphemus cocoon will be a much more daunting challenge than looking for Cecropia or Promethea. Polyphemus caterpillars spin a whitish-gray plump cocoon, about the thickness of a man's thumb or the size of a walnut. It is usually wrapped in a leaf since the caterpillar spins it while the foliage is still green, but since the creature does not tether the heavy cocoon securely to a branch, it is easily blown to the ground in winter. If I am very lucky, I will find one still dangling from a branch this early in the season. Once, several years ago, I had the good fortune to find a dozen or so of these cocoons and I used them in a little study. I scattered the cocoons in the yard to see if any would survive. Within a matter of days, all of them were shredded open by squirrels.

I should mention here that sometimes it is possible to get a good head start on searching for silk moth cocoons, well before hard frost and snow. By the middle of summer, I start looking down at my feet when walking along tree-shaded roads, driveways, sidewalks, or even paths through the woods. If I spot lots of dark round or squarish objects resembling seeds, I have a closer look. These are often droppings of large caterpillars feeding in the foliage overhead. Lepidopterists, the people who study butterflies and moths, call caterpillar droppings or fecal pellets "frass." The presence of frass betrays the secret habits, often well camouflaged, of what are sometimes very large caterpillars. Without frass, there would be little clue, save for a sharp eye looking above and detecting chewed leaves, giving away the presence of these jeweled caterpillars nearby.

One of my life maxims is that sometimes one must first look down to know what treasures possibly lie above. When I do this late in the season with regard to silk moths, I can find their almost fully grown caterpillars and watch them spin their amazing cocoons. It is an easy matter to collect a caterpillar, keep it going on a cut sprig of the food plant in a large jar, terrarium, or box, and watch it. When the caterpillar stops munching and stops making new frass, cocoon-spinning usually ensues.

But sometimes a pile of frass on the pavement leads me not to silk moth caterpillars but to sphinx moth caterpillars. The caterpillars of some sphinx moths can be an impressive size, equalling those of our larger silk moths (such as Cecropia and Polyphemus) or even bigger. But sphinx moth caterpillars can quickly be distinguished from these by the presence of a prominent "horn" at the rear of the body or a bump-like swelling with an eyespot. Adult sphinx moths, of the family Sphingidae (commonly referred to as sphingids by lepidopterists), have strong narrow forewings, thick powerful bodies, and a functional long proboscis used for sucking up nectar from the bottoms of tubular flowers. Their habits are very different from those of the silk moths, the Saturnniidae or saturniids. Sphinx moth caterpillars usually do not spin cocoons, although some make a thin silken webbing in forest floor debris in which to transform into the pupa. But most dig into the soil, shape an earthen cell, and pupate there. Obviously finding sphinx moth pupae is an immense chore.

The caterpillars of some sphinx moths feed on herbaceous vines and low plants, while others eat the leaves of woody plants. With the exception of recent reports of some silk moth caterpillars eating the invasive plant purple loosestrife, most species of these insects, with the exception of the Io moth, eat the leaves of woody plants. One of the most familiar sphinx moths in our area is the tomato hornworm, which gets its name from the fact that its large green caterpillars eat tomato plants—stems, leaves, green tomatoes, and all.

I find it therapeutic to look for trails and piles of large-size frass when walking in summer. Whenever I have spotted really large frass, I've felt a twinge of excitement: one or more very large caterpillars is above my head. The question is just how far above. I always figure I'm in luck if it is the height of a small tree or tall bush. But even if it is the height of a large tree, I will return to the spot when the weather has turned cold and the leaves have fallen. I might have an edge on finding cocoons if the frass was from silk moth caterpillars and not from sphingids.

I will not be going into the deep woods beyond the marsh today to scratch around in the freezing ground litter under the hickory and beech trees to find Luna moth cocoons. This is a formidable task at best. The Luna's cocoon, a dark brown, thin papery case wrapped in dead leaves, is usually found only on the ground, making it almost impossible to locate. I have only seen one of these cocoons in the wild in 50 years, and that instance was by pure chance when I was 12 years old. I can count on one hand the number of adult Lunas I have seen in the wild since then.

Unsurprisingly, that first discovery stays fresh in my mind. Prior to them, I had never seen a Luna moth in the wild or a living one up close under any circumstances. But I *wanted* to—did I ever—thanks to the encouragement of a kind adult. One stop on my paper route was the home of a writer named John Hersey, whose mother was the librarian at the Briarcliff Manor Public Library. One day she showed me an old book about insect natural history, pointing out in particular a chapter titled "A Barrel Full of Lunas." The story, of course, was about the author raising a batch of Luna moth caterpillars on hickory or walnut leaves kept in an old barrel. Little did I know at that moment that soon I would encounter my first and only Luna moth cocoon on the Hersey house.

On a biting cold winter afternoon while delivering newspapers after school, I paused to examine the dry ivy vines clinging to the concrete foundation of the Hersey house. A small clump of leaves concealed a dark brown, thin, and papery (but good-sized) cocoon. Carefully I peeled it away and carried it home in one of my pockets. Gently shaking the cocoon, I heard the pupa make a healthy thump against the chamber wall. Several months later, that beautiful male Luna moth emerged.

It's no wonder that wild silk moths have a huge following and that people snap up their cocoons for healthy prices. There is something intrinsically appealing about watching these cocoons, be it Cecropia, Luna, Polyphemus, and Cynthia (the latter is an eastern species whose natural range does not reach the Midwest), to see the adult emerge. But I do not feel at all comfortable with buying insect livestock, especially from other parts of the country, since I would opt to release the new moths into the wild rather than add them to a collection. And while we do not know for sure what the impact might be, I am skittish about setting free New York State Cecropia moths into the Wisconsin wild and vice versa. Even widespread species such as Cecropia and Polyphemus undoubtedly have evolved and adapted to meet the local conditions of their environment. Thus the genetic structure and composition of their various populations may be distinctive from one place to another, and I do not want to participate in tampering with this natural system.

I am very enthusiastic about cocoons and moths, even though I would not buy this insectan livestock from dealers. What gives me excitement is the hunt in the wild. My first and only Luna moth cocoon discovery attests to this lifelong enjoyment, as do my many years of searching neighborhoods and wild places near them for Cecropia, Polyphemus, and Promethea. My joy has come from finding their cocoons and letting them be, or collecting a few and setting the moths free in the same general vicinity in which their cocoons were found when they emerge.

There was a time during which I set out to collect as many Cecropia moth cocoons as I could find. While a graduate student in zoology at the University of Chicago 30 years ago, I became very interested in a research study on the pattern of Cecropia moth emergences being conducted by two entomologists, Gilbert Waldbauer and James Sternburg at the University of Illinois at Urbana-Champaign. They were finding a distinctly bimodal hatch pattern for Cecropia cocoons collected in their area. Chicago, located only 140 miles north of Champaign, might provide an interesting comparison. A bimodal hatching pattern, in which some portion of the cocoons emerged early and a second group a few to several weeks later, could be a means for the Cecropia moth to get an early start on the growing season without the entire population being subjugated to possibly unstable weather conditions. Or it could be that some Cecropia caterpillars made their cocoons and pupated earlier than others, causing the formation of the two-part emergence pattern.

Whatever its cause or causes, the double-barrel emergence trend in Cecropia intrigued me enough to scour the city in search of cocoons one winter in order to measure their emergence dates. Searching mostly in the vicinity of the Illinois Central Railroad tracks, I gathered up nearly 300 cocoons from a variety of trees and split the sample in two. Part of the sample stayed outdoors in a large cage in Hyde Park while I delivered the other set of cocoons by train to the Urbana researchers. With some differences in the proportions, the Chicago cocoons showed a set of two distinct groups similar to what had been seen in the Urbana cocoons. I also saw that male Cecropias tended to hatch slightly earlier than females within these two groups. This could have something to do with males needing time to scope out possible female cocoon locations even before the females emerge since unmated females usually will stay in one place and lure in males for mating. Of course, though, hatching of the two sexes does overlap. But because these moths do not feed and only live a matter of days or a week, mating must occur soon after females emerge from their cocoons.

Many people, including myself, have taken advantage of this mating habit as a means to obtain fertile eggs of these moths for rearing in the garden or in captivity. Placing a freshly hatched female Cecropia (or other species) in a wire cage at dusk on a warm evening will probably soon draw to the cage several males ready to mate with her. Only males of her own species will be attracted to her. If the screen mesh is large enough, the moths can mate through the screen. The male grasps the genital opening area of the female with his claspers and stays attached to her for several hours.

Once mated, the female moth is more prone to flight, needing to search for the appropriate food plants on which to place her eggs. But in captivity, a mated female will often place eggs on any available surface. The eggs can be gathered up and placed on the food plant. Some people put mated Cecropia moths in a large grocery store bag and then cut out the pieces of paper around a mass of eggs. These paper-covered eggs can be pinned to a maple, cherry, or red osier dogwood in the yard. The baby caterpillars hatch several days later and crawl off the paper and onto foliage to begin feeding. In some species the newly hatched caterpillar devours its empty egg shell as a first meal. No one knows the significance of this behavior.

I have done this sort of rearing many times over many years at several residences and always with the same results. Very few if any caterpillars "planted" in this manner in the garden survive to reach the time of cocoon spinning and pupation. Between watchful birds, carnivorous bugs, and paper wasps such as yellowjackets, saturniid moth caterpillars have little chance to survive, but some still manage it. I am convinced that overall, in the wild and elsewhere, caterpillars are intensely plundered as food by a range of creatures. I have never wandered the hills and found high densities of cocoons. Low numbers overall and low densities seem to be the rule for these exquisite creatures. And when I plant their eggs in the garden, I lose all or most of them within a matter of weeks. This is not simply a matter of overlooking their presence and erroneously concluding they are gone. I carefully tag the branches and note leaf-feeding damage from my caterpillars. When the damage ages and there is no sign of fresh feeding and no caterpillars, I assume death by carnivory. This seems a fair and reasonable assumption in the absence of direct observations. But I have also watched paper wasps cruising the foliage, looking to glean insects from it on many occasions, and I know that many other carnivores are often lured to their prey by the smell of the prey eating foliage. So the moth caterpillars have several strikes against them in the survival game. From such a state of affairs, one might quickly assume, perhaps erroneously, that silk moths are becoming rare or scarce. But assessing whether or not a species like the wild silk moth has become rare, regardless of the cause, is often very difficult. So many factors influence this species' perceived level of abundance, including weather, electric lights, and the locations of refuge within urban areas. In addition, we base our judgments about rarity upon sampling methods that not only have their own built-in biases but also are at the mercy of external factors such as weather and disturbances that serve further to bias our observations. A year or string of years of low numbers may or may not mean the wild silk moth is rare. This is not to say that we should not be concerned about silk moth numbers, for we surely should.

There are situations, however, in which the Cecropia moth has been very abundant in some areas. Frank Marsh, a biologist, did a master's thesis on the Cecropia moth population in southwestern Chicago in the 1930s. At that time the 30-square-mile area he investigated was filled with prairie remnants and lots of black willow trees, the moths' principal food plant. The densities of cocoons were astounding, much higher than at other places. Obviously there was little natural control on the moth population, suggesting the possibility that the flies and wasps attacking Cecropia caterpillars in this region were themselves curtailed by parasites, a condition called "hyperparasitism." Thus, hyperparasitism may be one factor explaining why these species might be unusually numerous in certain areas. Otherwise, one would anticipate that paper wasps, ichneumonid wasps, tachinid flies, birds, field mice, woodpeckers, squirrels, and screech owls control Cecropia and other wild silk moth populations quite effectively.

I have been out here now for three hours so it's definitely time to head back to the house for the feast. I have enjoyed cocooning, and look forward to doing it again near the winter solstice this year. Cocooning draws me in, pulls me up close to see a detail of nature in the bleak winter landscape. Wild silk moth cocoons tell me that this landscape, deathly cold and frozen as it is now, is very much alive. Winter's pale earthtone hues do not mean lifelessness or an end. Healthy silk moth cocoons, the few that make it, speak of life's continuance. The good snowfalls we have been having help in the search, especially for Cecropia and Promethea, since snow accentuates them among the twigs and branches, no doubt also making them easier targets for hungry birds and squirrels as well. As I mentioned before, wild silk moths are an important part of the food chain. They also are an important part of our national treasure, for they symbolize and reflect the deep stories of wilderness. Once again, I am speaking of the interconnections among all creatures in the design of a healthy whole planet.

186

I am glad to have been able to gather up a few cocoons today. I will keep them in the unheated garage until spring, away from predators. When the rising warmth of summer's debut brings forth the moths, I will bear witness to their bloom, celebrate their magnificence, and let them go free. This will be the moment not only to appreciate nature's gifts, the wild silk moths, and the perilous journeys most of them make, but also to think back upon the winter past and look ahead to summer's promise of a new crop of moths. More gifts, from a world that gives whether we have the sense to appreciate it or not.

I am glad that I am not a diehard collector. The cocoon hunt for me is a time to slip inside the beauty of the winter season to test my skills at finding some seemingly innocuous signs of life within the brittle landscape and brush. It's great when I find a cocoon, but it's also okay when I do not. The point of cocooning is to be experiencing a special time in nature, moving through the crunchy snow and brittle bushes. Finding something dangling from a twig or branch or tree trunk that appears to be a clump of dead leaves causes me to pause, have a closer look, and acknowledge the presence of quiescent life among what looks like nothing more than last summer's dead discarded chaff. Now *that* is the essence of cocooning.

A Royal Oak

I am walking across a barren cornfield in the dead of winter to visit a giant old oak tree. Where the land slopes upward to the west against the frigid ashen sky, that mammoth tree stands out, like some lone, stoic reminder of the sweeping hardwood forest that once blanketed these hills. Especially during winter, this oak, with its gnarled trunk the girth of four men and topped with twisted thick, steady branches, gives new meaning to the passage of time and nature's struggle to persist. In the summer, the oak's singular regality is compromised, blurred by the greenery of crops and a patch of forest a few hills over.

Spotting a huge tree on the bald head of a cornfield in winter is an odd juxtaposition, a link between the farmer's lot and the very ancient natural history of this land, but it is not an unfamiliar scene in the Midwest. These abandoned relic trees, stripped of their woodland compatriots and fast going the way of dinosaurs along with other native hardwoods, pepper farmlands, suburban landscapes, and city parks. The isolated, standing giant oak is thus a symbol of our heavily altered natural heritage. In open areas, old oaks boldly stand out as rugged giants, icons of well-seasoned strength and endurance. In our farmlands, cattle and horses seek them out for shelter. We are often married and buried beneath them. They give us cooling shade for a summer day picnic. People fall in love under them. Oaks give us a lot. For me the journey to the oak is an uplifting experience, especially in winter. This oak is my temple, my cathedral, a hallowed place. My spirituality is rooted firmly here along with the old tree itself rather than in deities of the heavens, imagined or real.

Some people might prefer to visit in summer, when the oak's sprawl of leathery leaves provides welcome shade from the merciless sun. I don't deny the oak's appeal on a steamy August day. But I much prefer it in winter, when the sounds of last summer's harvests of cicadas, crickets, and katydids have long since been muffled by the deathly cold. It's then

188

that I sharpen my focus on the intrinsic threads of hidden beauty that bind all life together. Going up the hill and standing with the tree on a wintry day gives me perspective on life's tenacity in the ever-changing face of adversity. I marvel at the ways creatures, even big trees, cope with winter and survive. I respect nature's ways of preparing its creatures to pass the seasons and to perpetuate their own kind over time. When everything seems so dead and forlorn in this cornfield, a wasteland whose silence is broken only by the howling wind, I am reminded that all is not dead but very much alive here at the foot of the tree. My spirituality jump-starts and feeds itself off the land. What I admire and revere in an enduring oak tree is the life it gives to many creatures and itself.

As I climb the rolling snow-bound summit toward the oak today, the lessons I have culled from past years rekindle my appreciation of nature's march through the seasons. There is little else out here on this frozen, bone-hard terrain to remind me of living and life. The oak's shadows, streaks of wavering bluish purple on the crusty snow, bring me very close to the center of life's seasonal patterns and rhythms.

But I am also uncomfortably reminded about the ease with which people topple giant trees. This big tree cannot hide from anyone, friend or foe, human with binoculars or chainsaw. In its own iron-tough strength and steadfastness lies its inescapable vulnerability to death and destruction. Surely an oak will eventually succumb to old age, multiple lightning strikes, wood-boring insects, or disease. But the premature death of trees, oaks and otherwise, is all too prevalent nowadays. People are killing a lot of trees, and we're not doing it for very good reasons. It's not enough that natural catastrophes, mudslides, earthquakes, hurricanes, and erupting volcanoes strip away huge tracts of forests overnight. People seem dead set on becoming the planet's worst natural catastrophe. A mighty giant tree cannot hide from our fury; it can only face us head-on.

I can barely begin to imagine what these rolling hills of now dormant cornfields were like long before white settlers came to this edge of Lake Michigan. The land was a mixture of open prairies and stands of hardwood forests. How and why this particular tree survived remains a mystery. Then again, maybe the tree was born even after the natural vegetation was pushed aside for farming. I do not know the precise age of this tree, but a good hunch puts it between 50 and 100 years. Whether the oak was born in a forest or in an open field does not really matter. Either way, its presence was inscribed on the hill long ago when an acorn, perhaps dropped by a passing animal, germinated, sprouted, and survived for a very long time to become a tree.

Maybe this acorn of long ago had to wait beneath a thick snow cover like the one today before the spark of life nestling in its belly could break open in nurturing moist sod on a spring morning. As a baby, the tiny

seedling was at first little more than an insignificant piece of this land-scape, and it would be many years before the oak—a witness to at least one world war, a human being walking on the moon, the birth of compact discs, the internet, and the demise of nature here and far afield across the planet—could truly stake its own rightful claim on the land and change the world in its own special way.

Being a seedling is a very chancy thing. Moth larvae and rabbits can ravage its first few tender leaves. But oaks fare better than other seedlings because the bitter tannins in their young leaves discourage browsing. As the tree grows, a balance kicks in between its enemies and its defenses, and the oak endures. It's the same tug-of-war that weaves together all of the pieces and players of an entire forest.

Tree survival is a matter of food and energy. Oaks grab the sun's light with their leaves, building stores of food-rich tissues that yield energy to produce flowers, seeds, more leaves, and roots. But the system is plundered by insects, disease, and other predators that siphon energy away from the tree. In a healthy forest, the system is kept in check and many of the players on this ecological chessboard survive. A healthy forest is the sum total of its plants, animals, and microbes, a complex concert of networks among species that make something bigger than the mere sum of the forest's beings. In nature, patience is a virtue. Nature does well at sowing its own seeds, of recycling its dead in due time. There is no waste.

Yet it would be unwise to look upon a forest as a fixed entity. Forests are always changing. Old trees fall down, opening up the forest floor, allowing new life to spring up—one of nature's most venerable ways of healing itself. This is all a very different process mind you, from what happens when people cut down trees and clear the forest. A healthy for-est deals well with its trees dying off slowly from natural causes. When people do the killing, a lot of other life is extinguished along with the slain trees. Healing is strained, forced, and downright difficult. This is not a trivial matter. The old oak tree insists that I reckon with the intercon-nections behind its silhouette. That in turn forces me to reckon with the darker side of my own species. We are part of the oak tree's bigger story.

When this oak became an adult creature long ago, capable of giving birth to its own crops of acorns, it reshuffled the dynamics of life on these rolling hills. Whether in forest or field, the tree, now at least 60 feet tall, changed the soil beneath it forever. The tree's breathing and ridding of its waste products fertilized the soil and its annual cascade of dead leaves and branches not only added a thick bed of food-rich mulch above the ground, but also a unique flavor to this life-giving debris. Its branches and summer foliage changed the air temperature and humidity beneath its lofty crown, encouraging other plants to sprout within its now expansive shadow. Like the oak itself, each of these plants attracted its own set of wildlife.

The real secret of a giant oak tree in winter is not so much what you can readily see and sense, but more what you do not see and must really push yourself to discover. Even in the starkness of the blinding white snow and the wind-pierced silence this morning, I can see the oak's partners—the legions of insects, galls, birds, and squirrels—and much more. I see and sense life, not death. I sense nature taking care of itself, healing and preparing for spring. I see the lesson at the heart of the oak: that its value lies not in its physical attributes—sheer size, strength, and endurance—but in its ability to support other life.

Gazing at an icy limb, I see the oak six months from now. Its foliage, I hope will host a family of leaf-green katydids the way it has other years. The katydid's flat, slate-gray eggs are already securely affixed to the oak's branches; the babies will hatch when new foliage appears in late spring. Several species of birds will forage regularly through the branches, seeking spiders, moth caterpillars, and beetles to feed their own fledglings. Beneath my feet, the ice, and snow, and far down in the soil, cicada nymphs wait out the cold today; soon they will resume feeding on sap from the oak's fine meshwork of thread-like rootlets. And by late summer, the oak's crown will sizzle with chorusing cicadas, their sharp, steady buzz filling the sultry afternoon air. After dusk, as summer slips toward autumn, katydids will sing from the very same crown. Maybe a queen bald-faced hornet, herself a hardy survivor of this long winter, will choose a branch here to begin building a paper nest that will throb with the drumming of many hundreds of frenetic wasps by summer's end. Certainly a red-tailed hawk will perch on one of the large dead limbs, not to nest but to scan the ground below for field mice. No doubt a squirrel or two will streak through the corn from that distant forest to plunder acorns, scattering seed that holds promise for a new oak to appear somewhere else on this gentle hill or the next one over. And I cannot begin to list all the rich assemblages of microbes, fungi, mites, sowbugs, and other creatures that are dependent upon this tree. Many creatures, mostly small, shape the destiny of a baby tree as it becomes a giant oak.

So, even in a monotonous midwestern cornfield, an old oak tree is a venerable oasis of glorious life—life of every imaginable shape and size. Remember again, though, that more than 80 percent of all animals are smaller in size than the length of a paperclip. Remember too that in smallness there comes a wealth of biological diversity and ecological ingenuity—of worlds within worlds that underpin the more obvious signs of our natural heritage, like giant oaks and whole stands of old-growth forests anywhere in the world. Herein lies the real lesson about life on earth. Every living being, from the geological past to the present, and those yet to be, depend upon other creatures, and most of these are very small. I cannot *see* most of the beings that make this oak tree possible; yet I know they are here and that the oak tree, even in winter, is doing its part to nurture their existence. This is the essence of biological diversity. Ecological soundness. And species wisdom. People need oaks; and today, perhaps more than ever, oaks need people.

I have been most fortunate to have been able to visit this oak for many winters past. I hope I can do so many more times in the future. Admittedly, my motive for coming is peppered with selfishness. I need the sense of spirituality that this tree, and trees in general, provide me. For all too often nowadays, I feel as if the hallowed realms of wild places are vanishing, destroyed by a rapidly expanding modern civilization and its urban sprawl, luxury condos, more malls, and burgeoning populations. If only people could see the bigger picture, learn to think of human beings as a vital part of their ecological tapestry, they too would seek out their own winter cathedral to pay tribute to a great old tree. From its foot, a human can look both out and up—toward what can and should be, if we simply let trees and all they tell us be held sacrosanct now and forever.

Winter Moon

I am tired after the five-hour drive into the North Woods from the city, but I head outdoors anyway. It is close to midnight, and the full moon, suspended in the misty blackness, shines so brightly that I can make out the threaded branches of the aspens and birches lining one side of the clear path down to the lake.

It is moderately tempting to stay inside and curl up on the couch in front of the fire. A North Woods winter, after all, can be downright tough, a formidable barrier to life's basic demand for warmth, food, and protection from searing cold. At these high latitudes, life has little choice, few options. There is no way to detour around winter. Nights like these always lure me out to celebrate that fact. After all, there are few enough of them. Many winter nights here are complete white-outs, with dense clouds erasing our view of the moon entirely and making the tree lines and lake nothing more than a fused wall of darkness revealing no etchings of life's story. So nights like this one are doubly special. And, perverse as it may seem, they often reveal more of the land than even daylight does.

As strange a juxtaposition as it might appear, this silvery bright moonlight always compels me to reflect on the many tropical dawns I have witnessed in Costa Rica, dawns that ignite the day's first chorus of screaming rainforest cicadas. In an uncanny way, the awakening sun secretes an aura, a vibrancy that also defines this winter moonlight tonight here in the North Woods. Perhaps the striking ambience between the two very different times and places is not all that strange. Seeing this moon tonight, with its reflected light drenching the frozen lake, promises the warm summer sun and the myriad insects a northern summer will bring well beyond this cold, biting time.

No matter what the season, the North Woods is truly a marvelous product of nature's forces—hallowed ground to my way of thinking. Its rolling landscape was carved some 10,000 years ago by mighty glaciers sculpting the hills, lakes, and wetlands. While heavy logging has obliterated much of what once was pristine wilderness, there are still impressive stands of forest with oaks, poplars, maples, firs, and aspens as canopy trees. In both summer and winter, I have sloshed through clearings where forest has given way to tamarack swamps and bogs. A rich fauna still abounds in this mosaic of habitats covering this rugged landscape. Some 250 species of birds nest or at least visit here. So do wild turkey, grouse, white-tail deer, brown bear, porcupine, wolf, and both red and gray foxes. This place too is the home of many Native Americans. Other groups have settled as well. Altogether, the place is a beautiful piece of nature's handiwork.

So I'm standing outside in it for a while tonight. My view from the deck sweeps over the expansive plate of flat lake ice that seems to stretch for miles into a distant line of trees not visible now. The air is very still and there is no forecast of snow. I actually wouldn't mind if it did snow, especially one of those special North Woods snowfalls where the huge flakes fall straight down, making soft brittle noises as they land on the tree branches. But tonight is a night for the moon.

Winter here typically means plenty of snow and ice anyway, but lately there have been some lean winters up here where moisture is concerned. At other times the season is rife with icy rain. Days of heavy overcast and steady freezing rain paints a very dreary, worn landscape. Winter rain coats the snow with a frozen crust, giving a dazzling sheen to the terrain whenever the sun finally peaks through. Footprints leave near perfect depressions in this kind of snow. Freezing rains coat the trees with a crystal patina, weighing down the branches almost as much as wet snow, making them creak, crack, and twist loudly in the wind. When freezing rain comes, I stay clear of the deck and watch my steps very carefully when walking along the road. But the season this year has so far eluded the winter rains. They might come toward the end of this winter, but for now the snow is abundant and the sky is clear, good weather in which to grasp the personality of this place.

I enjoy the contrast of viewing this place at night while remembering it in daylight and seasons past. My view into the lake is a wedge of open space with three large pine trees and a line of young aspens scattered along the left. To the right the landscape slopes upward with a dense thicket of tall aspens and birches. These two borders on either side break up a complete view of the lake's horizontal expanse, but I catch glimpses of it anyway through the tree branches.

I'm reminded of the hot August day I spent here searching for the pair of loons that have turned up every summer recently. I lamented the advent

of the jet skiers who have also found this slice of northern paradise and cold-bloodedly tear up the quiet waters, frightening the loons and other wildlife. Despite their annoying presence, I can still stand here and imagine what this place must have been like before houses appeared all around the lakes and the area became densely populated. This was indeed the land of the loon, beaver, osprey, muskie, dragonfly, water strider, pink lady slipper, and so much more. The deep chill of this night holds summer in its hand. In the ethereal steam of the moonlight across the flat frozen lake, in the blackish latticework of bare branches breaking up this scene, I sense the hot glows of the summer just past. Being able to do this has much to do with being given the opportunity to become familiar with this place, one summer following spring, one winter skimming off fall, like a rock skipped across the ice.

The moon is incredible, huge and sharp, a perfect entity hanging in silence over the lake. By now the ice must be a good two feet thick with another foot or two of snow topping. Though numbed and fatigued, I find these moments in the dark very therapeutic and good for the spirit. Occasionally I glance back into the cottage, glimpsing the red-hot roar of the logs burning in the fireplace. Warmth, of course, is what stirs up life and keeps it going. No wonder it looks so appealing. But out here too, in the cold embrace of winter, with the play of the moon's light accentuating the landscape and bringing it to life with a meshwork of tree branch shadows and huge puffs of piled snow on the evergreens, the embers of life are still glowing, perhaps not with a warm red glow, but surely very alive and well beneath the snow and ice.

Snow, snow, snow, snow, snow. This is what life needs at these latitudes come winter. A snow-less winter or one of light, occasional snow spells death for many creatures that crouch down low in the mulch and brambles or dig in the soil. Just imagine gale force winds and brutal cold without the thick, warming blanket of snow. Snow warms up the earth beneath it, helping the creatures there—from bacteria, spores, seeds, mites, isopods, great spangled fritillary and checkerspot butterfly caterpillars, luna moth cocoons, sphinx moth pupae, wooly bear moth caterpillars, mice, and many other species—to survive the long winter, giving them a collective, creative edge in the struggle to stay alive. Up here in the North Woods, winter will, I hope, always be the season of deep snow. Endless cold, knee-deep snow, numbed fingers, cracked and dry skin, ice-caked noses biting wind gusts, layers of damp, sweaty hiking clothes, little sun, and no primary colors anywhere in sight—I wouldn't have missed any of it for anything. But what I enjoy best about winter is silence. Winter lets us listen to silence, and silence has a lot to say. The absence of many sounds gives deeper meaning to what we see in the winter woods, day or night. A thickening carpet of falling, fluffy snow, a glittering down of sparkling diamonds in the moonlight, is the richest voice imaginable, especially when interrupted by creaking old branches rubbing against each other as the land sleeps.

When a winter season is mild, an absence of snow deprives these creatures and the earth of the moisture needed to nourish life. Snow, snow, snow, snow, I say—the heavier the better. It is not just a matter of helping to save what lives beneath it, but also of providing a cushion, a bed, for the materials of life that winter winds and ice blow downward. Shredded tree bark, twigs, branches, last-minute seed escapees from still-tethered fruits and pods, and animal carcasses all land here.

This is the time of the year when the stage is truly being set for summer. Then we will expect to see wildlife, from butterflies and lumbering beetles to songbirds and foxes. But this happens only because snow has helped the links in these food chains to make it through winter, allowing the landscape to replenish itself with new life come summer. Snow, snow, snow, snow, snow: the savior of summer.

Here in the North Woods winter, all of life becomes deciduous, even the evergreens, in one way or another. In preparing for the season and getting through it alive, life sheds its many diversified masks and layers, but first nestles into a snug place its sustainable core and soul, the seeds that will bring new life when the land warms up again several months hence. The penetrating, steel-hard moonlight tonight highlights the illusion that winter is a time of death. And surely it can be. When water is no longer liquid and food is scarce, much of life cannot go on. What it easily exposed in the bath of celestial light is the death of the outer rind—withered, dried, and curled by the cold—an illusion of death and an apparent end. But what is hidden and not at all obvious in this seemingly forlorn scene of sharp angles and patchy black and white lines and blots are the very much alive propagules of life's continuance, those vital links through the cycle of the seasons that allow life's ancient saga to flourish, not for our sake, but for its own well-being.

This is the basic truth that leaps to the forefront of my thoughts when I am standing outside in the cold under the glare of the moon. As it exposes that bold sheen of lake ice and snow at night, when everything else seems muted and dark, that glistening sheet gives up its secrets to me. The moonlight, so powerful tonight that it makes the fresh snow layer sparkle and shine everywhere it touches the landscape, draws our attention to that flat disc of incredible whiteness, and the lake appears alive as a cradle, a womb of life. The ice is a very protective fortress, keeping creatures safely ensconced beneath it. So while this winter cold may convey a strong sense of death and a life-saving instinct toward warmth, in death there is already the assurance for new life.

I see less obvious signs of wildlife in winter here not because they aren't present, but because fewer creatures are active in this tough season. It is tough even for me. But, whenever I so desire, I can slip back inside the house and embrace the warmth of the fire, safely ensconced and protected from this cold. The animals cannot. In fact, if I did not have this option and if I were ill-equipped to handle it, I would surely perish in this cold. Humans—from the earliest Native Americans to people today—need a source of flame in winter in order to survive. And while some indigenous cultures have learned to stay active in long winters, even they need shelter from subzero winds. Long ago people gathered around fires and today we burn fossil fuels to stay warm. Fire increases the chance of survival in winter by several magnitudes. Some other animals have learned to invade warm dwellings in winter: a field cricket chirping on a warm fireplace hearth when the first snowfall comes is a very pleasant thing indeed. A wise one as well.

When the land turns warm outside, life returns, coming out of its shelters and crevices. Sometimes this happens even when it is suddenly warm in the middle of winter. Creatures are waiting to warm up. So winter is physically tough but ecologically benign. Summer, with its active webs of life, is ecologically tough. But staying alive is the biggest challenge for all no matter the season.

Still, I sense a great hope, an optimism for life, out here in this deathly cold. I see beyond this night to many months ahead to understand the essence of winter. Winter is indeed the season of renewed promise and a time for me to wish the very best for all the creatures with whom I share the earth. This is especially a deep message here in the rugged beautiful winter of the North Woods. All of the players are here, close at hand, under the ice and snow, waiting and ready to spring to life. This is what I sense as I look at the moonlit trees and frozen lake. Just as strong eddies of wind in the past weeks created the peaks and valleys of the sculpted layer of snow now wind-packed beneath the trees, so too winter helps me paint a portrait in my mind of nature's complex weave.

Frozen water, be it fine mist, snow or deep ice, reminds me of life's heritage. Winter is a good season to think about our world being mostly water and not terra firma. We call this planet Earth, but perhaps it should be called Water instead? Not only is there more extant ocean and lakes than land, but our own bodies are about 70 percent water too. Life evolved in water. Human babies, like the young of many other creatures, develop inside an envelope of water. The arthropods left the seas millions of years ago and evolved into the highly successful insects, arachnids, millipedes, centipedes, and land crustaceans. Vertebrate animals left the seas to give rise to amphibians, reptiles, birds, and mammals. Conquering land, breathing air, and supporting the body in the absence of water's helpful buoyancy were major challenges. New opportunities, including the development of wings, lungs, complex life cycles, and the capacity to control body temperatures, gave land-bound animals a grand new journey.

Many of them went back to fresh water to spend part or all of their lives, not so much because they had to, but because it was a viable option. Standing here on the frozen deck, glancing across the thick moonlit snow, and spying the snow-covered rock-hard lake, winter exposes its basic element. The season merely locks up water for a while, denying us access to its precious qualities. For more than one reason, we need the thaw. But out here in the brutal cold, with my body struggling to maintain its life-balancing temperature, I think of water's gifts. Water cannot be taken for granted. Water is not infinite.

The challenge at this time of the year is to look for signs of life beyond this mask of frozen water, or at least to be aware that much of what will grace this landscape next summer is already here. Sometimes I feel I learn the most about a place such as this one by being quiet. In the naked silence of a cloud-free night, the land speaks to us, but we must be quiet to hear it. This is a popular haven for snowmobiles; the heavier the snow, the more of them. I wish them no ill will. But I like it best up here when there is true silence because what I enjoy the most about winter is listening to the land conversing with us. Of course, the land is dialoging with itself and not solely with us. We are not that important a participant here. Yet I believe we can be included in its conversations.

Even on a wind-free night such as this one, there are sounds here. Not people sounds. There! A branch just crashed down off to the right. It didn't make a loud noise. Rather, its fall to the ground was muffled by the snow. Most of what I hear is the deathly silence broken with the crush of wind through branches and the clatter of swirling snow and ice. The sounds I heard at night in summer are no longer here. There was the whippoorwill then, the eerie early evening cry of the loons, and the faint chirp of an occasional cricket. In spring, I enjoyed the calls of woodland frogs in the temporary depression on the opposite side of the house.

I remember, too, the sounds and sights of these North Woods as the first snow of this winter season was just starting to fall. The mulch creaked and crunched beneath my feet as I trudged across a low hill across the road from the cottage. As the big flakes came down, they made loud rattling noises when they hit the crisp, dry leaf litter. Their sounds filled the afternoon air with a disjunct and atonal dirge. As they continued to cascade down, the woods appeared to be draped with a covering of cotton mist. What had been a tapestry of sharp lines and crispness was being transformed before my eyes into a softened and steadily blurring wall of whiteness. The earthtone flooring beneath my feet and around me as far as I could see was slowly obliterated by this lazy snowfall. I had the feeling that shortly, for sure by daybreak, I would be seeing the last of autumn's signatures on the land for another year. And by dawn of the next day, sure enough, the light snowfall became an envelope of thick, dripping mist, a smoldering white cotton veil strangely suspended somewhere between snow and water by the interplay of near-freezing temperatures. The air blew around the cottage in sweeping swirls. Winter had settled in.

I found a place deep in the woods that day where I sat on a log and said nothing. And learned something very important: when you are very still, you begin to hear the woods, even against the backdrop din of falling snowflakes changing the ground from brown to frosted. I heard chickadees scratching bark as they hopped along tree trunks and saw at least two chipmunks scurrying through the leaves on the ground. As the snow continued to fall and dusk beckoned, I moved along to an open area bordering the woods. Sometimes you have to go to the signs of life at this time of the year rather than sitting down in silence waiting for them to expose themselves. Nearly always it takes work and patience to see winter signs of life's existence. Lifting some loose rocks atop an old stone wall, I found a small cache of acorns. A frayed orb weaver spider's web tethered two reedy goldenrod stalks together with strong silk. No spider showed up, but I knew that somewhere nearby, down in the dried thatch or attached to a stalk perhaps, was this massive spider's papery thin but secure, silken egg case. A small clump of dried milkweeds stood nearby with several split-open seed pods attached. In some of the open pods I saw the silky tufts of seeds yet to be blown off by winter's winds.

On my way back to the cottage I passed a tall pine tree with an old nest of an osprey perched on its broken off top. Many times I have seen ospreys flying over the lake in summer. By now the snow was forming a thick coat over the ground, deep enough for me to see fresh deer tracks. Not long after that I even noticed the faint etchings in the snow where a group of pheasants had walked slowly across the opening made by the trail. Perhaps they had passed through only moments before.

Tonight, sitting out here on the deck bathed in frigid moonlight, remembering the sights and sounds of this place, I try once again to sense the interconnections of creatures that establish a healthy lake and forest. The earth on which this cottage sits carries rich payloads of microbes, fungi, and very minute arthropods and worms, all of which plunder the leaf mulch at its interface with the soil. These processes, by which these hidden tiny creatures feed from the rotting mulch and its byproducts while at the same time giving off substances seeping into the earth, help to feed the forest trees and shrubs. Every autumn and winter, tons of leaves, seeds, and branches are blown to the forest floor by winds. Branches big and small in the forest canopy snap off under the weight of heavy wet snow and ice.

Spring thaws over centuries make mush of this natural debris to provide food and homes for many insects and other arthropods. The wetness of these woods much of the winter and spring encourages the growth of lichens that can be seen, even in winter, alive and well on the trunks and branches of the aspens nearby and on the sodden wood railing of the cottage. Looking closely come daylight, it is possible to see even the tiny whiskers of lichens clinging to the planks of this deck, beneath the snow.

Not only does the forest accumulate a rich bed of fertile mulch, so does the lake. Branches, twigs, and leaves coat the bottom of the sandy lake in some places more than others, creating a nutrient center that fuels the food chains under the water. The osprey and bald eagle live here because the lake has fish on which these regal birds feast. The fish are in the lake because there are insects and other small animals, not to mention plants rooted in the submerged mulch and debris, to feed them. The loons thrive on the lake because they can successfully dive for plants, crayfish, and dragonfly nymphs. Dragonflies live on the lake and in it because there are plenty of midge larvae and other small insects living on the bottom of the lake. Midge larvae recycle the decay products of the leafy mulch on the lake's floor.

This lake has a couple thriving beaver lodges too because there are still plenty of birches and aspens ringing much of the lake in spite of the many clearings made for human homes. Beaver dens are good for the life in the lake because they provide shelters for some kinds of fish. Around the lake the deer population stays healthy because the forest feeds and shelters them. The patchwork of open meadows and marshes surrounding some of the lakes in this area support field mice, skunks, and opossums. Together with chipmunks, squirrels, and unguarded baby birds, these creatures feed the red foxes and red-tailed hawks sometimes spotted near the cottage. The forest's welcome repertory of songbirds thrive on a rich array of seeds, berries, and insects.

The sapsuckers and woodpeckers in these woods, even in winter, are here because of the decay cycle that starts not in the mulch, but well above the forest floor. Legions of wood-boring beetles and ants festoon the damp bark and heartwood of trunks and big branches near the top of the forest. These beetles and ants weaken the wood but also nourish the woodpeckers whose rapping on a silent winter day sometimes resonates quite loudly if the wind's direction is right, or when it is absolutely still.

Though woodpeckers are not affected by snowcover, animals more dependent on hunting for food on or near the ground are. A rich snow blanket helps creatures that go underground for the season, including raccoons, woodchucks, weasels, chipmunks, and some mice. These animals either hibernate or go into a shallow torpor, lowering their body temperatures to near freezing in the former condition or to 5 to 20 degrees

Fahrenheit for short periods in the latter. While snow certainly cuts off the food supplies for many animals, it also serves as excellent insulation under which the temperature stays just a bit below freezing. Thus many creatures, ensconced beneath the thick snows of the North Woods, are protected from brutal arctic blasts of far below freezing temperatures as well as hungry predators on the roam. When snows cover up brush, an air space at the bottom of vegetation allows some animals such as small rodents to find food. This of course creates a potential hardship for hawks and owls patroling the snowy landscape, and when conditions are really bad for these aerial predators, they often head south in search of better hunting grounds. This is more true for hawks than it is for owls, which tend to stay put and switch to hunting small birds such as chickadees. Horned owls will even go after rabbits.

In short, thousands of years of adaptation have equipped native species of animals to survive the rigors of the northern winter; however, there are some creatures present in these North Woods whose geographical range is being stretched to the upper limit, and this makes winter a real struggle for them some years. Take the Virginia opossum. Its naked tail and naked ears give it away as a southern species. It is no match for these northern winters. Opossums are basically subtropical beasts, so seeing one dead from frostbite in the North Woods is not at all surprising. What appears tonight from this cold moonlit deck to be so rugged, then, is in fact also fragile.

The endurance of the huge white pines, oaks, and maples—the stalwarts of what was once pristine forest—is precariously dependent upon a multitude of tiny, largely hidden creatures. Bacteria, fungi, protists, worms, and arthropods are the creatures that nourish the thin soil of this place, giving it the food bulk needed by big trees. Without the underpinnings of small life, there would be no big trees and the forests they form. Nor would there be many of the big animals we identify with these woods, such as the white-tail deer, bald eagle, red fox, porcupine, and legions of songbirds. I call this the big illusion of wilderness and nature. Whatever appears at first glance to be strong and enduring and independent is often the most vulnerable. Big creatures sit at the very pinnacle of complex assemblages of many lifeforms, most of which are quite small and often totally unassuming. When the land is disrupted and the vital bonds of life uniting these small beings into some semblance of orderly structure and dynamic design are broken, forests and their wildlife collapse. There is thus a well-earned greatness in the smallness of most of this planet's citizens.

So I stand here on the deck under a late-night shower of soft moonglow and celebrate all that still lives beneath the snow and ice. Here on this biting-cold night, I can see the porcupine, perhaps now sleeping close

by, once again foraging for berries across the landscape next summer. A few brittle dead leaves rattle on branches near the cottage. Splintering limbs make raspy groans under their weight of snow. Somewhere, perhaps under the shingles of the cottage roof, sleeps a numb tortoise shell butterfly and maybe even a foundress bald-faced hornet. All of these things and a multitude more are the welcome promise of this land's proclivity to breathe with new life come warmer weather three or four months hence.

The clouds are moving in and the brilliance of the moon will soon be smudged into the darkness as it moves across the sky. I feel snow on its way and that too is a good thing. I can practically feel the changes underway, moon and earth shifting positions. It is not always easy to sense change. Sure, I know the seasons change, and days fade into night and night becomes day. I know the feel of that first hard frost, and of winter's heavy snow squalls. Come March, I anxiously await the spring thaw and the earth to soften once again. I am no stranger to the sauna heat and dampness of an August day at noon. I can reconstruct in my mind the beauty of the seasons from this deck. But there are times when I yearn for knowing about other dimensions of change, ones well beyond reach.

As I stand here, I wonder what this scene was like a century, a millennium, or 10,000 years ago. What I see from this deck, even at night in winter, is what is left today of a long, complex history of the changing complexion of the land. Beautiful as these woods and rolling landscape are, the life here now is an anachronism of what it once was in ancient times. Deep in the North Woods, nature holds on in pieces and fragments of its former self. People have taken away a lot from the land. Gone are many of its old-growth trees and some of the creatures that depended on them. We hunt out the woods and we fish out the lakes. I am not saying this is a bad thing. I believe in hunting and fishing for food and I believe that, given the altered condition of the land causing over-supplies in some game species at times, these activities can still be good for the land if they are managed carefully. I worry about what we do without thought far more.

What I like about being out here in these woods in winter is the sense I get of the land's contours. In winter, its personality leaps out at you. I am glad that the aspens, birches, and pines are still here, and with them an array of animal life. Nature has reseeded this land itself. And in this act there is an insightful clue for our own destiny. It is best to harvest from nature just what is needed. It is unwise to clear away immense areas of the land or plug up swamps and wetlands simply to suit ourselves. Trying to live in harmony with nature can cause us to reassess our needs too.

A fine snow is starting to fall straight down now, and the moon is being blurred by a veil of clouds. The heavens have disappeared for this night.

In the stillness and freshness of new snow, in the silence of the woods and ice, I know that life is continuing, subdued for sure, but with its presence accentuated by the sketchmarks of aspens against the gray winter sky and an occasional glimpse of a chickadee or two flitting from branch to branch. A melodious sonnet of quietness warms my spirit and enlightens my mind. There is indeed much to be thankful for up here in the North Woods in winter. A conversation with the wintry land from the deck of the cottage on a night flooded with moonlight—and then closed with gently falling snow—tells me it is so.

Commencement

I have been walking across these hills now for close to an hour. It is one of those slate-gray April afternoons. Here and there are patches of rapidly melting snow, as if winter's battleground has shaken loose, throwing up its arms in tenacious defeat. While the air feels warm, there is a biting edge of cold hanging over the land. Winter struggles to hold on, spring teases by holding back. Aside from those dissipating scabs of snow clinging to low points, the place is brown, bare, and tired. Some people call this in-between time of the year a fifth wheel—the mud season.

In spite of some recent bouts of spring-like weather, the mood of this dull scene might appear to be nothing but cruel cold and death. But this is not really so. At these moments, I am encouraged in my quest by the thought that "life goes on." Throughout the tough late winter, when many of these brown and bare contours speak of death, life's determined continuity endures. This land is filled with survivors; in spite of its highly modified cover, life breathes here, even now.

The winds are blowing hard, a heavy rain storm is brewing, and the deluge will be here before dusk. It is too warm for more snow. March and April near the western rim of this great lake are typically cauldron months of blustery, shifting weather, and right now this landscape resembles a battlefield. The rows and rows of broken and beaten reedy brush gives way in the distance to a faded thin line of wispy trees.

This time of year, to be quite frank, simply cannot be corralled. In some years, the move from winter to spring is nothing short of peculiar, even volatile. There can be a long stretch of mild, sunny weather bringing a welcomed thaw and plenty of dripping everywhere. Then this pleasantry goes away. As if from nowhere, the sky fills up with billowy, black clouds, terrifying lightning, and thick rain showers. And it is still cold, especially at night. Others years bring protracted gentle rains, just what the land really needs to soak it thoroughly and bring forth new life. Slow rains are always better than fast downpours. But this transition can be ugly—a slate-gray horizon shouting loudly of despair. The mud season seems to be life's bleakest moment—much bleaker than winter's deathly grip. Even human emotions run hot and cold, back and forth, in this mixed-up time when it is neither winter nor spring. At first, winter recedes and the thick snow cover vanishes. But then, in a matter of days, a carpet of light snow-flakes suddenly re-blankets the landscape—a thin coating that will dissi-pate in a day or two when temperatures swing upward. Then the warming air exposes once more the scars of winter on the flattened, brown land-scape. But winter's treachery is not gone for good. A sudden deep freeze turns the patina of thaw into a sheet of ice, thin in some places, thick in others.

It is frustrating to not be in winter or spring. We can take either season, but an uncolored purgatory is hard to take. Enough of these skies stuffed with sweeping ribbons of high clouds. Give me bright sunny days and clear, star-studded nights. Finally spring's insistence prevails. The crust softens into muddy slush, and spirits rise with a promise that this mantle of gray will vanish for good this year. Off in the distance comes the trilling of a wren, a welcomed omen that winter truly has been kicked aside for another year.

The wren's trill is a plea to stop moping about grayness and mud, to push ahead beyond an ambience of mourning and tragedy. It is time to put aside setback, personal losses. This is not at all an easy thing to do, but it must be done. Life goes on. The lone wren on the now barren land-scape proclaims it so. This is the magic stroke when life is at its best. When everything seems bleak, ugly, and beaten down by winter, life rises to the challenge. All of a sudden, the skies open, the grayness slips off, and a magnificent blue sky sings of life yet to be. Life does go on. Soon a smoothing sweetened healing will arrive in the form of downy green spreading out across these pockmarked hills. But right now, there's no way to be certain that winter is really gone for good this year. Perhaps that dry Yankee wisdom of Robert Frost's "Two Tramps at Mud Time," " . . . winter is only playing possum," is the best thought of the day.

Patches of new growth are emerging. Here and there, a fine layer of nature's green rouge is pushing skyward, giving birth to a fresh meadow. Even as the land sits, stoically battered, whiplashed and spanked by win-ter storms, new life is already taking hold. This is a very good thing. For in all the lands and places where I have walked through the seasons, every epilogue is truly a prologue. The end of winter and the arrival of spring fuse and dance through the mud season every year.

Soon the first wave of spring wildflowers will pop up in broad carpets in that distant woods. Honeybees, and more important, dozens of native bee species will be charging up to gather the season's first, fleeting stores of nectar and pollen. Lots of flies will show up on the mulch and some sluggish grasshoppers will appear in the dried tufts of grass. Before things really heat up is in fact an excellent time to bring along a hand lens to practice the skills of picking out ants, bees, or flies against the softening earth and mulch. Becoming an apprentice aficionado of mud season's small creatures is inexpensive and gives huge returns.

No crickets or katydids call yet. The cicada's song is still several months away. But by this time, the mourning cloaks have mated in the woods and batches of their eggs are already placed on shafts of swamp willow. And soon a foundress paper wasp will be sunning herself on that fencepost.

My boots squeak in the mushy earth as I move down the slope toward the woods. Tomorrow or the next day this soft, pliable earth may once again be hard and crusty if the weather turns itself back into a last gasp of deep winter. Spring is a time of quiescence and action all at once. Nothing is the same one day to the next. The cycle of the northern seasons especially are tumultuous, even tempestuous, affairs. Within weeks, the farmers who plant these hills will again worry about rain. Will it be too little or too much? A good winter filled with plenty of snow and a spring rich with rain holds promise of good bounty, both for the farmer and for nature. This is the time of the year when I too hope for plenty of rain. No matter if it is still cold. Rain softens the earth, awakening the myriad life forms that live unnoticed below my feet. The soil and its overlay of thatched grass and mulch become a hotbed of life by early spring. Literally millions of insect eggs, fungal spores, protists, worms, mites, and bacteria are waiting right now to spring into life. I am walking upon a living skin.

Spring storms are good for the land, but I am afraid that many creatures, especially the legions that go unnoticed each summer, are caught in the throes of a terrible ecological storm from which there is little or no real recovery. I do not know this for sure, but I am concerned. I do know that we have less and less natural areas available as the years pass. I know too that fewer butterflies and songbirds show up each year. From ancient times to now, human beings have tinkered and tampered with nature. People have pushed back wilderness, made fires in old-growth forests and prairies, hunted out the woods, and fished out many streams. They have dumped untold payloads of harmful chemicals into fields, forests, and streams. Wetlands are in deep trouble. Many of our land-use systems also change the climate, especially when massive areas of forests are cut down. A planet devoid of its wild heritage, an ecological desert adorned with expanses of turf grass, pavement, planted gardens, and parks, cannot sustain in the long term those chains of myriad life essential for a healthy biosphere.

I walk on toward the woods. It is tiring to wade through this muck, but it is good exercise and the land will speak to me, which will make the slogging worthwhile. Near the edge of the forest, my footing is much firmer on the matted down, thatched grass. The shade cast by the trees still prevents some of the snow from melting. There's a knot of haggard crows in one of the trees. They blend in well with this leaden, shadowless afternoon. If there was some real sun pushing down through the clouds, I would almost expect to see a mourning cloak butterfly in this place.

A lot of life is sleeping here. That gray object high in one of the trees is last season's abandoned nest of the bald-faced hornet. I am amazed that a good part of the original nest is still intact. Usually by this time winter winds and ice storms shred them, but this one has mostly escaped that fate though part of the outer envelope is missing. I can barely make out the layers of brood comb cells now exposed but always concealed inside a nest with living wasps. Myriad life holds on in these islands of forest clutching these hills. Its promise, to be present again in its full form and guise, is hidden right now in these woods and along its edges, assuring me that life goes on. Life is sleeping, drumming beneath the debris.

Winter storms have had their way in some instances. Tangled limbs lie piled atop one another, fashioning a maze of interlocking dead branches. Inside it, the grayness of this day melds with the earthen hues of the thick brambles. It is a good place to breathe deeply and smell the essence of the woods on this time cusp between winter and spring. Inside it the scents of the land rise up in the vapor of forest decay. Not bad decay, but a good healthy rot. Over time the maze, if little is added to it, will dissolve into the mulch. When the maze is hammered by rain and sleet, its return to the earth is hastened. The branches become mulch and the maze, defined as it is by the spaces between the branches, disappears.

Before that, though, its tangle of branches will provide a three-dimensional structure which animals will use to make their nests. This is especially helpful for songbirds. As the maze is exposed to cascades of snow, ice, and rain, this bombardment changes the personality of the brambles, creating new opportunities for wood-boring beetles, ants, and the creatures that hunt wood insects such as the hairy woodpecker. The downed branches will be attacked by bacteria, fungi, protists, and a variety of wood-tunneling and wood-eating insects. Some of these insects have symbiotic creatures within their own digestive tracts that assist in eating decayed wood. In turn they will be stalked by other hunters. Out of rot and decay is born the substance of all life. This maze of sticks, seemingly innocuous and dead, is instead an ecological hotbed of life.

It takes many years for a maze of branches to disappear. Right now this one stands about four feet high. Perhaps within the next year its belly will cave in, lowering it a bit. But every year too, more sticks will fall from the top of the forest, adding to this maze and making others. Some creatures, when the land warms up, will take wood from here. This pile of tree limbs, many with the bark now spliced and peeled away, is a good source of nest-building materials for paper wasps. Dead wood, shaved off by foundress wasps in tiny fibers, will become a huge paper nest, the protective shell of a new colony that will thrive in this forest over spring and summer. The maze is good too for wandering caterpillars searching for concealed places for becoming chrysalises and for spinning cocoons. When I visited this particular pile of branches last fall, I noticed a woolly bear caterpillar curled up underneath a section of branch on the bottom of the heap. And for the past few years, a cluster of bracket fungus has been flourishing on one of the thickest lower branches in one corner of the maze. When the maze is covered with thick snow, it also becomes a cozy, protective cocoon for field mice, rabbits, and some birds, hiding them from the hungry hawk circling overhead. Creatures make good use of this pile of branches, coming into it, staying a while, and then leaving.

No matter how many times I visit this little woods and wonder about the maze, I am still awed by how little I understand of these wild places near the edge of this great lake. Every year, every season, this mystery grows, becomes more complex, more inspiring, and I feel ever more responsible to help keep the promise of life alive.

There is a real connection between the healthiness of nature and the healthiness of society. Natural wastelands, including wrecked wetlands, shaved forests, dead lakes and streams, breed cultural wastelands. Human beings need the sense of place, insight, and inspiration that only nature can provide. Nature and culture are thus married partners in the quest of humans for calm and happiness. If we destroy one, the other cannot survive.

A patch of forest and its natural litter or rotting leaves, branches, and seeds tells me much about life's inherent continuity when it is left undisturbed by people. The death of foliage, whole trees, branches, animals, and other organisms break down into substances that promise new life. This can be a helpful lesson for human beings. The greatest loss a person feels is the demise, expected or unexpected, of a loved one. Nature may help us to understand, to cope. Nature teaches us that winter cleanses the landscape's palate of myriad life, but not without these creatures sowing the soil, mulch, and rotting or living plant tissues with eggs, seeds, and spores (all well furnished with safeguard antifreeze) to survive the long winter. This is creative death in the sense that it is death without disappearance. Death is renewal. This is all that seems to matter in the continuance of life in its myriad design and diversity—its drive to go on. Birth, growth, sex, and death. And then renewal; call it resurrection.

Out-of-doors, in this mushy, dripping time of the year, is a good place to think about these things. I want more spring and summer seasons filled with myriad life. Emotionally the challenge is far more awesome. Can there be solace in knowing that the death of someone close is a part of nature and that both the body and spirit of that being becomes a part of nature? When I walk across these hills as winter turns into spring, when I feel against my skin the whiplash of wind and rain, when I see the sun straining to poke through that thick mantle of gray clouds high above or view the thin line of these isolated pieces of forest, and when I stand inside a pile of dead tree branches inside the woods, I am connected with the rest of my kindred creatures who live here. The pile of rotting branches, the forest: these are pieces of a place of worship, my cathedral for connecting physically and spiritually with what I believe is the greatest gift of this universe, myriad life.

I am not saying that this is an easy thing to feel and believe. But how do we feel about nature? That is, are we comfortable, even in love, with the idea of nature, but at a safe distance? In our everyday living, do we abuse, beat up, or kick it aside, and kill the many faces of nature close at hand? Or do we embrace these diverse manifestations with little or no value judgment? Is the best brand of nature that which we see on well-edited television programs and in books? Or do we truly take the time to venture outside to hone our skills on what to see, to learn the details, to gain new insights, even in our yards and gardens, and a new respect for myriad life? Can we become heartfelt citizens of nature?

Nature is not about peace and beauty; it is about brutal sex and war. But nature surely has beauty—beauty of design and arrangement. Remember always the interconnections. When once we begin to understand the brutality and beauty of nature, the intellect and heart become one. I am not at all suggesting that we should canonize nature, even though it is surely sacred, priceless, and irreplaceable. But to become whole persons, we must always seek to better understand and respect nature, not for commercial gain but simply because myriad life exists.

A healthy, collective philosophy about nature begins with individual practitioners. We cannot profess to love walking in the woods, breathing fresh, crisp air and listening to hidden frogs, without an ethic that leads us to better understanding of what is here right now. Can we, as a society, slow down enough to see small creatures when we venture through a pile of fallen branches or stir up mulch on the forest floor? Must we always look up? Can we not look out horizontally and look down more often? Seeing nature beyond trees and other plants comes slowly, but can truly be painless, fun education. Catching the sudden movements of small creatures in leaf mulch or in a stream takes time and perseverance. The rewards can be mind-boggling. We need to be less concerned with getting done with a walk and more dedicated to ingesting what small pieces of the complex puzzle of a field or woods we can notice along the way.

If you can get yourself past the brash, shifty, unstable weather one day to the next, venturing outside in this transition cleanses the mind of everyday stress, those gremlins of civilization, and refills it with a sense of awakened drama as the land changes. This can be the very best of therapy. You re-awaken, become restored, as the land around you wakes up and changes its guise. Wisdom is seldom a store of facts. Wisdom seldom comes from books and well-meaning teachers. Wisdom *can* come from seasoned insights hidden in the land. Try a challenge: how many insects can you find on a raw afternoon? Lunacy, you say? The effort might surprise you. In the mud season comes physical, mental, and spiritual rebirth; venturing out into it on a raw, biting day kickstarts the process internally. This is not a matter of a quota of new facts about nature, but about a process, a booster shot of invigorating energy, to be wholly absorbed outside yourself. This is the best brand of wisdom, that which gives us a sense of our place in the universe.

Remember, please, the spirit. Always the spirit; do not ignore it. I am not speaking about religious custom. Rather, I speak of natural spirituality. This spirit is all too easily trampled over, or cocooned into full retreat by the noisy issues of modern living. When you walk outside in the cold and look for signs of life in the mud season, the natural spirit will come back and settle in. It was never really gone at all—just muffled and harnessed beneath a numbing coat of daily ups and downs, like myriad life muzzled under the ice of a frozen lake resisting the thaw.

The real challenge for me always has more to do with process, with becoming a sleuth in search of new information or challenging old dogmas. In order to better understand the panoply of life, tackle the challenge of finding an insect, or watch what a certain caterpillar does on a plant over the course of an afternoon puts me definitively in *this* place at *this* time. Isn't it marvelous to watch a cicada emerge from its earth-crusted shell on a tree trunk, and to learn whether or not it will be attacked by marauding ants? Again, the quest is to become aware of the interconnections. Always the interconnections. It is a good thing to sense the closeness of insects and other small creatures in seemingly ordinary and familiar places. Your world is theirs. Their world is yours. Within the stretch of your arm can be found many small creatures in and on the earth. Life breathes in the softening earth of mud season, in the thaw of the pond. Life goes on. You need to be outdoors in all of the wonderful seasons, even if you only go as far out as your own backyard. And there you need to look and listen.

Let me quickly add that having an ethic about nature in no way disqualifies the myth of the natural man. Humans have always been and always will be avid hunters and modifiers of the landscape and the ecosystems it supports. The human journey is largely a matter of technological progression, all threaded together with the same basic instincts, urges, and aspirations to control the environment. People will always be converters of the land, changing its natural contours, disrupting its ecosystems, and removing its wildlife. Any healthy ethic about nature and the land for people will not evolve the human species away from these tendencies, because people will continue to change the land, air, and water. But nonetheless, we can seek to balance such aspirations with a renewed sense of attachment to our natural heritage and the myriad life about us. Seeking out the small creatures of ordinary places helps us find this balance. If we can just learn to value them as much as we value ourselves, then life—we may all hope together—will surely go on.

Bibliography

Allman, L. 1996. *Far from Tame: Reflections from the Heart of a Continent.* Minneapolis: University of Minnesota Press.

Carter, R. E. & C. Kenway. 1995. *Cabin Fever.* St. Paul, Minn.: Galde Press.

Coniff, R. 1996. *Spineless Wonders.* New York: Henry Holt & Company.

Dethier, V. G. 1992. *Crickets and Katydids, Concerts and Solos.* Cambridge, Mass.: Harvard University Press.

Dillard, A. 1974. *A Pilgrim at Tinker Creek.* New York: Harper's Magazine Press.

Fisk, E. J. 1990. *A Cape Cod Journal.* New York: W. W. Norton.

Grishaw, P. 1988. *The Necessity of Empty Places.* New York: St. Martin's Press.

Hubbell, S. 1993. *Broadsides from the Other Orders.* Boston: Houghton Mifflin Press.

Leopold, A. 1966. *A Sand County Almanac.* New York & London: Oxford University Press.

Margulis, L. 1998. *Symbiotic Planet: A New View of Evolution.* New York: Basic Books.

Margulis, L. & D. Sagan. 1998. *What Is Sex?* New York: Simon & Schuster.

Swain, R. B. 1991. *Saving Graces—Sojourns of a Backyard Naturalist.* Boston: Little, Brown.

Teale, E. W. 1937. *Adventures in Nature.* New York: Dodd, Mead & Company.

Waldbauer, G. P. 1996. *Insects through the Seasons.* Cambridge, Mass.: Harvard University Press.